To Jerry & Elizabeth
this story of long ago
& far away —

Geraldine Kennedy

HARMATTAN
2/18/94

Also:

From the Center of the Earth:
Stories out of the Peace Corps

Edited by Geraldine Kennedy

HARMATTAN

A Journey Across the Sahara

Geraldine Kennedy

Clover Park Press • Santa Monica • California • 1994

Clover Park Press • PO Box 5067 • Santa Monica, CA 90409-5067

Some names have been changed to protect the privacy of individuals.

Lines from *CLEA* by Lawrence Durrell. Copyright © 1960, renewed 1988 by Lawrence Durrell. Used by permission of Viking Penguin, a division of Penguin Books USA Inc.

Excerpt from *The Blue Men Rise*, Copyright 1964 Time Inc. Reprinted by permission.

Lyrics from *Dites-moi* which appear on page 202. Copyright © 1949 by Richard Rodgers and Oscar Hammerstein II. Copyright renewed. Williamson Music owner of publication and allied rights throughout the world. International copyright secured. Used by permission. All rights reserved.

Lyrics of *The Riddle Song,* arranged by Tennessee Ernie Ford and Jack Fascinato, used by permission of the publisher, BayShore Music Corp.

Lines from *LONELINESS*, by Clark E. Moustakas, Copyright © 1989, 1961. Reprinted by permission of the publisher, Prentice Hall/ A division of Simon & Schuster, Englewood Cliffs, NJ.

The lines from *my father moved through dooms of love* are reprinted from *COMPLETE POEMS, 1904-1962,* by E. E. Cummings, Edited by George J. Firmage, by permission of Liveright Publishing Corporation. Copyright © 1923, 1925, 1926, 1931, 1935, 1938, 1939, 1940, 1944, 1945, 1946, 1947, 1948, 1949, 1950, 1951, 1952, 1953, 1954, 1955, 1956, 1957, 1958, 1959, 1960, 1961, 1962 by E. E. Cummings. Copyright © 1961, 1963, 1966, 1967, 1968, by Marion Morehouse Cummings. Copyright © 1972, 1973, 1974, 1975, 1976, 1977, 1978, 1979, 1980, 1981, 1982, 1983, 1984, 1985, 1986, 1987, 1988, 1989, 1990, 1991 by the Trustees for the E. E. Cummings Trust.

Library of Congress Catalog Card Number: 93-073120

KENNEDY, GERALDINE
HARMATTAN: A JOURNEY ACROSS THE SAHARA/ GERALDINE KENNEDY
1. TRAVEL–SAHARA DESERT–WEST AFRICA
2. ADVENTURE–SAHARA DESERT–WEST AFRICA
3. AUTOBIOGRAPHY
4. SAHARA DESERT–HISTORY
5. WOMEN–AMERICAN WOMEN–TRAVEL IN THE SAHARA
1994

ISBN: 0-9628632-1-1

The text of this book is set in Palatino on acid-free paper
Jacket design by Sylvia Keulen
Manufactured in the United States of America

To
Jim

HARMATTAN

Här•ma•tan´ (rhymes as if: *har—baton)*

The legendary hot, dry wind that sweeps south from the Sahara and along the western coast of Africa, ladened with clouds of dust.

[Similarities with a number of languages:
- Twi — *haramata*
- Fanti — *harmatán*

both above possibly derived from:
- Arabic — *haram*, an accursed thing, from the stem of *harama*, forbid, similar to *haruma*, to be forbidden]

Contents

Author's Notes

In the first months of 1964, we five went on a journey. We moved a step at a time, from the last place to the next, 4,000 miles across a continent and the great Sahara Desert. This book is the story of the somewhat random intrusion of our transient selves upon each other and upon the people among whom we passed. Like the Harmattan winds that accompanied us, we moved through each place, stirring it a little, taking a part of it, and leaving a part of ourselves behind.

It was a period of hopefulness for us and for the young nations we visited. Colonialism was passing, everything was possible. We lived in the present, intensely, learning, testing, improvising our way. In the crucible of Africa we faced the unknown and met ourselves. It was a wonderful time.

The Jerrie Markos who crossed the Sahara became the Geraldine Kennedy who wrote about it. Over 30 years, large parts of this book were revised, set aside, and other parts added. It often seemed close to ready for publication, but real life intervened, distracted.

Now a generation has passed and my children have their

mountains to climb, seas to sail, and foreign cultures to fathom. With their joyous curiosity and exceptional tolerance, they are exploring parts of the world I've never seen and discovering themselves. One day I realized that this is where I came in. The gene pool had made its way around to another adulthood. I wanted them to know this story, to think about history. It was time for this book, my last remaining, sheltered, stay-at-home child, to be sent out into the world.

The real people represented in this book by Victoria Dahl, Kate Gruber, Darleen Saffran, and Pat Pollock, and I had lived in Africa eighteen months before the journey, as teachers with the first group of eighty-seven Peace Corps Volunteers in Liberia. In 1964, our crossing of the Sahara was news and we were all, briefly, public figures. In the many years since, my companions and several other recognizable characters have established separate, private lives and so, to not bring them unexpected intrusion, I have changed their names. The places and events, however, remain true to the best of my memory and records.

I am most appreciative of the talented friends who have read and commented on the manuscript over the many years it has been in process, especially Barbara Doutrich Weeks, Patty Perrin, Jim Heaton, Carole Coleman Michelson, Eve Bowers MacMaster and Kate Kennedy. The time, encouragement, frank insights, and prodigious knowledge of commas they provided have made this a far, far better (and shorter) book. Thanks also to John Coyne for readily opening his *formidable* address book, and for his selfless support of writers.

And now for Jim, who first suggested a book before the desert crossing was complete and never lost faith. He shared the years and the children, has read *Harmattan* in all its mutations and more times than anyone ought to. This is for you.

Geraldine Kennedy
Santa Monica
September 1993

Introduction

For those in a hurry, here is the bottom line on *Harmattan*, Geraldine Kennedy's new book: Get it. Beg, borrow or steal it. Read it. You will laugh. You will learn. You will be inspired. Nothing better reveals the spirit and courage necessary to create a new world for the 21st Century.

Reading this book let me relive a marvelous moment in my life—the moment when I first heard that five, repeat, five, American Peace Corps women had traversed the Sahara Desert, unsupervised, unaccompanied, and successfully astonishing the entire US Foreign Service in Algeria and the Secretary of State in Washington.

The five young women of *Harmattan* never aspired to heights of valor or fame. They undertook their adventure just to show they could do it, just to test the limits of their abilities and imaginations, just for fun. They traveled with almost no money, no contacts with the politically powerful, or financially wealthy, or brutally strong, or morally corrupt. They perservered against daunting challenges and gave us a story to make us proud.

Our country has been through much since that euphoric period. Political scientist Zbigniew Brzezinski describes a dangerous drift in our culture which disturbs me as well: "Western secularism in its present shape is essentially a cultural wave in which hedonism, self-gratification, and consumption are the essential definitions of the 'good life.' The human condition is about more than that. The defense of the political individual doesn't mean a whole lot in such a spiritual and moral vacuum..."

"Spiritual and moral vacuum." Those are the operative and threatening words in Brzezinski's analysis of our plight today and of our potential collapse tomorrow.

The young women of *Harmattan* present a different possibility for America. Their life in Africa inspires us because they exhibit what America needs—courage, unselfishness, compassion, good humor, and a spirit of adventure. More important, I believe *Harmattan* demonstrates that we of the western world can reach deep within ourselves and into the deepest recesses of our culture and religious beliefs for an understanding of the current crisis of the West.

Our recent president had trouble with "the vision thing," as he termed it. He knew that something was missing in our society. He was right. Geraldine Kennedy's story tells our ex-president, our current president, and the rest of us what "the vision thing" is, and how to express it in one's life.

Kennedy may well believe I have exaggerated the importance of her book. She probably did not intend to write a morality tale for these days and years. But I believe she has. The qualities of character displayed by the five heroines in *Harmattan* reveal many of the qualities we need in order to create a safer, and more civil world.

Let me be specific.

All the protagonists are women. They travel without weapons or traditional protection through a world where women are virtually never seen in public. They are physically weak, they are ignorant of the desert, even of paths to follow. They have no vehicles of their own, practically no money, no knowledge of the Arabic language or any other native desert tongue. Yet they succeed where—dare I say it—most western men would have failed. How? By brain power and by spunk and by respect for the many different people they encounter. They are willing to be themselves in an environment clearly unprepared for their presence and hostile to public female assertiveness. Fear, genuine fear, is never far from their minds. Yet they overcome the threats by their courage, their resourcefulness, their willingness to take the risks involved.

Thirty years of effort in providing US citizens with experiences like those gained by the five Peace Corps women in *Harmattan* has brought our country immeasurable understanding of other people and cultures. It has cost the taxpayers less than the cost of two modern submarines, less than "Star Wars" (now defunct), less than the <u>annual</u> budget of the CIA.

Why do we spend so much time and money on making war and spying?

When are we going to spend equal or more time and money and brain power to create peace?

We need millions of Peace Corps Volunteers and others like them, educated at home and experienced abroad, knowledgeable and dedicated to the task of re-inspiring all Americans to the moral foundations on which this nation was first dedicated and built. Then and only then will there be no danger of a collapse tomorrow.

Fortunately, the women of *Harmattan* never gave up and, thirty years later, have produced a tract for our times.

Bravo! Geraldine Kennedy. Bravo! Darlene, Victoria, Kate, and Pat. I hope you and your story live on and on. You have pointed us all in the right direction.

Sargent Shriver
Chairman and CEO, Special Olympics International
Founding Director of the Peace Corps

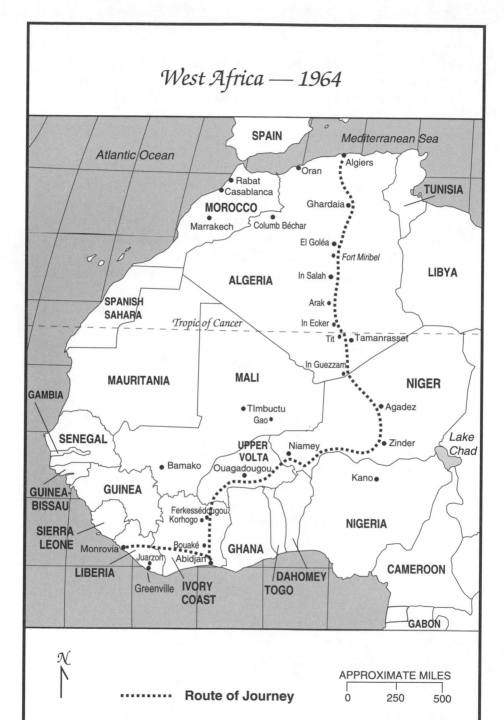

West Africa — 1964

SPAIN

Mediterranean Sea

Atlantic Ocean

Oran ●
Algiers ●

Rabat ●
Casablanca ●

TUNISIA

Ghardaia ●

MOROCCO

Columb Béchar ●
Marrakech ●

El Goléa ●
Fort Miribel

LIBYA

ALGERIA

In Salah ●

Arak ●

Tropic of Cancer

In Ecker ●

Tit ● ● Tamanrasset

SPANISH
SAHARA

In Guezzam ●

MAURITANIA

MALI

NIGER

GAMBIA

Tlmbuctu ●
Gao ●

Agadez ●

SENEGAL

Niamey ●

Zinder ●

Lake
Chad

Bamako ●

UPPER
VOLTA
Ouagadougou ●

GUINEA-
BISSAU

GUINEA

Kano ●

SIERRA
LEONE

Ferkessédougou ●
Korhogo ●

NIGERIA

Monrovia ●
Juarzon ●

Bouaké ●
Abidjan ●

GHANA

CAMEROON

Greenville ●

IVORY
COAST

DAHOMEY
TOGO

LIBERIA

GABON

N

•••••••••• **Route of Journey**

APPROXIMATE MILES

0   250   500

1

Nous Cinq

Zinder was that place on the edge of the Sahara where they kept and told the desert stories. They knew of the men lost— sixteen Arabs in three trucks swallowed last spring—and those spared, praise Allah, to return to Zinder. A strange sort of anticipation permeated life there, a foreboding of misfortune inevitable as the wind swirling dust through the alleys, against the ancient ageless mesquite, under skirts, and over piles of peppers and yams.

The Harmattan blew. Resignation replaced hope. Endurance meant survival.

Despite the wind, winter was the preferred time for travel in the desert. Death, the people said, accompanied the summer trips of fools.

Here we were, the five of us, at the start of February, 1964, clinging to the speck of luck that had brought us to Zinder in the right season. During the past weeks we had traveled nearly two thousand miles overland from Liberia, through the Ivory Coast, Upper Volta, and across Niger, making spur-of-the-moment choices, forgoing easier destinations, and dropping alternate routes as if they were stones along the wayside. The band of five we had haphazardly become stood alone on the edge of the great Sahara Desert.

We arrived in Zinder long after dark. The cool air of a beautiful evening had done a great deal to improve our spirits. The Trans-Africain bus turned into a walled yard and parked in a row beside several others. We were among the first off, waiting for the driver and his assistants to unload, watching for clues as to where we would spend the night. This time, unlike the previous night, they took everything off the top of the bus— every carton, bag and bicycle—things the passengers couldn't possibly need for an overnight stop. It seemed an unnecessary effort when it all would have to be hauled up again in the morning.

A certain finality in the manner in which bags were claimed and carried off into the darkness prompted us to ask what was happening. The driver suddenly appeared to be a lot less jovial.

"*Mademoiselle*, on Monday my bus and I return to Niamey," he replied without a wink.

"But we are going to Agadez!" "Good. Agadez is very interesting. Here are your things. Good luck. Good-bye."

"Just a minute…" Here we were again, in the midst of noise and confusion, not understanding what everyone else seemed to know well enough to take for granted.

"*Monsieur*," I shouted after him as he climbed up for the last package. "Is there another bus to Agadez?"

"*Oui.*"

"*Ah bon.*" So that was it. "And when does it leave?"

"Friday."

"I must be really tired," I told the others, "I'm sure he said the bus doesn't go to Agadez until Friday."

"But this is Saturday. That's a whole week. Maybe there's another word that sounds like Friday, but means something else, like tomorrow, or three p.m. Know what I mean?" Victoria struggled to make sense of it.

Once again, as it had been repeatedly over the previous weeks, Victoria's longing for rational (American) behavior was thwarted. We all hated not understanding what was happening. Africa continued to define itself and confound us. It was hard enough to come to terms with it in Liberia, where we lived and worked in English. But through weeks of travel, Victoria's frustration intensified with, what was to her, the maddening incomprehensibility of French.

"Ask him again."

The driver's careful explanation in whole sentences did not change the result. In addition, we learned that there was no *campement*, only a French-run hotel not far away. We had come to rely on the network of *campements*, primitive but cheap lodging left behind by the French Army. Hotels always meant higher prices.

The driver, plainly tired and relieved to be off-duty, ushered us out of the empty bus yard, locked the gate and walked off in the dark.

The world was black. I had never seen anything like it. Not a lamp or candle, or a sliver of moon. Only stars. We were enveloped in every direction, overhead and out to the horizon in the entire galaxy of dancing stars. It was at once merry and awesome. I smiled very loud to thank them all for coming out on our behalf, for shielding us from the fear of this unknown place. Dancing seemed the only appropriate response.

"Jer, are you crazy! People are sleeping."

I felt marvelous for the several whole minutes before reality struck.

"How are we going to find the hotel?"

Out of the darkness a voice offered to help us and a young man moved into the flare of light created by one of Gruber's short-lived matches. She struck another and held it between his face and hers.

"*Bonsoir*, friend," she replied mixing languages as if he would surely understand.

His emergence startled us, yet we accepted his offer with little hesitation. We were beginning to get used to such encounters. Almost as if they had been scripted, young men seemed to come out of the wings at the moment we needed them. People reached out to us. Without them, we would have been doomed. We were able to move our vulnerable selves from place to place only with their acquiescence and often with their protection. Each day we learned a little more about gratitude.

We awakened the innkeeper who pointed out it was after midnight. Without many more words we took two rooms.

Tomorrow we would think about the cost. Tomorrow we would plan our next step and worry about transportation. This night we would sleep soundly and not think at all.

I sang at the top of my lungs and loved the way the sound reverberated about the tiled shower alcove. Under a hard spray of cold water I scrubbed vigorously. Water is wonderful.

Another morning in a new place. I did not even know what the world looked like outside our Zinder hotel room. We were again just *nous cinq* (we five), without involvements, without ties to anyone else.

Despite my eagerness to get outside, I held to the protective habits we'd acquired as we traveled. The first rule was to never ignore what the present offered. Take water or food, or the time to write a letter, or to organize belongings, or gather information. And here in this room was all the water one could hope for. I quickly moved from washing myself and my hair to all my dirty clothes, until everything I touched became cold water clean, white tile shower clean, white enamel sink clean. I packed my remaining things and spread the wet clothes about the room to dry while we went out to find a meal and meet the day.

Even at that early hour on a Sunday morning there were several men lingering over their newspapers in the patio restaurant of the hotel. They watched as we stuffed ourselves with fried eggs, *croissants*, and *café au lait*.

A number of problems had to be addressed. The most pressing was where to go for the rest of the day and that night. It would take at least that long to find a way out of Zinder. The hotel was extremely expensive for us, and the gruff old Frenchman who ran it had given us until 10 a.m. to get out or pay for another day in advance.

"It's out of the question," I argued. "Why pay him in advance this early in the day? There must be some other place to stay."

"What if there isn't, and we come back later to find all the rooms are taken?" asked Victoria.

"That isn't going to happen."

"What time is it?" asked Darlene.

"I have 8:30."

"Wait a minute, you guys, my watch says 8:42. That's almost a quarter to nine. This is a very accurate watch..." Gruber went on.

"All right! All right!" Pat interrupted. "Whatever time it is, I say we get our stuff out of the rooms and start by trying to find those two Englishmen we heard about on the bus."

"What were their names?"

"I wish I'd paid more attention to that conversation. I'd like to find those guys just to get some information in English."

Two Europeans who had been eavesdropping on our conversation, but who did not seem to understand English, moved over to our table. They asked in French if they could help.

Thanks to them, within an hour, we contacted Graham Pireney and John Mains and were invited to stay at their home on the outskirts of town. They were the friends of Malcolm Goude, whom we'd met on the bus, and, like Malcolm, they taught in Niger as members of the International Voluntary Service, the British version of the Peace Corps.

The flat land lay at a slight tilt and the road to their house rose steadily among massive boulders, like giant grey eggs strewn across the landscape as far as we could see.

"I'm no geologist," said Graham, "but I'd guess they've something to do with glaciation." They looked like terminal moraine, but that theory was challenged by their size. They averaged 20 feet in length by 10 feet in diameter. Could they have remained from the last glacial period, pounded year after year by the wind, exposed to extreme temperatures and still be that large? They were as fascinating as any natural wonder I had ever seen, and yet I'd never heard of them. No one had declared them a national treasure. No busloads of tourists came to photograph them. They were simply there, and the people lived among them.

We knew we were welcome at the home of Graham and John, although when we saw the size of the house we wondered with them how we would manage. Half a duplex was theirs, three rooms in a row, the mirror image of the other half, home of an African teacher. Open concrete grillwork, the only break in the severity of cement floor, block walls and flat roof, made up one wall of the front room. Intended to take the edge off the searing heat of summer, the perforated wall was surely designed by someone who had never spent a winter in Zinder. A room that could not be closed away from the outdoors could not be heated. And in February, the lovely flow of air was likely to bring frost. Insects, reptiles, and rodents had easy access. Pale house lizards regularly scurried across the upper walls and ceilings. I gave them clear passage because it was said they ate mosquitoes. Rats were another matter. Graham's stories of their abundance did nothing to relieve my dread of them. The front room, I noted, would not do for sleeping.

Our hosts kept the second and smallest room for themselves. Even though it had solid walls and a firm door, they slept in hammocks with mosquito nets hung from the ceiling. A clothesline stretched diagonally across one corner substituted for a closet. Two other hammocks kept shoes, some canned food, and a few books up off the floor. The room had been prepared as if it suffered regular flooding.

More of the concrete grillwork had been used to make a partially open corridor along the front of the building. It was through this short corridor that we hauled our baggage to the third room.

Word of our arrival spread quickly and a steady trickle of people came by to look at us. Lots of kids, some neighbors, and a few of John's and Graham's fellow teachers just stopped by, said how-do, and moved on to report how we looked and what we said.

Children came to frighten and amuse us. Adorned in masks and feathers, their bodies hidden between large straw mats, they twirled and stomped.

"They'll be expecting something now," John whispered.

"What do you mean?"

"*Un cadeau.*" (A gift.)

"What's that?" asked Victoria.

"A tip, like Liberian *dash.*"

"Shall we?" Pat asked.

"If you do, you'll have every kid in town getting rigged up and coming over here," John said.

"Tell them," we decided, "tell them that we are pleased with their dance and their welcome of us to their country. But that we are very poor and very stupid in the ways of this place."

Even with the parade of visitors, the day seemed suspended in tranquility. We five were beginning to learn how to be together so much of the time without devouring each other.

Tea drifted into Fanta and then into soup and bread. We passed the afternoon at the table in the front room, talking, reading and writing, a perfect Sunday afternoon and an important pause to consider what the past weeks had meant. We had moved so often, with so much time put into the effort there never seemed to be enough for writing. I scribbled furiously in my journal, noting also that it was February 2, Groundhog Day in Pennsylvania.

By and by we made a supper of Spam fried with ketchup and relish (referred to as barbecue) and ate it over rice.

Among those who came to inspect us that day was Tamati, the teacher who lived in the other half of the duplex. A small middle-aged African in the white shirt and suit coat that were almost a uniform of the middle class, he treated us with great formality. Upon hearing that we were short of beds, he remembered, alas, that he would be away that night and his wife, who was young and from the country, did not like to stay alone. So it would please him very much to offer two of us a place at his house.

Pat and Victoria agreed to go to Tamati's the first night. Once they and one blanket were gone, Darlene, Gruber, and I arranged ourselves in the bed in the storage room. The two of them on either side, and I in the middle. Their heads at one end of the bed, and mine at the other. At first this seemed as if it were just asking for a lot of foot in the face, but it was scientifically the only way to sandwich the three of us into the space. By the next morning I was only too willing to take a turn at Tamati's and agreed to go in Pat's place.

We could not forget that Zinder was the last chance to turn back. If we were to cross the desert, we had to leave very soon. The pressure of time was always with us, even in the land of no-time.

Putting together our supplies for the desert crossing grew into a vexing and tiring chore. A great deal of bickering accompanied every decision to add a needed item to a load that was already more than we could carry.

We were spared having to acquire medicines in a foreign language by having brought a good supply with us from Liberia. These included vitamins; Aralan, an anti-malarial; sulfa; Terramycin; Miltown; Benzedrine; APC; antihistamine; Kaopectate and paregoric—which mysteriously could be used to deal with both constipation and dysentery—and iodine tablets to put in our drinking water, thereby hoping to eliminate the need for paregoric.

Gruber owned an all-purpose Girl Scout knife that had eight separate tools, including can openers, knives and a screw driver.

We also carried a small assortment of Band-Aids, a thermometer, a bottle of rubbing alcohol, scissors, eye drops, calamine, an Ace bandage, and Dial soap with hexachlorophene to ward off bacterial and fungal skin infections. A snake bite kit, whose anti-venom was virtually useless after fourteen days without refrigeration, stayed with us for its symbolic value, one of the amulets we allowed ourselves.

We took comfort in relying on our little pharmacy to shield us from bad stomachs, fever, headaches, rashes, malaria, and general anxiety. A Saint Christopher medal, sent to me by a friend of my mother and pinned inside my purse, would remind the patron saint of travelers to protect us. Anything else would have to be left to Allah, whose territory this was. We proceeded, we later learned, as only the cavalierly healthy and blissfully ignorant can.

Little else in our bags uniquely addressed this journey. Among the five of us we carried a few changes of clothes, most of them better suited for the tropics: toiletries, sunglasses, gum, cigarettes, cameras, two rolls of soft toilet paper, two blankets, one pair of socks, a few books, writing paper, a wash cloth and small towel each, a tube of thick white skin cream, ever after known as *crème*, and five quarts of water. The water issue continued to stir tension as Victoria persisted in refusing to carry her own supply.

In Zinder we organized, made lists, and tried to feel in control of our situation. We bought two very large baskets. In one went blankets, sweaters, hats, and some of the water bottles. The rest of the water, a small enamel cooking pan with a lid, five plastic cups, and five tin spoons went into the second. The space left in the second one would determine the amount of food we would carry.

The crossing was expected to take ten days. The food we carried had to be edible without needing refrigeration or more cooking than could be accomplished in our one pan over an open fire. The list came to ten cans of tuna, five cans of sardines, two one-kilo canned hams, eight packages of dehydrated soup, tea, oatmeal, powdered milk, one pound each of white and brown sugar, six boxes of English biscuits, a small jar of pickle relish, three cans of peaches, and three long loaves of French bread. We added two rolls of stiff brown toilet paper after we were unable to find any soft.

On Monday morning the five of us set out for market to gather the supplies and to find a way into the desert. The Harmattan blew, enveloping the horizon in haze, obscuring the sun, muting colors until people and animals and buildings took on the monotony of the earth.

Only the flies seemed immune. They clung to their blackness with the same tenacity with which they clung to every warm creature. How hideous was their pervasiveness, their resilience. While we continued to drive the flies away from our eyes and mouths, the people watched. Were they smiling at our futile efforts? This small gesture separated us from them. We would be rid of flies. We would protect ourselves against the assault of nature, control it with all our energy. They would coexist. Accept.

All the while, the buzzards of Zinder, their backs humped, their necks crooked, perched on rooftop parapets. They clustered in twisted acacia. Waiting. Ever vigilant. Sinister. Now and then one would leave its perch, ride the wind and suddenly plunge to earth with a shriek. We winced only slightly, adjusted our wraps and strode on with conspicuous vigor.

The conditions in Zinder gave us some idea of what we would face in crossing the Sahara. Darlene had reached the height of her fears and lobbied openly for us to turn back. Despite her earlier training as a nurse, she hadn't acquired a trace of equanimity. She took every opportunity to rerun the litany we had by then memorized: her rash, her cold, we were running out of money, it was taking too long, there was too much uncertainty, it was physically hard work and never comfortable. And then the "what ifs." What if one of us really got sick? What if we encountered bandits? What if we became stranded? What if we came to a place where we couldn't communicate in any of our languages? What if we hadn't planned properly for food and water?

In going north from Zinder we were leaving our touchstones behind. Could we pass, just the five of us, as complete strangers among all the different people of the desert? Could we go safely without our own vehicle, without institutions we could rely on, without arms or protectors?

Darlene's rash spread.

"I can understand it if you don't want to go on. You have some good reasons," Victoria began, taking her aside. Victoria sat very still in her stiff Mandingo shift, her spine poker-straight. She tilted her head just a bit and smiled as she continued. "You can take the bus back to Niamey, or maybe get a small plane to Kano."

"I guess I could."

Darlene, hearing encouragement in Victoria's calm words, quickly added, "We could spend a few days in Lagos. They have lots of shops with great imported stuff…and a great Peace Corps hostel. We could get some decent food…"

I listened carefully to their conversation. I wanted to cross the desert, but I was unsure of the resolve of the others. There had been much joking and testing over the past weeks. If we had at first been inspired by exotic fantasies, little of that remained. How much doubt had Darlene's whining stirred? Would fear of the unknown and dread of cold nights win out?

"But Darlene," Victoria went on in the same solemn soft voice, "I don't think anyone else wants to turn back."

Darlene glanced at the rest of us, a deep pink slowly rising across her round face and down her chins.

"And," added Victoria, "if anyone does want to go back, or go somewhere else, I don't think she would expect anyone else to give up this trip for her sake."

That was it. The group was now a being in its own right, protected by the members it sustained. We each knew—we said it outright—that if anyone left the group, she did so alone. The group was going across the desert. None of us could jeopardize it.

How amazing that we had come to this—a group. Just a few weeks before, some of us wanted nothing more than to get away from each other. We said it. Planned it.

I lived in a small house on a mission cut out of the Liberian rain forest with Victoria Dahl and Darlene Saffran, two other Peace Corps Volunteers. We taught school on the insular mission compound, providing an enduring subject of curiosity for the students and a tenuous counterpoint for each other.

Victoria and I split the high school English and social studies classes, and Darlene taught the second grade. Although she was keenly sensitive about not having attended college, Darlene turned out to be an inspired second grade teacher. She brought energy and order to the sessions and imagination to their delivery. She used games and rewards, and filled the walls of her drab classroom with pictures carefully snipped from our magazines. Some children cried when they were promoted to the third grade.

Victoria Dahl valued tranquility and order. She was long and lean, like me, but she had blond curls, blue eyes and pale rosy skin. Her gaze was direct. Her full, broad smile warmed and affirmed everyone but herself. Her sweet songs brought calm to all but herself. For a brief but important time we were friends and confidantes.

Through it all we shared willingly, unwittingly, joyfully, resentfully. We shared the space, the chores, costs, friends, secrets, decisions, students, discoveries, pains and stories. Together we waited for mail and separately we dreamed of loves who were back home, in the city, or up-country farther in the bush.

As we approached the end of our second rainy season—and nearly a year and a half in Liberia—we'd had enough of sharing. The school term would soon end and we'd have a long break beginning with the Christmas holidays. We renewed our firm agreement to spend the time away from each other. I had been talking to another friend, Pat Pollock, about traveling to the desert, perhaps to Timbuctu. No one we personally knew had been to Timbuctu, a good enough reason to go there.

In the afternoons the Liberian sun closed in, boiling out body fluids only to have them trapped by the thick and present air. I took to my bed for siesta. The clear pale blue walls of our bedroom challenged the heat. Very white curtains caught the slightest breeze.

Close-by odors of sweat and mildew commingled with the underlying essence of the tropics—inexorable decay.

Limp hair matted on my forehead. My body lay heavy and my mind dull in the hot and humid afternoons. Or was it in the afternoons at sea level? Or the afternoons so close to the equator? Or just in afternoons meant to be so? So hard to focus.

There would be no sleep in the bright room, only a half

consciousness, a waiting for sunset and a time for the goblins of nightmares to take distorted proportions, for the squeals of a few children on the field to swell into the drone of an incessant swarm.

I dozed, losing count of the rhythmic swoosh of cutlass against grass made by the workmen who slashed to keep back the bush. Their line moved in grace and unerring cadence across the mission and back to the beginning, for by the time they reached the end, the beginning had grown up again. The bush, of which there is always more, and the slashing, for which there is always need, these were the absolutes. To this metronome of their own making the men chanted—tales, shouts, smiles, scoffs—a song of life understood and unchanging.

What did they sing of the teachers with the white skin who crossed the field from the classrooms to hide out in their little house until the sun fell?

It was on such an afternoon that Kate Gruber appeared.

"Hi, gang!" She squinted through the bedroom window screen.

"What's new, Gruber?" (Kate suited her very well, but with seven Katherines in our Peace Corps group, she had become Gruber, a name of her own.)

"Oh, nothing, you guys, I mean it's OK, everything's fine-o." She let herself in.

I pushed my pillow up against the wall and slouched down into it. A pale house lizard scurried high across the wall, froze and scurried again.

"Did you bring our mail?" I asked Gruber.

"Oh man, you guys, I almost forgot to give it to you." She reached into her rice bag and pulled out a wad of letters, notices from the office, and our weekly *Life* magazine.

There was a thin letter for me from Jim Kennedy, a Volunteer who lived nearly two hundred air miles down the coast in Sinoe County. Between his occasional trips to Monrovia, we held together a fragile friendship with letters. At first, once in a while, but now, more and more regularly, he sent me books and a shopping list. I sent him books and the supplies he couldn't

13

get in Sinoe. Something special was happening and sometimes I went to my corner of the bedroom to write page after page in my journal, trying to understand it.

I slumped deep into my pillow, ignoring the others as best I could, and savored the profound intimacy of written words.

Jim wrote that he expected to come to Monrovia during the school break. I did want to see him before leaving the country on vacation.

I also had a fat envelope from Pat Pollock, who lived in a small town north of Monrovia. She had done a series of felt pen drawings promoting desert travel, reminding me of our discussions about a trip to Timbuctu. How clever she was. I was reminded of how much Pat loved language. But her aspirations as a writer suffered in the conflict between who she was supposed to be, who she wished to be, and who she was. I recognized that smoldering confusion from my own Catholic upbringing, and found her interesting.

Gruber drew her legs up under her and nervously plumped a pillow onto her lap. She was three years older than I, but so childlike in her manner I felt grimly mature by comparison.

"Oh man, it's so neat! And this would be a perfect opportunity." Gruber took several maps from her rice bag and spread them on the bed. "If you had just seen the movie you'd know. Man, it was impressive. We just have to go." Gruber had been in the States on a medical leave that summer and had seen a new film, *Lawrence of Arabia*.

She had gone on to read *The Seven Pillars of Wisdom* and then several books about the Sahara, fueling her enthusiasm for traveling to the desert. But with Victoria?

They seemed such unlikely companions. Gruber, who babbled on in embarrassingly adolescent ways, whose deluge of words one wanted to plug, if only long enough to shout, "Get to the point!" And Victoria, spare and deliberate in speech, each of her words painfully selected and qualified, each emotion contained until it could be digested, analyzed and carefully, so carefully released. I watched Gruber struggle to make herself understood. Poor Gruber.

Darlene padded across the room leaving a trail of wet powder from her bath. She peered briefly at the maps.

"Nice, if you can afford it," she said, and went on gathering her hair curlers.

I drank from a warm Fanta and drew patterns with my finger in the condensation on the bottle. Victoria sat on the edge of her bed, thin and straight, especially her back, so the remarkable straight line of her spine ended only in the little tilt of her cantilevered head.

Gruber had a handsome, open face framed by brown hair so wonderfully coarse it held a cut and never went limp, no matter how humid the day. It was rare to see such coarse hair on a white person. She once showed me a picture of President Kennedy and asked me to analyze why he looked young. "It's in the eyes," she said. "See those narrow puffs along his lower lids? They crinkle up when he smiles. Just like mine. No matter how old he gets, he'll always look youthful and merry. Just like me." Sure enough, Gruber had the same narrow puffs along her lower lids.

I listened to Gruber and Victoria speak of Timbuctu, Gao, Mali. Their plans were similar to Pat's and mine. An interesting coincidence. Yet, it was a big desert.

But it was only November. There was much to be done before any of us could set off. And ordinary and life-altering events none of us could ever imagine were yet to occur.

The ninth grade asked to make a play from Clement Moore's story of how he came to write *A Visit From St. Nicholas*, which they found in our reader. There was something incongruous about dramatizing this nineteenth century character, whose tale was now so much a part of the imagery of English and American Christmases—my imagery, my Christmases— and setting it in the chapel of a Southern Baptist Mission in tropical Africa. The children did not care about incongruity. They liked the idea of a sick child with a clever story-telling father. They liked the magic of a gift-giver who rides through the sky on one special night. They liked the sound of the language. I did, too.

We agreed to the extra hours for rehearsals and haggled

over roles and behind-the-scenes responsibilities until everyone was satisfactorily included.

The tenth grade class began more casually with talk of their President Tubman's coming inauguration—his fifth—and led one student to compare Liberia's relative political stability with the dramatic changes taking place in every neighboring African country. *Time, Newsweek*, the BBC, the Voice of America, even the Voice of Moscow, reported enough coups and uprisings to make it seem as if the whole world outside of Liberia sputtered and burst like randomly exploding firecrackers. Their curiosity drove me. We had a vigorous, far-ranging discussion of civilization, processes, government forms, literacy, oppression, stratified societies, and national vanities—all defined, qualified and concluded with examples and elaborate scribblings on the blackboard and map. The students argued, scoffed, and sighed in wonder as points were made or discredited. It grew to a great palaver.

Every Liberian was a wordist. Issues were rarely resolved, but resolution was not the chief aim of palaver. Instead, there was the pure joy of words, the skill of an intricate, not necessarily logical, argument to be relished. Liberians of any age could go on for hours (sometimes to the dismay of Americans, who wanted a quick response) refining a point, circling, enhancing. I saw extended, exhausting palaver diffuse anger and prevent blows. I saw it force patience on people not ready to make decisions. Sometimes my head swam from the dance of words.

We were not living, after all, in the world of science and logic, but in a world of witchcraft and oral history and truths gleaned from testing the spirits of nature. We and the Liberians acknowledged one another's strange ways. With the full confidence of our upbringing and history, we each knew that we possessed reality, had been endowed with wisdom, and could best deal with the unknown. But all the while we and they watched and listened and softly noted there were one or two things we could learn from each other.

The discussion went right through social studies period and well into English without a break. In the end we determined that the miracle of a truly democratic society was its tolerance of diversity. With adequate means for the expression of opinions and the redress of grievances, violence was not necessary. Change, occurring in increments, could be borne. Power shared was power safely accounted for. I went so far as to say that violence for political purposes was not even a consideration in a civilized democratic state. It was a simplistic but honest conclusion. I had no idea how soon I would be confronted by my naiveté.

By the middle of November noticeable gusts of wind and nighttime lightning storms signaled the impending change of seasons in Liberia. While some of the students found this twice a year drama frightening, even ominous, I welcomed the excitement.

The weather of a tropical rain forest is unremittingly monotonous. We who had been reared in a temperate climate craved variety.

The change from the rainy to dry seasons was marked by the arrival of the Harmattan. This legendary dry wind swept south from the Sahara, laden with fine dust. It blew for months over a band of grassland and forest several hundred miles wide. By the time it reached coastal Liberia, the Harmattan had lost much of its force but continued thick and sluggish.

Liberia's red laterite earth, which makes such a good road surface because it packs and drains well, also powders easily. After a single day without rain, billows of red dust trail every vehicle and settle on the vegetation banking the roadway. After several dry days tires sink deeper into the crumbling laterite and the Harmattan keeps the dense billows suspended and carries them far afield until no object remains uncoated.

We had looked forward to a stop in the daily downpours, longing for clothes and beds that were not always damp, eager for a respite from the battle against mold and mildew. The Liberians dreaded the dry season. "The people suffer so," the children said.

It did not take long to understand that suffering. The sun beat down ferociously, the humidity remained high and red dust caked our house, our things, us. We were irritable, unable to concentrate, easily slighted, and anxious. We rarely felt clean.

On that particular Friday evening, the last of a day's welcome rain sank into Liberia's sodden fields and clung to the edges of broad waxy leaves. Darlene and Victoria had gone to Monrovia. Randy Moore, our neighboring Volunteer, pulled his battered bike onto our porch. Two seventh grade boys crossed the field from the dormitory.

The boys were not my students. I knew them only by name and sight.

"Miss Marka, Mister Moore, how do."

"How do."

"You people heard Kennedy shot?"

He stood, a lean and awkward adolescent grown too tall too quickly, his thin shoulders sloped, his face quiet with the bewildering message he carried.

They swore they heard it with their own ears. Someone came and fixed the radio so I too heard it with my own ears. The man was dead. The sky had fallen.

In the weeks that followed President Kennedy's assassination, life within our house became oppressive. We had all had enough of the constant closeness and sharing. We needed time apart and counted the days until we would go our separate ways during the upcoming vacation.

Pat wrote, pressing me for a time to plan our trip. Of course I would go with her. I had agreed. Yet to plan for it was far from my mind. I had so much other unfinished business.

The children asked for more class time and extra lessons to prepare them for the final exams. In their eleventh-hour anxiety they looked to me to relieve their fear of failure.

We tried to cope, each in her own way. Victoria withdrew to type her careful lessons. Darlene took baths. And I wrote in my journal.

Sometimes even journal writing was not distance enough. I had to get away from the the inner-focused mission compound and our stultifying household. I walked up to the road and waited under the little magnolia at the entrance to the mission.

Damp and sweaty, I hailed the first money-bus that passed and crowded in among the other damp and sweaty bodies.

I knew every mile of bone-jarring washboard on the way to Monrovia. Clusters of thatch-roofed mud houses dotted the roadside. From the ever-smoldering hearths plumes of acrid smoke twisted heavily upward. Bare-breasted village women, wrapped in *lapas* from waist to ankles, pounded cassava.

A few large drops of water spattered against the windshield and within seconds the rain came in torrents blurring the women, the smoke, blurring whole villages.

The money bus left the laterite road at a paved causeway which crossed the St. Paul River to Monrovia. It rattled through Bushrod Island, letting off some passengers, and continued beyond the port to Waterside where a Texaco station at the foot of Mechlin Street doubled as the bus depot.

I tied on a rain hat and leaped from one high spot to another as best I could, dodging rushing water and flooded potholes as I hiked up steep Mechlin to the corner of Front Street. It was only a few blocks, but I had to pause to catch my breath before climbing to the second floor Peace Corps office.

Friday was a good time to be around the office. The local volunteers were in for their mail. The out-of-towners were in for the week-end. People swapped stories and arranged for places to stay. Doc had his usual line waiting for stool checks.

The cloud burst had surprised everyone. This was supposed to be the dry season, we all said knowingly to one another. I collected all the mail and notices for our household and went out to the stairwell for a first reading of my letters.

Jim would not be coming out of Sinoe early in the school break as he had expected. Instead, he invited me to visit him. I was disappointed, pleased and confused. I had counted on his visit. The change ought not to have been so upsetting, but, close on the heels of the assassination, the horrid weather and the unending little irritations of daily life, it seemed more than I could manage. Suddenly, the last straw was laid upon me.

I left the office in Monrovia in late afternoon, working out my bewilderment in a raging inner conversation. I didn't see the port or Bushrod Island or feel the thud and rattle when the bus hit the washboard road. My head began to throb. A wave of nausea. I couldn't shake the bright spots before my eyes.

At some point I realized that the money-bus was stopped dead across from the little magnolia at the entrance to the mission. How long had we been there?

I lay on my bed with fever, the back of my neck taut, the pressure in my head intolerable, unrelieved by the pills. Victoria was there. I could not see her but I knew her presence, still and straight on her bed, staring upward in intense concentration.

Hours passed. More pills. Pain. Hallucination. Victoria did not move. The sun cooled. The oblivion of deep sleep.

"Thank you for staying."

"You really care for him...I cannot conceive of it...Except to know that at this second in time how utterly alone you are."

I loved Victoria.

Another Thursday, another letter from Jim, going on about teaching, change, bloody turtles and mamba snakes, the silence of his house in Juarzon during holiday, until I could burst. "Merry Christmas, luv," he wrote. I clung to the words.

There was no hint that my letter got through. But now my health was better. I could act. I could go to Sinoe to see him.

My friends were as pleased as I, if not for my sake, then at least to have my moping, miserable presence out of their hair. Darlene giggled while I packed, Victoria sang. Pat agreed to get the visas I needed for my passport so that she and I could leave for Timbuctu as soon as I got back.

A slow market wagon took my excited and impatient self to the airfield. And on Christmas Eve, a free soul arrived in Sinoe, a tin of fruitcake and a bottle of wine in hand.

A few weeks later Jim and I sat in his blue Jeep in the midday sun waiting for my overdue plane. I was leaving and thinking of the crazy demands of long separations and intense days together. There was never any normal time—just not enough time or too much. I hated to go, needed to go. Nothing was very clear. Except that I would much rather be the one leaving than the one left.

On January 10, I returned to Monrovia to find that plans had changed. Darlene had persuaded herself that she could afford a few weeks' vacation and was joining Victoria and Gruber. Pat hadn't taken care of my visas and, in my absence, threw in with the others. Despite my letters confirming that I would return, she said she believed I would remain in Sinoe, leaving her without a traveling companion. Pat was determined to depart in two days, on Sunday, and had arranged for the others to pick her up at her house on their way overland to the Ivory Coast border.

It was impossible for me to get the paper work done by then. I was to follow as soon as possible and catch them in Abidjan, a plan to which they all nodded, but with great skepticism. In a few days it became clear that I could not be ready in time to follow overland.

Thus, despite the outrageous cost of over $50, my trip to the desert began alone on an Air Liban flight to Abidjan at 4:15 p.m., Thursday, January 16, 1964.

By late Monday, February 3, we had become a tentative group of five with one aim—to cross the Sahara. Thanks to the efforts of our hosts, Graham and John, we had contacted a French merchant by the name of Monsieur Joyce, who had stores in Zinder and Agadez. He was in the process of loading a truck to supply his Agadez store. It was our best possibility for reaching Agadez, but neither we nor M. Joyce were completely sold on the idea.

Among the admonitions one picks up about the desert is to never travel with just one vehicle. The only safeguards to completing a journey were those you took with you. Only a suicidal fool would not insist upon a convoy. We had been told this repeatedly, especially by other Americans. It was good advice. It also kept a lot of people out of the desert, especially Americans.

M. Joyce was sending one truck. One at a time was all he normally sent. It would leave when ready and there would not be another for several weeks.

For his part, M. Joyce had simply never known of women, European women, whites, riding a truck in the desert. If there had been only two of us, perhaps. Two could ride in the cab. But with five, *"Impossible!"* He threw up his hands. With five, at least three would have to ride on top of the load. That would be quite out of the question for European women.

When we reminded him that we were Americans, he nodded. "Of course, one can never understand these Americans."

To help our decision, M. Joyce offered to let us see the truck, which everyone referred to using the French word, *le camion*. I am sure he meant to discourage us by pointing out its discomfort.

Victoria thought it rude to examine *le camion*, as if doing so in some way questioned M. Joyce's integrity. Here we were, amidst the man's grocery shelves, needing a ride, yet debating whether we ought to go out the back door and look at his truck.

I bolted off with John and M. Joyce, leaving Victoria and Pat to finish filling the food basket.

"Look at the size of it!" I gasped. Squeezed into the little loading yard behind the store, *le camion* appeared mammoth. I stood beside it in the dusk, measuring its chest-high tires against myself. This was it. A proud Berliet, the French-built "Mack truck." Its shadow alone could protect us from the ferocity of the desert.

M. Joyce introduced the driver, a young Arab who was supervising the loading. It was all I could do to contain my excitement, to appear calm, experienced, intelligent. I walked about questioning and inspecting in French.

"And this tank?" I pointed to a fifty gallon container bolted under the belly on the passenger's side.

"Mademoiselle, the water."

"Ah, oui, l'eau. Potable?" (Safe to drink?)

"Certainly."

"Bon."

I poked and nodded and frequently said, *"Ah, oui,"* in a

nonchalant, knowing way. All the while I felt I would burst from the thrill of it. The tires had been checked. Yes, there were spares aboard. A tank on the other side held more gasoline. Yes, there would be other passengers. The load consisted of drums of peanut oil and beer. They were being carefully positioned with consideration to the problem of shifting fluids.

"*Ah, oui.*" I nodded.

At supper we discussed our options. John and Graham had exhausted their sources. If we were to cross the desert, we had to get on with it. The choice dangled before us, but we did not have to make it that night. Instead, we lingered about the table with our hosts, as if we had known them over a long time. We spoke of England and America, Liberia and Niger, of the Beatles, witchcraft, our students, French singer Françoise Hardy, the assassination, of how each of us had come to be in Africa.

With Victoria's clear gentle voice in the lead, we sang. Hot stew and wine helped stave off the night air. We felt mellow and warm despite the draft through the open lattice wall.

"I say, do you hear a knocking?"

"Perhaps the wind?"

For a moment we listened to a vague pounding at the back door. John called out, but there was no reply.

"Well now," he said returning to the table, "you've got it all worked out have you, where you'll each sleep tonight?"

"I guess Victoria and I will go to the neighbor's," I said.

"Oh, yes, Tamati. He'll be by later."

The sound came again. This time it was more distinct, a heavy thud at the back door.

"I'll go this time." Graham rose. "If there are any spirits about, John'll frighten them off. But one look at me and they'll know I'm the friendly harmless sort."

A short dark-haired fellow with the beginnings of a beard came in out of the cold night. He wore a thin short-sleeved shirt and a kerchief about his neck. The rest of his belongings were tied in another kerchief at the end of a pole. He looked like Stanley Goldblum.

"Stanley Goldblum!"

"Stanley! What are you doing here?" It was not a very imaginative question. Stanley was one of our Peace Corps group in Liberia. He had the distinction of having built, with his own hands, the only known solid mahogany out-house in the country, or perhaps the world.

"I take it you all know each other…?" Graham began.

"Well sure, we're all friends, from Liberia," Stanley said for all of us. He strutted to the only empty chair at the table, Graham's chair, leaving Graham with the open door in his hand. Graham did close the door as a great cold gust rushed in. But it was too late. The temperature indoors would continue to fall.

"I'm starved. Something sure smells good. Anything left in that pot?" Stanley described his trip to Zinder, boasting that he had not spent a *franc* on food all day, having allowed the trucker who brought him to buy his breakfast.

"Yeah, I came in on an oil tanker. The guy is going on to Agadez in a couple of days. Figure I'll go with him if nothing better comes up."

"Off to see the world, are you?" Graham noted politely as Stanley dug into the plate of stew he had set before him.

"With his knapsack on his back." I could not resist.

"Sure am glad to find you guys. Hate to pay money just for a place to sleep," Stanley said.

"How did you find us?"

"Stanley, are you following us?"

Upon arriving in Zinder, Stanley had searched for a free place to stay and a meal. He learned that there were "English" at this house and that some of us had been inquiring about transportation across the desert. Stanley assured us that if we had secured a ride, he'd be glad to come along, to look after us. That way he figured he wouldn't have to worry about his meals. He didn't mind eating whatever we had.

I held my breath, thankful that no one mentioned our plans or M. Joyce's truck. A grey chill of night air crept among us. Whatever good feelings had survived Stanley's coming were done in by the arrival of a very drunken Tamati.

Behind him followed his beautiful tribal wife and their child. The woman sat apart, upright, neither intimidated nor embarrassed by Tamati's drunkenness. Indeed she seemed to want us to know that she was not his chattel. He may "know book" and be her elder, but he was a fool. Her rank and her pride were her own, written in the silver ornaments of her people which adorned her arms and neck.

She paid no particular notice to the child, whimpering from time to time in her lap. The flies had been to this child's blood-shot and oozing eyes. Perhaps if he had been clothed in more than beads, perhaps if he hadn't shivered so conspicuously, if his eyes hadn't been quite so large, perhaps then we wouldn't have realized that a child survived here on his own. There was abundant joy and affection, but no coddling, no preventative efforts to intervene between an individual and destiny.

Had this taut young woman shivered as a child? Were her independence and her pride secured in knowing that she had survived?

She spoke no French. There was no need. She missed nothing. The shy nods, the self-contained demeanor, and the glint in her eye that said she could easily enjoy getting into mischief were compelling to watch. I regretted not being able to speak with her.

Between Stanley's boasting and Tamati's drunken harangue, the mood of the party rapidly deteriorated. Tamati's wife took the baby back to their house and gestured for us to follow. Pat, Gruber, and Darlene went to our room. I tried to wait up for Victoria, who had gone out for a walk with a Nigerien (from Niger) teacher. By and by, John and Graham went to bed. I grew very tired, but did not want to go next door to Tamati's house alone. When Victoria did not return, I woke up Darlene to go with me. We tried to say good-night to Stanley and Tamati, but they had become so engrossed in themselves and each other's stories, they did not notice.

In our warmest clothes and wrapped in blankets, Darlene and I made our way to Tamati's side of the duplex. It was a very dark, moonless night. A dim bulb in the corridor behind his lattice wall was our only guide. We moved carefully, waiting for our eyes to adjust to the darkness. All of Tamati's doors were closed except one, which opened into a darkened room. We assumed it had been left ajar for us.

"*Madame*," I called in a loud whisper. "*Personne ici?*" I had that phrase down very well and loved the sound of it.

There was no reply.

"Where do you think we're supposed to go?" I turned to Darlene.

"Pat said it was the second door. That's the open one. I think she said the woman stays in the last room."

We crept nearer and with the faint light from the hall could make out the edge of a bed in the middle of the room.

"I guess this is the place."

Beyond the pale triangular patch of light in the doorway, the room was completely black. We moved quietly, feeling our way along the edge of the bed. We found ourselves being as discreet as possible, whispering, sensing that we should not create a disturbance. Yet there was no one to disturb.

I took off my shoes and lay down with great care. I had tried to be considerate of Darlene by staying near my edge of the bed. It was a little annoying to find I was leaning against a large lump.

"You're really fast," I scolded. "Will you move over and give me a few more inches?"

"Move over? I'm standing behind you!"

"Well SOMEBODY is in this bed."

"Ooooooo," quivered Darlene, "let's get out of here."

"Wait a minute." I put my face close to the body in the bed and forced my eyes to help me. "I think it's Tamati's wife."

"What should we do?"

"She did invite us to come tonight. Probably doesn't want to sleep with that old drunk and came in here for protection."

"What about us?"

"The fact is, we don't have any other place to sleep. Go on around and lie down on the other side of the bed."

After a few seconds I heard Darlene call my name.

"What is it?"

"The baby's over here."

"Oh, brother. Sleep on your side. Try to not wake them."

A longer silence followed, broken only by the creak of the bed as Darlene positioned herself. We lay motionless, the woman and baby between us, breathed easily, and drifted to sleep.

I'm not sure how much time had passed when we were jarred awake by a commotion in the corridor. That raucous voice could only be Tamati. He fell against the wall, staggered to regain his balance, bellowing all the while. His body momentarily blocked the light as he passed our door on his way to the next room.

Darlene and I took quick breaths of relief, but then...

"He's coming back here!"

"What can we do!"

"Be very still."

Tamati stumbled in and slammed the door tight behind him. The room was completely black. Darlene and I spoke more quietly than we breathed.

"We've got to get out of here."

"How?"

Tamati tottered near the foot of the bed alternately mumbling and raging to himself as he tried to undress.

"Just get ready."

A giggle came up from the middle of the bed. The woman had not been asleep at all. Now she lay there, enjoying our predicament. Tamati staggered against the bed, oblivious to our presence.

"Have you got your shoes?" My right arm gingerly searched the floor and grasped both sneakers while the left clung to my blanket.

"I can't find mine," Darlene said, terrified.

"You've got to." I was about to tell her my plan when there was a great thud. The bed shook, all its springs reverberating.

"What happened!" Darlene was about to die of fright. The woman in the bed snickered. I held my breath.

"Tamati just fell on my foot." I very slowly and carefully moved my free foot into position. "When I say 'go', run for your

27

life."

With a firm grip on my shoes and blanket, I drew up my free leg and let go with a kick that dumped Tamati on the floor.

We flew out the door, past the lattice wall, over the gravel road, and into the Englishmen's house before our bare feet ever touched the ground.

The day of our decision to go into the desert began soon after dawn when we gave up on a cold and sleepless night and tried to warm ourselves with cups of hot tea. Although we had not yet agreed out loud among ourselves or with M. Joyce that we would ride his truck, everything we did that morning prepared us to leave.

We washed our clothes quickly in cold water and laid them over a wall to dry.

We took pictures of John and Graham and the boulders that mystified us.

To our relief, Stanley left in late morning to catch a ride on the oil tanker to Agadez, an old Berliet that, he told us several times, had a large "D" painted on the roof of its cab.

We put together our last shopping list. Turbans and socks were essential, soft toilet paper a welcome extravagance. By the time we set off for market the afternoon wind churned streams of dust and dimmed the sun. Pat went to M. Joyce's store, while Victoria and I amused the market by choosing cloth for our turbans. We could not be sure the people smiled because women were about to wear turbans or because we chose hot pink and bright blue cloth. The vendor also sold us a type of skull cap which went under the turban to anchor it and give it the proper shape. There were no socks.

The buzzards twitched and stretched. We hurried to finish our shopping. The merciless wind created a premature dusk and spread agitation throughout the marketplace. Victoria went through a stack of lightweight cotton blankets that would make good ponchos. They were all of the same design—grayish white with red and orange bands at both ends. Printed into the fabric we read: MADE IN THE PEOPLE'S REPUBLIC OF CHINA.

"That's Red China!" Victoria's voice dropped at the mention of a place that officially did not exist for us.

No doubt about it. We read it in English. Why, in this land of French, Arabic, and dozens of tribal languages, none of which was English, did the blankets from China have only English words on them? Was anyone watching us touch them?

No time to dawdle over the thought or the purchase. The Harmattan lashed us. The blanket vendor hurried to fold his stall.

There was good and bad news from Pat. Soft toilet paper and facial tissues were unheard of. But the *camion* was ready. Among us at that moment went up an excited gasp, a strong smile, a frightened sigh, and a great cheer. This last was mine. We would leave once the wind died down, in just a few hours. In addition, M. Joyce had given Pat a letter of introduction to a good friend of his in Agadez, a Catholic priest who had guest rooms where we could stay.

Now there were just the little things, odds and ends, to fuss over while we waited. Anything to keep busy, to stave off the fear and the giddy excitement. Graham gave us a lesson in wrapping a turban. Over the basket bulging with food we tied a *lapa*. We cut holes in the center of our "made in China" blankets in order to be able to pull them over our heads. We gathered our clothes from the drying wall and shook the sand from them. We had a last look through the house to check for anything that might have been forgotten. Everything was packed, clean and tight. Everything was ready.

Once again we came to a parting, to leaving behind. But the twinge of sadness at each *adieu* was overwhelmed by the pure excitement of the unknown to come.

Camion seemed such a gentle word for the tough truck idling in front of M. Joyce's store. The drums of peanut oil and cases of beer were tightly packed, but on the top layer they filled only the periphery. A space about six feet wide by ten feet long and two feet deep had been left in the center. Heavy grey canvas tied to the sides of the truck covered the cargo. It had been left slack so that it took the shape of the load. This trough was where we and two other passengers would ride. Three-quarter-inch diameter steel cable secured the load and a taut length of cable pulled around the top of the outer frame of the truck gave us a hand grip.

There was room for two in the cab with the driver. One of those places went to Darlene without debate for the rest of us were eager to ride on top. We believed it was important to also have someone in the cab who could communicate with the driver. Since we did not trust Darlene to be able to handle it, Gruber unhappily got stuck in the cab for the first part of the trip.

John and Graham gave us a last chance to reconsider, shook our hands and wished us well.

With the driver's help we positioned our baskets and suit-cases for their stability and our comfort. We watched the other passengers make their own little niches and adjusted ourselves here and there so that we might seem as accomplished at riding atop a desert *camion* as they. We settled down in the front of the trough in a half circle, our feet to the center, our backs protected almost to our shoulders by the outer wall of cargo.

The dust-churning wind of the afternoon had settled to an invigorating breeze, blowing dry and clean across our faces. It could not have been a more optimistic departure. At last *le camion* moved forward and we gave a final wave to the little band left standing in front of M. Joyce's store.

As we turned up the hill on the way out of town, we saw a lone figure, head bent, with a pole over his shoulder. At the end of the pole was a bundle. It had to be Stanley.

Months later we learned that the oil tanker had gone early in the morning, without Stanley. He had spent the day, at first not believing it possible to have been left, trying to find it. When the truth was confirmed, he tried without success to find another ride. He stayed with the Englishmen a few more days before giving up. By and by he returned to Liberia without ever getting into the desert.

But we five were on our way across the Sahara. Zinder disappeared in our trail of dust. *Le camion* was the tallest object in a relentlessly flat world and we were on top of it.

2

Friends and Strangers

On top of the *camion* leaving Zinder I felt higher than I had flying over the forest from Monrovia to Abidjan a few weeks before.

From the plane it had still been the Africa I knew, clumps of dark green, bounded by red laterite roads and the occasional bare earth and dry tan thatch of a village. At the inlet of Grand Bassam, ocean and land conspired in a confusion of shallow dead-end waters and island swamps.

A hundred years earlier forbidden Africa sucked the boats of outsiders into its mystery. From the decks they strained to see into and beyond the black-green forest fortress. They quieted their breaths to better listen for familiar sounds of life. Later, seeing beyond would mean more forest and they would cover their ears to keep out the whine of mosquitos, familiar sound of death.

The plane circled Abidjan and swooped along the clean curve of harbor, low over the crowded zinc roofs of native Treichville, up again over the delicate pastels of air-conditioned Cocody. I longed to see Abidjan with my own eye, yet I approached with caution, forewarned by the difficulties of so many of my friends.

A brisk sure step, I thought, as I imagined how I must look coming down the ramp in my cocoa linen blouse and the black skirt I had made for mourning. Chin up, look a little off to the side like a well-traveled woman, mysterious, sophisticated and so accustomed to going here and there. Control and confidence echo in each step of my high heels on the near-vacant airfield.

I was glad to be alone, to not have to speak, to be insulated in quiet so that I could see everything.

Two fan palms shielded symmetrical plots of flowers before the entrance to the terminal. My eyes strained to take them in, to let them sink back through months of dormant senses. Someone had taken care to measure two equal distances from the path. Someone had chosen to plant flowers in exactly that pattern. Another had carefully made forms in which to pour the concrete curbs that edged the plot in perfectly straight lines. I was overwhelmed. This had been a conscious act of human intervention, design, and control, conceived and executed simply to create a spot of beauty.

I almost stopped there. But I had not finished enjoying the detachment of passing through, and without the slightest break in my stride, I walked into the terminal.

A slick-haired Lebanese man complained to me in French of some inefficiency in unloading the baggage. This was it. Sink or swim in this language with no one to toss out an English life jacket. I listened hard to the French. I let him continue without telling him I could not trust my ears. The beautiful correct sentence forming in my mind was blocked by a giant lump of fear from reaching my mouth. When his grumbling stopped, I managed a very matter-of-fact, *"Ce n'est pas Paris, monsieur."* At least I hoped it sounded matter-of-fact as I raised my chin a bit and tilted my head off to the side as I thought I ought in order to maintain my image.

"Oh, are you from Paris?" He perked up.

"No." I was in for it, doomed to a conversation.

"Then, from where?"

"From Liberia."

"Yes, but where is your home?"

"In Liberia, in the country." It was ever so much more exotic to be from Liberia than from McKeesport, Pennsylvania.

"Really? How unfortunate that we did not meet on the plane, for I have also just come from there." He was really talking fast now. "Is someone meeting you? Is it your first time in Abidjan?" He smiled too much. "I would be honored to offer you a ride to your destination." Those were all the things I thought I heard. Listening intently to French was hard and threatened to intrude upon my lovely vacuum.

I stood up straight in my high heels and looked down into the place his oiled, black hair parted. *"Pardon, monsieur, mon fiancé m'attend."* That's how we sometimes did it then, getting rid of one man by having another, even a fictional one, waiting off-stage. It was decisive and could not be misunderstood as coyness.

By the time I got outside it was already dark. To watch a sunset in the tropics one must be alert. Day moves to night quickly, without lingering. Electric lights had been turned on, not so many to be harsh and offensive, just enough to grace the shapes of darkness.

Taxi drivers watched for fares. One picked up my bag without a word and started across the road. I was left with my mouth open in the shape of "ma friend" as I realized I did not know the French equivalent.

"Monsieur, monsieur le chauffeur!" I called after him. It had not disturbed me that he assumed I wanted a taxi and had gone ahead. But we hadn't agreed upon a price. His pointing to the meter roused a distinct discomfort in my cool security. One trusted a man's word in agreement beforehand, but suspected the accuracy of a mechanical number box. What to do?

I told him he had a very beautiful country, for it was breathtaking, a beauty of aesthetic order and symmetry that seemed so un-African to me. Miles of divided paved highway later, we met French round-abouts and the miraculous cloverleaf of overpasses suspended against the sky. For a moment I almost swooned, filled with too much excitement and wonder.

Abidjan began to look less and less like Monrovia, where

anyone could be located by a few inquiries. I didn't know the neighborhoods. The Peace Corps address was only a P.O. box number. If my friends from Liberia had arrived and if there was a hostel as we'd heard, they'd be there. Where to begin?

It seemed a good idea to start at the Embassy, something I could say and the driver recognize, much to the satisfaction of both of us. Set abruptly off a curved silent street, walled, discreetly lit and identified, the American Embassy looked formal and aloof. The only other moving things were shadows cast by light filtering through slowly swaying branches. Where were the people and animals?

While the taxi waited, I walked quickly up the paved driveway to the guard cubical. The marine on duty had arrived in the Ivory Coast that week. He could not speak French, did not have an address for the Peace Corps hostel, and couldn't reach anyone by telephone because it was after business hours. The only hopeful note was his assurance that I could use the bathroom and easily get another cab. By the time I dismissed the cab, the staggering fare left me with sixty cents of my original ten dollars' worth of *francs* and confirmed my distrust of taxi meters. It was time to look more closely into the resources available to the Marine Corps.

Before the duty officer had searched many pages of addresses and numbers in his black book, another very clean and very young marine appeared out of the dark courtyard behind the iron gate and joined us in the pool of light from the guard house. He had been called out to direct me to the ladies' room. On the way he summarized the peculiar traits of the Ivoriens, listed all the important people he had ever met, evaluated the world situation from the two poles about which it revolved—the Marine Corps and the Peace Corps. He talked fast, pausing only to point out the cooler of safe drinking water where I stopped to take two APCs, our too-common headache tablet, and a tranquilizer.

My friendly informer also knew the location of the Peace Corps hostel, and on this, his first night off in ten days, would be glad to take me there. My esteem for the Embassy as a source of intelligence was restored.

Riding again through the tepid air was a joy. Glass shop windows and wide wet boulevards glittered in reflected light. How plain Monrovia was by comparison.

"And there are a lot of Americans, some great places to go." The marine was also enthusiastic about Abidjan, but in his own way, which was different from mine.

I did not want to pay attention to him. I wanted to see this place, to just inhale it, to be still and let it happen.

"Down that street, over there, there's a social club with ping pong tables, and they plan activities…" he went on.

"Oh, yes?" While I floated through the streets of Abidjan, he marched.

"Then there's this softball team some of us guys started…"

I could not reply. I had forgotten the proper American responses. I only wanted to feel the breeze. You must be still to catch it. I wanted to tell him about the glints of reflected light, but the ride was too short and his voice too loud to hear.

The taxi left us on a side street in crowded and run-down Treichville. Behind a tall iron gate, we stepped into a dark narrow alley. We made a nervous joke about the obvious effort that had been taken to disguise the entrance to the building. A white-robed *gardien* hobbled and cackled out of the darkness and waved the stump of a switch to threaten us. Like many watchmen, too old to watch and too feeble to interfere with any trespasser, he could only create a great racket.

With a flourish, the marine put my large bag on his shoulder and ran up the stairs. Half a flight more to the first floor lit only by slivers of yellow seeping under doors; turn away from the mixed odors of African and French cooking up to the next landing of cool air. Another turn back to the building. I clomped on, high heels scraping each step. We ran the whole way, up and around, into the building and away to the city. By the top, the fourth floor, I was out of breath and wet with sweat. To the right, at the end of a dark corridor, the marine knocked on an unmarked door.

It opened to a room packed with beds and mattresses on the floor. Over them lay opened suitcases and a number of Peace

Corps Volunteers.

"Markos!"

"Here am I."

"I swear, you actually made it. How did you do it?"

As pleased as I was to have found them, I immediately sensed my arrival was an awkward surprise. Instead of applause I was greeted with side glances and strained smiles. Pat and Darlene made an uncomfortable joke. Victoria came from the next room looking tired and unhappy. Only Gruber seemed in the least glad to see me.

They were just about to go out to dinner. I dragged my bags in, away from the doorway.

"All the beds in this room are taken," Victoria said. She did not say it kindly to relate information, but defensively to guard a precious resource. It was a warning not to expect any past friendship to translate into favors.

Pat stood by, averting her eyes off to the side of her green tinted glasses, while the residual vision in her brain watched my reaction. I didn't know whether this chill was meant for me or whether I had just fallen into an ongoing scene at the wrong time. I acted on the innocent bystander theory and chatted with enthusiasm, still heady with satisfaction at having gotten there on my own.

While we were absorbed with ourselves and our news, the marine left without any of us noticing.

The Hôtel Ivoire was new, in-ter-con-ti-nen-tal, and very grand. It was not our usual sort of place, but it did not take much prodding to move the group toward an extravagant night in Abidjan.

We had drinks in the hotel lounge in front of an enormous purple wall and dark carved wood doors. Gruber was ecstatic about the aesthetic.

"What courage!" she said repeatedly. Her artist's eye relished every dramatic detail. It was a wonderful space, so lush and air-conditioned. Some of the testiness I'd sensed at the hostel faded in the uncommon pleasure of coolness as we told each other the stories of the past weeks. We kept to the funny parts and embellished them with astonished faces and exaggerated gestures.

Darlene had succeeded in dividing up the bulk of her seven cartons of cigarettes and fifty packs of gum among the other three. She meant to use these gifts to bribe the "natives" if we got in trouble. I had suspected she would not want to carry all that stuff herself. I gave out the mail from Monrovia, the last any of us would have until our return. Someone mentioned that we were together as a group for the first time.

"Now we are five."

A sigh.

"A toast to *nous cinq*."

"To us five!"

A nervous laugh.

"Let's eat."

The group of four was leaving in the morning. I could join them or be left on my own again. Their past few days together had formed them into an oddly joyless bunch, yet they were determined to push on. We all seemed to be going in the same direction, yet not one of them would stay an extra day. It was, I thought, rigid, selfish and petty of them, meant as some perverse form of punishment for my having survived independently.

If I continued alone, baggage would be a problem. The camera was too heavy. It was a 24-hour trip on the train to Ouagadougou. Going alone intensified my need to get control over the language. I was deeply uneasy in French and stunned by the sudden, total immersion. It was no longer a fun exercise. People actually communicated in this language. While they thought and talked it, I laboriously translated.

I had come to Abidjan for my own reasons and to see my old friends. I would not leave without attempting that.

Near dawn I was aware of the others leaving for the train. They had left a message which only said they would try to stay with Ruth Depweg, an Ivory Coast Volunteer who lived in Bouaké, about eight train hours to the north. This would break up the long trip to Ouagadougou. They did not say how long they would stay in Bouaké or how to find Ruth.

At the hostel, other friends from Liberia shared their breakfast with me, and we set out to tour the city and find my Ivory Coast friends. The humidity weighed heavily and we rested often. Once, in a park, we sat down on the grass, right down on the grass on the earth of Africa. This was not done in Liberia. We were caught off-guard by the tug of dormant memories. A person could get homesick doing that.

We had supper at a neighborhood restaurant with my friends. Course after course of French food, rounds of red wine, crusty bread and cloth napkins—all for a third what it would have cost in Liberia. I understood why the neighborhood restaurant was an extension of their homes. It seemed so adult. We talked for hours. In addition to the usual problems of adjustment and the difficulty of living in the tropics, the new Ivory Coast Volunteers had to contend with the French. Only a few years out of colonial control, the French were dealing with the loss of their master status. Now, in fear of losing their privilege to Africans and their jobs to this handful of fresh Americans, they dug deep into their cultural arrogance to harass and isolate them. It had been rough and many Volunteers hadn't lasted. Why had others withstood and grown? Would I have prevailed as well?

One day's seniority won me a cot in the main room of the hostel and I lay awake listening to the late night sounds of the city. In a few hours the train would leave for Bouaké and I ought to have been asleep. But that night I faced the open balcony, the air was sweet and I was so awake.

Before full light of morning I stood at the depot. Figures muted by the dawn drifted past. The edges of patterned shirts and bundles ran together, an undulating still-life.

I moved forward in the ticket line. My baggage and I formed an island of clarity among the obscure forms murmuring and shifting about the platform. I struggled to get them in focus. I had to work hard to make up for the sleep I'd missed. Concentrate, I told myself. Concentrate.

It was my turn. I sensed the crowd growing larger and louder, but somewhere outside the little circle of myself.

An impassive Frenchman stared through the ticket window.

"Bonjour, monsieur."

Silence.

I knew exactly what I wanted to say. I had rehearsed it. It was important to be very clear.

"Monsieur, I wish to buy a ticket to Ouagadougou, third class. But this evening I want to leave the train at Bouaké. Now, must I buy two tickets or will one…"

"Eh?"

I couldn't do it again. I had to concentrate. *"Alors, je veux un billet..."*

"Eh?"

The crowd pressed in, louder and angrier. I was taking too long. I leaned into the window and said v-e-r-y c-l-e-a-r-l-y, *"Un billet à Ouagadougou."*

"Un. Dougou." He shouted, pulling a long strip from the rack behind him and quickly filling in the blanks without pausing.

"Troisième classe."

His hand chopped the air. Bits of ticket flew about the cubicle. More grumbling from the anxious line pressing behind me. The artery on the side of the vendor's neck nearest the light throbbed and above his collar he reddened with the rising sun. He waved me away with a comment about the stupid English and something about wasting his time.

"Pardon, monsieur. I can't hear." Sometimes it was just as well to not hear. "How much is a third class ticket to Ouagadougou?"

I had no idea what he replied but put down more than I expected the fare to be and fortunately got some change.

The train approached slowly, then bolted in a series of reverses and forwards. All the passengers charged back and forth, following the train *en masse*, jockeying for positions from which to board. I was in the thick of it. Back and forth, clutching my belongings. By the time the train finally stopped, I found myself at the rear door of a passenger car. I heaved my baggage onto the open landing and hoisted myself up, damp and out of breath but quite awake.

Two young men put my large bag in an overhead rack next to theirs and I slid under it for a seat by the window. The train lurched several more times. Between lurches more passengers boarded until nearly every seat was occupied. The two fellows (students or civil servants, I guessed, by their manner and their Western clothes) tested the windows and settled in beside and facing me. They called my bag a *valise,* a quaint word I thought, which, after I heard it several times, I adopted. By and by the train pulled forward and moved steadily on, away from Abidjan.

The colors of the forest in morning, so pure and intense, saturated the landscape. Heavy dew hung from the deep greens of farms and orchards. The smoke of morning fires hovered about the conical thatch roofs of forest villages.

I had never been to these villages. I would have been thought a foreigner in any of them. Yet I felt I could get off the train and be at home. How intrigued we are by the wilderness, how we cherish the untouched, long to experience the secrets of wild places, or test ourselves against the unknown. Yet we find our emotional home in human-created order, in the acts of our own doing, the places of our own making.

We recognize the patterns of other cultures, the simple arrangement of shelter and possessions and processes that say "this is how we do it" more readily than the messages of the wilderness. The passing village offers greater comfort than the primordial forest.

Along the train route, the Baoule, the Agri and the Abro, people I had only read about, adapted their ancient familiarity with the tilling of soil to the present-day plantation. The traditional plot, like those still prevalent in Liberia, tended by women with sticks and protected from birds by a few children with stones, was cultivated to stave off hunger. But north of Abidjan, within reach of the train, lay these grand plantations of coffee and cocoa, crops for cash. Magnificent native hardwoods had been removed for delicate rubber trees and row upon row of pineapple and banana.

A tropical rain forest devours everything it touches. It laps up roads and consumes the sites of whole villages. It is insatiable. All the more wondrous to look upon the phenomenal industry of a people who would dare to plant their seedlings in careful rows and clear and tend the earth around them with such a vigilance that not a blade of wild bush could encroach.

I saw all of this from the train. We were within reach of the land, yet safely contained, our little community of passengers sharing the passing of places. Even though it was like no other train I had ever been on, with its wooden slat benches filled mostly with tribal people (white people did not usually ride third class), its aisles crammed with baskets of produce, crates of chickens and two hobbled goats, it seemed right to be there.

I exchanged nods and smiles with a sturdy tribal woman across the aisle. She seemed an old hand at this sort of travel, confidently arranging herself, an infant, several small children, and a large basket from which she fed the children throughout the trip. On top of the basket she kept a potty which she discreetly covered and carried out of the car to empty each time a child used it.

Throughout the morning, the train made numerous regular stops and at each one dozens of people rushed to the windows to sell things to the passengers. A tall boy in short khaki pants balanced a two-foot stack of folded cloth on his head while his arms signaled, bargained and traded high into the window. Others sold trinkets and carvings of ivory and ebony as well as a good many of lesser woods stained black with shoe polish.

Bananas, oranges, pineapples, coconuts, platters of greased cakes, giant twisted breads, fried plantain, cooked hot meat—a feast passed under our window. Arms waved and reached out. People shouted to the vendors in numerous languages and each appeared to understand the cost of things by a flash of fingers or the nod of a head.

At the first stop, my seat mates bought a coconut, a pineapple and some cakes which they cut and shared with me. We had nearly polished them off by the time we reached the next station. It was my turn. I still hadn't the vaguest idea how to carry out the bargaining, but my appetite and courage were whetted. I resorted to my old method of offering something and waiting to see what I got in exchange. I put a small coin in the hand of the banana woman and discovered I had bought five bananas for about a cent! Those were the first of many bananas I purchased that day, but they were the sweetest and I readily shared them with my companions.

Between the sharing of food and the frenzy at each station, we introduced ourselves and chatted a little, but conversation was limited by my halting French. We passed the morning smiling, adjusting the window, shopping at the depots, reading and gazing at the landscape. The sun warmed then roasted us and each mile north carried us away from the great humid forest, nearer the arid scrub lands.

As the forest thinned and faded to grassland, the station platforms as well became sparsely occupied and pale. The sweet thick aroma of dense vegetation disappeared along with the vigor of the vendors. Dust dominated everything. One could buy a woven grass mat or perhaps some grease cakes from a woman crouched passively beside a basin of brown yams. But there was no more fruit, no clever carvings.

By early afternoon most heads drowsily nodded to the heat and the gentle clack-clacking over the tracks. Suddenly the train jolted, screeched, and stopped dead. There was no road, no depot, no wayward passenger flagging a ride. For a few seconds the rail cars trembled from the eruption of people and baggage spewing out into the bush that engulfed us.

I tried to ask what was happening, but no one would stop to answer.

"*Allez, allez, mademoiselle! Vite! Vite!*"

"I don't understand." Once again a key piece of information seemed to have escaped me.

"Come on!"

"Wait. Why? What's happening?" I just could not go running off into the bush.

"Hurry, hurry! *mademoiselle.*"

I did understand what I saw next: my *valise* being passed

out the window by one of the banana-sharing fellows to the shoulder of the other. I grabbed my straw bag, stuffed the remaining food into the pocket of my shift, and leaped from the train just as my bag disappeared into the bush. The second fellow hurried me along to where many other passengers were running, and I saw the bush open to a fairly wide path. I was able to jog along just fast enough to keep sight of the second man as he ran after the first. Now and then I caught a glimpse of my red plaid bag flash beyond a distant bend in the path. I was growing short of breath. I could not keep up the pace for long. After about half a mile, the path abruptly opened to a small clearing where another shiny train sat in the sun waiting for us.

My bags were thrown onto the nearest car, and I scrambled up the embankment and hoisted myself into the open door, no platform or step to help. A stone-faced French conductor stood by as my African companions spoke privately to each other, glanced quickly about the car, then leaped from the train and ran along the embankment. That was the last I saw of them.

One look at the interior of the car explained why they had run off. This, with its high-backed leather upholstered seats, was certainly not third class. I wished I had not been abandoned here. Still short of breath, I tried to discuss my predicament with the conductor. I said a lot to that stone face, trying to elicit some positive response, all the while hoping he would not toss me and my baggage back down the embankment and force me to find my way alone. He was not at all interested in my story. Perhaps it was my ticket he awaited? I looked up halfway through rifling my bag to assure him that I would find it. He was gone.

I sat on the edge of what should have been a most comfortable seat, trying to determine what to do in order to avoid being found out, being hassled, paying more fare, and most of all, to avoid a laborious explanation in French. While I considered my options, I overheard that another train had been derailed and blocked the track. That had caused our evacuation to this one. I could not determine from my eavesdropping, however, whether the derailment had happened seventeen days before or on the 17th. The latter would have meant that the other four might have been on board.

There was no sign of any intent to check my ticket. It was hardly noteworthy to have a white woman traveling first class. Still, I was uncomfortable and after all uniformed officials were out of sight, I dragged my belongings through the train to a less pretentious car and settled in for the rest of the trip.

Long shadows of acacia fell across the tracks as the train arrived in Bouaké. Up a short hill from the station, the patio restaurant of the Hôtel Provincial was well situated to monitor the comings and goings of the town. The colonial French, I had come to realize, lived a life of perpetual annoyance and studied arrogance. Those in provincial towns had the time and inclination to hone these postures to a razor's edge. They gathered at places like the Provincial, sipping aperitif hour after hour, complaining of this and that, waiting for what the train will bring. With hard eyes they claimed never to have heard of the Peace Corps, knew of no Americans in Bouaké, and could not remember whether four white women had arrived the day before. I knew it was not true.

I had not felt as tired before I encountered them. Now the long trip, the heat, the drastic loss of humidity, all the effort to communicate and understand by myself, the weight and clumsiness of my baggage wore me down. I did not want to make any decisions, to solve any more problems.

The day was passing. Perhaps an hour or two of light remained.

I finished my drink, down to the last speck of ice, and hailed an Ivorien taxi driver with whom I shared my dilemma. I used all the identifying phrases I could think of: Peace Corps, white women, Americans, teachers, Ruth Depweg. He did not appear to have any helpful information. I wasn't sure he understood what I wanted. However, for a price, he would take me to his cousin, who knew many things. It was a dubious solution but I clearly could not walk the streets of this strange town, looking for someone I did not know who might be putting up four people I did know who may or may not be here. I was willing to give the cousin a try before finding a room for the night.

We rode about until I began to recognize streets and landmarks we'd passed before. I suggested we skip the cousin and go to a neighborhood with a school and foreign residents, a place with ordinary teachers' housing. As the driver put me down on a modest residential street, I took a minute to be satisfied with my ear for catching a bit of the French African *patois* and with my first reply in imitation of it.

A young woman played with several small children in a nearby yard. She smiled excessively and nodded as I approached, not the sort of response I had come to expect from the French. Indeed she was not French, but Arab, a nurse to the children. She tried to tell me something but her French was more limited than mine. She did not speak English nor I Arabic. Still, she was not willing to let me walk away, but with much smiling and nodding pointed to the bungalow next door and insisted that I go there.

The house was locked. No one answered my calls. Through the window I could see stacks of books and clothing draped over most of the furniture. I sat on the porch to consider my situation and consoled myself with the bananas and biscuits left from the train.

The sun had dropped to a clean orange ball. The dry air blew cooler. Half a dozen people silhouetted against the horizon moved slowly toward me. As they came nearer, one of them stopped the others, spoke and pointed at me. They continued a little faster now, waving their arms, their talk agitated. I hastily gathered my things and, knowing I could not escape, went to the road to meet them. I concentrated on all the words I needed to explain myself.

"Jerrie!"

I squinted into the sun. To be sure, among the group were Pat, Gruber, Darlene, and Victoria.

At the moment it was clear to each of us that we were not seeing an apparition, Gruber rushed forward.

"Oh, wow! You made it. That's great. Hey, you guys, isn't it great? Jerrie made it!" Once again, Gruber alone seemed to welcome my arrival.

"How the hell did you do it?" Pat smiled her wry little smile and shook my hand.

Of all the streets the driver might have chosen, of all the porches I might have rested upon, I had come to exactly the right place.

They were returning from a swim at a club pool and looked extraordinarily fresh and clean to me. But despite sun-tinged faces and wet hair, their spirits sagged. That is to say, all except Gruber, who badgered them with her unbounded enthusiasm.

Darlene was so frightened by thoughts of strange places she broke out in a rash. She monitored and reported its inch by inch progress across her body as evidence that she could not travel far, especially in these uncertain and primitive circumstances.

Ruth Depweg fed us and added stories of her life in Bouaké, so different from ours in Liberia. The pervasiveness of French influence overlay the native cultures like a coat of paint, a thin but most visible veneer. It was the language of schools and commerce, the linkage among diverse peoples, the part that made things work, in a Western sense. The French were another Western tribe, like us, and we could admire what they produced for they were things we produced: roads, railroad, telegraph, electric power, systems and processes, an order we readily recognized. One could not ignore the French in French West Africa, even in former French West Africa.

Again and again we would see how difficult it was for the Peace Corps Volunteers, or any third country nationals for that matter, to function and maintain a personal identity and integrity in French Africa. Frustrations developed out of trying to teach African children and have African friends while saving face with the unavoidable French colonial middle class, who believed in proper places for everyone.

The dry air of the savannah affected us severely. We'd learned to live with the humidity of the tropics, lessons of no use here. Instead of mildew, we had dust; instead of fungus, cracked lips and rough skin. Parched eyes and runny noses would be with us until we returned to Liberia.

Once the sun was high and hot we did not venture outdoors. The afternoon passed as we lazily napped, wrote letters, washed underwear, and prepared to leave. I stretched out on a cot to finish a *Time* magazine I'd carried from Liberia. Just as I drifted to sleep, my eye caught an article about the problems the government of Mali was having with the nomads along its borders. This was the area we were about to enter. I read aloud:

> Lukewarm Moslems, the Tuareg twist usual Islamic custom by insisting that their men go veiled while the women's faces remain bare. It is not a bad idea since most Tuareg women are handsome—at least before marriage. Obesity is a sign of beauty among the Tuaregs, and many tribesmen force-feed their wives on macaroni and goat's milk.

"So?" Someone was actually listening to my reading.

"So if we get into trouble we make friends with the Tuareg by selling them our pleasingly plump pals."

"Very funny." Darlene flushed and scratched at her rash more furiously than ever.

"It might not be too bad. Afterwards you could write a book, *I Was a Tuareg Wife*, and become famous."

Despite Mali's internal problems and our apprehension about the possibly hostile political climate, Pat and I had generally intended to head north into Mali through Mopti, then on to Timbuctu and to try for a desert crossing from Gao. Now it wasn't clear who was traveling with whom or who would continue at all. I didn't push it. I wasn't sure what answer I wanted.

We noticed a number of *pistes* on the Michelin map. From various explanations of *piste* we discerned that it was something between a path and a rough road. We would later learn it could be far less than either. A network of *les pistes* as well as other informal information we had gathered made Gao one of the best places from which to enter the desert. By moving in that direction, whether or not we actually got into the desert, we had the consolation of going to Timbuctu and circling home to Liberia through Senegal and Guinea.

Each of those possibilities would be dealt with as we reached them. First I wanted to visit my friend, Carolyn Dillon, a Volunteer teaching in Korhogo, a town 65-75 kilometers east of Ferkessédougou, the closest train depot.

As the 5:30 p.m. departure time for the train to Ferké neared, I looked to Victoria or Pat to be getting ready. I had expected one of them would take this trip with me. They had, after all, displayed the greatest distaste for the company of the others and for being part of the group. Neither of them said yes. Nor did they actually say no.

"What if there isn't any transportation between Ferké and Korhogo?"

"What if your friend isn't there when we get there?"

"We can't waste a lot of time taking side trips."

They were good at it, but I was going to Korhogo.

"Does anyone want to come with me?"

"Sure. How about me?" This instant response was from Gruber. "Me go too, ya?" she offered eagerly.

That child, that tag-along, the practical jokes, the harassment. What sort of visit could I have while looking after her?

"Why not!"

The car and driver we hired got us from the station in Ferkesédougou to Korhogo in about an hour. Carolyn was as rare and wonderful as I remembered. She spread her broad smile across Gruber and me and we felt we had come home. We talked for two days, covering all the important things we were experiencing: love, Africa, our friends, love, teaching, the French, the assassination, the Liberians, the climate, the Ivoriens, love and our friends.

Carolyn cooked in the French style, many separate courses on separate plates: the *hors-d'oeuvres,* the soup, the meat and rice, the salad and bread, the cheese and fruit, red wine and mineral water, red and white checked cloth napkins. Cloth napkins. Fresh mint from a patch outside the kitchen door went into the tea just before it went into us and put us fast asleep.

Like so many West Africa towns, Korhogo tolerated the co-existence of old and new, of native and foreign culture. Amid concrete block houses, a post office, school, scores of dust-raising Citroëns and all the bicycles, transistor radios, black briefcases, and imported Western paraphernalia necessary to identify a modern provincial center, a traditional Senofu village remained serenely aloof. High mud walls linked its round houses and made the whole an inner-focused compound in the manner of its ancestors.

Gruber and I sat for a while in the merciful shade of a mesquite at the edge of the marketplace and watched what activity we could in and out of the Senofu village. A single bird scavenged a morsel from the conical thatch roof of a small granary, one of the round houses of the outer wall. I longed to cross the square and see the life inside the fortress.

The Harmattan was up, blowing dust from the desert. Across the parched land the air was so full that every breath brought more dust into mouth and nostrils and eyes. We stayed under the mesquite until our eyeballs felt as if they would flake from the hot dry air and blinding glare. We sat as long as we could, but no one invited us inside the Senofu village.

Seeing how ill-prepared we were for the climate, Carolyn gave us two wool army blankets and a magnificent Senofu hat with a densely woven broad brim and conical crown (like their roofs) trimmed in red leather and silver. Blankets and hat, bread and roses, a shelter from the cold and hyacinths for the soul.

Once again, Gruber and I stood shivering at dawn on the platform in Ferkessédougou. I put on a brown wool sweater which I'd never needed in Liberia. Gruber took a picture of me as a waif in my thin brown sweater under the magnificent hat Carolyn had given me.

When it did arrive, the train coming up from Abidjan was very late and already crowded. Baggage and animals filled the third class aisles. We squeezed onto the edge of a bench, but knew we could not spend the rest of the day balancing our bags on our knees. As the train lurched forward, we were thrown against other passengers while our things slid from our grasp.

This would not do. We tried to make our baggage as small as possible and began to haul it from one car to the next. There simply were no places. In fact, each car was beginning to seem more crowded than the last until we found ourselves climbing over an aisle of baggage, passing our things to each other over the heads of other passengers, jostled by the train, frequently losing our balance and falling on anything or anyone in the way.

Clinging to the tiny platform between cars, we shouted over the rumble and clack of the train.

"Should we go back to the first place?"

"Through all those people!"

"The last bunch was really angry."

"What's ahead?"

"It doesn't matter. We can't stay out here!"

To our great relief the next was a second class dining car, where we could apparently stay as long as we bought refreshments. The car was outfitted with booths of upholstered benches, facing each other across large tables. It was nearly empty.

Before the waiter returned with our first drinks, we stashed our bags under the benches and claimed a booth. The table made it possible to write letters and sketch. The air was so dry my small sheets of paper crackled. I was afraid they would snap apart when I folded them.

We ordered *une Coca Cola* at a time, each one as if it were the first. The waiter was amused and kept our supply steady. But he had no interest in taking away the empty bottles.

Fourteen, eighteen, the bottles accumulated on the table and the floor under it. High on Coke and so bloated, we could barely maneuver our more and more frequent trips to the toilet. As the day wore on and shifts of passengers filled the car for meals, we hung on and ordered yet another round.

The land grew steadily more barren as we traveled farther north into the interior of the continent. Sometime in the afternoon we crossed the border from the Ivory Coast into Upper Volta. There were longer periods between stops and far fewer things appearing for sale at our window. Yams, chewing gum, a cooked meat offered at the end of a stick and referred to only as *oiseau* (bird). We did buy some flat cakes that resembled a glazed Danish pastry, only to learn after taking a bite that they were grease cakes with no sweetening. We were not hungry enough to eat them.

Trees in villages of round houses clumped around water holes. Between them stretched a flat beige earth, clad only in the stubble of parched grasses and small tangled shrubs. A trail of dust marked the movement of each living thing. Just before Koudougou we passed over the Volta Noire (Black Volta), which was not black at all but a muddy green.

Gruber and I maintained our territory in the dining car by slowly but continuously drinking and eating throughout the day. As it grew dark, we called for the dinner and ate every bit of the four courses with wine. Two Syrian men changed booths several times until they were across from us. We all smiled and nodded, but none of us crossed the aisle. After they had gone, a somewhat perplexed evening waiter told us they had paid for our dinners.

It was nearly 9 p.m. and very dark as Ouagadougou was announced. It had been a long, absurd day, but we were wide awake, stuffed, and pleased with ourselves.

"How are we going to get up from this booth and off this train?"

"Waddle."

"I can't bend over. I'm going to make one more trip to the john."

"Too late. We're slowing down for the station."

Gruber was a good sport and shared the excitement of dealing with a complete unknown. Upper Volta was a blank page. No Peace Corps project. No contacts. The skeleton American delegation was rumored to be unfriendly to travelers. Our cord was cut, or rather had run out, in this strange place.

The faces of people waiting in the station blended with our own reflections in the window glass. Pressing toward the exit, we could hear shouts of *"taxi"* and see several men bobbing up to attract passengers. One young black man in a white shirt and dark suit swung from a hand rail at the exit, calling for our attention as others pushed past him trying to disembark. Amidst a lot of noise and confusion we heard some unexpected familiar words.

"Darleeeeeen, Vic-tor-i-a, Pat!"

"Did you hear that?"

"It's that guy hanging on by the exit."

"Do we know him?"

A taxi driver walked off with my suitcase. The young man joined us in intercepting him.

"Your friends I have," he said.

Another unknown face in another unknown place. Mustafa leaped in front of us gesturing wildly. Most of his English vocabulary tumbled out in no particular order. "Darleen, Pat, they ride, Victoria, my car, no, you ride, Peace Corps, friends will come, OK..."

We got Mustafa to speak slowly in French. It was clear that he knew our three friends, and it seemed they had sent him alone to meet us because his car was very small. After a moment to discuss it privately in our most obscure Liberian English, Gruber and I agreed to go with him.

It was not far from the train to the outdoor restaurant where Pat, Darlene and Victoria were finishing their supper with several of Mustafa's friends. We all toasted the reunion of *nous cinq* and were feasted upon by mosquitoes.

It was no better inside our room. There were no nets for the beds and we could see the mosquitoes pour through the slats of the shutters in search of our warm bodies. I hated the sound of mosquitoes. I hated their incessant buzzing at my ear. How I wished the French cared half as much for screens as they did for cloth napkins.

The Buffet Hôtel was bright white inside and out. And although our room was spare, it was warm at night and very cool in the day, as any good desert dwelling ought to be. A gentle sun filtered through the lattice work that partially filled the arches along the balcony outside our room. We breakfasted on fat cups of coffee with hot milk, fresh *croissants* and grapefruit.

The enemy mosquitoes retreated in the mornings to let us treat our wounds. The treatment of sores and bites had become as much a part of our daily routine as brushing our teeth. We cleaned the swollen and crusted bites on our bare arms and legs with rubbing alcohol and plastered them with calamine lotion. We coated the worst of them with a tetracycline salve.

Ouagadougou was especially lovely in the mornings when the streets were swept, the tile and brick patios washed, and the gardens watered. It had a grace and unity that allowed the grand pastel homes of the official and colonial to coexist with the square earthen compounds of the rest of the people.

The capital and largest city of the new country of Upper Volta, Ouagadougou had been the administrative capital of the French colony until three years before. At the end of the rail line from the coast and linked to several other key Sahelien and West African cities by all-weather roads, it was well enough situated to prosper. Yet, with only about 70,000 people, it remained a city of human proportion, a place to walk about under the shade of acacia.

We five, however, seemed to be among the few who walked. We found ourselves, along with an occasional squawking Peugeot or Citroën, darting amidst thousands of bicycles. The roads hummed with the gentle whirr, which transported market women, students, government clerks, and artisans, with their loads of yams and peppers, black *valises*, transistor radios, books, goats, brooms, and babies. The bicycles conveyed a sense of energy and independence, a wonderful, purposeful *mêlée*.

At the grand outdoor market hundreds of red and black print head scarves, the fashion item of the day, dangled from dozens of stalls between baby shirts and bright colored *lapas*. At 175f ($.70) the scarf was a painless first purchase. We strolled down the long aisle of robes just when the sun divided it exactly in the center, with the shady side dramatically cooler than the sunny side. Everyday A-shaped robes hung in rows like paper doll cut-outs, their sleeves stiffened by hangers reaching out across the aisle. The more inspired merchants grouped their robes by size and color. I bought a straightforward brown

Mandingo robe on the cool side of the aisle for 550f ($2.20).

Darlene found plastic water bottles for about 50f each ($.20). A simple item, one might think. Yet a water receptacle turned into a litmus test of our values. Victoria could not be bothered about something so common, while Gruber was appalled that we could be perfunctory about something so important. A simple plastic bottle with a threaded cap seemed adequate to three of us, but Gruber required a meaningful container and went off by herself to search for one. Victoria ignored the matter altogether.

There was no doubt that the bottle Gruber proudly and repeatedly displayed for us was extraordinary. It was made of brown canvas bonded to rubber and thus was collapsible. It had a three-part cap: a wide opening for filling, a center section with a medium hole for careful pouring, and a top section with a very small hole through which a fine spray could be squeezed. It was this last feature that most appealed to her.

"How much?" The rest of us surrounded her.

"Well, everything can't be judged in monetary values..."

"How much?"

"1,300 *francs*."

"Gruber, that's more than $5—for a water bottle!"

"All right, you guys. You'll see. When we're bouncing along and you try to drink out of your bottles and you can't because they're spilling all over you, you'll see how neat mine is."

The lobby of the Buffet Hôtel also functioned as a dining room and cafe for the society of Ouagadougou. Sipping Fanta in its shady patio, Pat, Darlene, and Victoria had been overheard speaking English and were thus discovered by the Voltain student, Mustafa. It was a fortuitous meeting. He was going to the States in a month and was eager to try out his book-English, which turned out to be more intelligible than their French. This especially pleased Victoria, who had no French at all.

Mustafa and his friends adopted us and treated us as their personal and honored guests. Among those we saw most regularly were Amadou, playful and always merry; Claude, reserved, the complete civil servant; and Jean-Marie, a few years older, the one the others deferred to. They answered our questions and helped us understand something of the tribes and politics of Upper Volta. All of them were very curious about the United States and the time we spent together ran into one long conversation.

We toured the countryside in Jean-Marie's week-old car and talked of the price of automobiles, the Peace Corps (which had not yet been invited to Upper Volta), how snow feels, women smoking, capitalism, colonialism, the loss they felt with Kennedy's assassination. We rode horses at an acacia-shaded stable at the edge of town and did our best to convey the texture of a different life and place. But how could we really convey American life and changing seasons, the materialism, the complexity, the wealth?

Eating in the restaurant of the Buffet Hôtel, we were watched with a cold eye by the French who gathered there. It was another instance of the suspicion and hostility that we met throughout former French West Africa from the colonials who had stayed (or been left) behind.

I loved French, the j's, the r's, the inflection, the grace of a language built on vowels and soft consonants, the speed of it. But I was beginning to not like the French. Until Ouagadougou this feeling was distant, vague. It grew out of the haughty ticket seller at the depot in Abidjan, the snobs on the veranda of the Hôtel Provincial in Bouaké, the social pressures the French put on Peace Corps Volunteers, the way they stared at us and rarely extended a friendly courtesy.

The former colonial countries tended to look down upon Liberia as a backwater. Yet we were finding that Liberia's cosmopolitan racial and social mix made it far more relaxed insofar as our personal status was concerned. To be sure, there were tribal rivalries, there were country people and city people, there were Lebanese merchants, Israeli builders, German importers, Swiss miners, American bankers and rubber planters, every sort of missionary, and the entire host of international organizations. But Liberian society was open, with enough protocol and respect to maintain identity and dignity, yet without the rigid separations that lead to exploitation, suspicion and resentment. Perhaps having a black ruling oligarchy suppressed the tendency of white foreigners to cultivate public attitudes of superiority.

We would search for the reasons long into the night.

On the Thursday afternoon of our stay in Ouagadougou, we learned the bus we planned to take to Niamey had left that morning and there would not be another for a week. It was unacceptable to stay in Ouagadougou another week. So much of our time and money would be spent that we could not hope to cross, or perhaps even enter, the desert. At supper that evening we five gathered in a niche of a densely planted outdoor restaurant to discuss our predicament.

From a table partly obscured by a Mimosa in early bloom, two German fellows sent us a bottle of wine.

"I'd be satisfied to take it easy and just go to Timbuctu," offered Darlene.

"What does it say?" Victoria asked, leaning over to see the note a waiter delivered from the Germans.

"Greetings from the people of Germany to the people of the United States. Sincere regards for a pleasant meal. Who are you?" Pat translated for us.

"Cute." Victoria smiled and nodded at the Germans.

"Let's not get distracted. We're in a pickle if we don't find a way to Niamey."

"Have you got a pen?" Pat asked.

"Hey, you guys, we can't give up yet," pleaded Gruber.

"I agree," I said. "Anybody can go to Timbuctu anytime."

"Does anybody really want to get something going with these guys?"

"OK, OK. Just write thanks for the wine," Victoria conceded. "So what are the possibilities?"

The next day we put the problem to our Voltain friends and asked their help in making contact with a trucker. They were not enthusiastic about the idea, pointing out the discomfort, the uncertainty, the fact that, "to be sure," neither they nor any persons of quality they knew would consider traveling by truck.

This last argument was not persuasive. I was not about to miss the Sahara Desert because the mode of transportation was inappropriate to my "class." Only Gruber was strongly with me on this point. But she had seen the movie, and visions of Lawrence making it in Arabia by going native were convincing. Victoria felt there must be good reasons for their advice and we ought to heed it. Darlene would rather not have gone on at all, preferring to pass the weeks shopping in the big cities of the coast. Pat spoke to all sides, wanting to go on, but not sure about the trucks.

Later that day Mustafa brought us an offer. Jean-Marie, he said, would drive us to Niamey. In fact, he was, at that moment, arranging for insurance on his new car so that it could be taken across the border into Niger.

"Thank you, but it's too far, too much to ask of you, we can't accept."

"Ah no," he insisted, "this is a good time to make the trip— very dry—and we have friends to see there."

"But we must leave tomorrow," I said, knowing how slowly and unpredictably the wheels of African bureaucracy grind.

"Yes," he said, "Claude has a friend at the ministry who is helping."

Among ourselves, in our cool whitewashed room, we debated the alternatives.

"Why should they want to take us?"

"Maybe they just want to help."

"They have been great all along."

"But we've only known them for a few days. How would we even know where we're going?"

"Don't be ridiculous!"

"I think we should consider all the possibilities."

"Well then, what makes you think we'd be any safer in a truck?"

"Anyhow, it would be five to one."

"You don't think Jean-Marie is going to drive alone?"

"All right, five to two. No more than that can possibly get in any car I've seen in this town."

"Speaking of that, just how are we and all of our stuff going to fit?"

"Good question."

"We can't do it."

"Well, if they show up here by 10 a.m. I'm going to accept their offer."

"Whatever we decide, I think we should all stick together."

Niamey was to the east. We could reach it in a day's drive. That was what we knew of the trip ahead as we massed for the last time before the Buffet Hôtel. Jean-Marie, Mustafa, Amadou, their bags and transistor radio, our four suitcases, backpack, two large straw bags, three purses, and the five of us faced Jean-Marie's two door sedan. We no longer thought of danger or folly or alternatives. We thought small and stuffed ourselves into the car.

As the overloaded little Fiat thumped its behind, which was our behinds, over every washboard mile, we learned the way to Niamey, inhaled, in fact, the entire length of it into our being. The all-weather road, it turned out, had nothing to do with paving. It simply meant it probably would not disappear completely in a flash flood or sand storm.

From the edge of Ouagadougou we picked up an escort of dust. Churned by our own tires into a high, long billow, it followed us the whole day. Every moving thing was accompanied by its own dust: from the rise-rest, rise-rest shuffle dust of a market woman's sandals to the low rolling dust of a ball chased along the ground by the stick of a jogging boy. In the hierarchy of poof, cloud, billow, mound, storm, wall, or coat of dust, our vehicle raised a mass that held its own among the most determined of them. We got good at waiting until the last second, then quickly closing the windows against oncoming vehicles, charging through their golden-beige glare.

Jean-Marie, having been accorded, without debate, the driver's seat to himself, soon became the envy of us all. Mustafa and Amadou measured out equal shares of the front passenger bucket seat, their bags under their feet, the transistor radio across their laps. In the back, I opted to have my legs prickle asleep and become numb with Victoria on my lap, rather than have my back bent and my head repeatedly bang the roof of the car were I to sit on her lap. Darlene and Gruber shared the back seat with us, the one at the window holding Pat, the other in the center with all the purses in her lap, straddling the transmission hump.

A fine grit settled on every surface, penetrated from hair to scalp, and through the fabric of our clothes. Dust invaded our eyes and nostrils. Our throats rasped. Every effort to wipe away the dust only rubbed it in, and exposed new areas into which it could filter.

From time to time we stopped, shook ourselves out, revived our circulation, and drank some of our water. At one place we bought bread, at another meat on sticks cooking over an open wood fire. This and a can of corned beef turned out to be food for the day for all of us.

The sun was low by the time we crossed into Niger and we were halfway between the border and Niamey when we were stopped at the customs' checkpoint of Lamorde-Torodi. Until now the trip had been physically difficult, but jokes and good nature had made a merry time out of misery. The line in front of us, native traffic, passed slowly but easily through customs. We were asked to pull off to a side area. Assorted inspectors and agents of diverse ranks paraded by, nodding at our perfect papers, yet dumbfounded by the group of us. The first inspectors called out their cohorts until I'm sure everyone on the post got a look. We were getting nowhere. They didn't have any questions. They didn't indicate, in any signs I understood, that they were waiting for a bribe. We certainly weren't that amusing!

Eventually one of them called for our luggage, which received one cursory inspection and then another. We grew more uneasy. What if this was the day one of them decided to make a name for himself? How many of them could read any of the papers at which they stared so intently? What if the tribe of one of them were the historic enemy of the tribe of Jean-Marie? Outlying border posts were ruled more by caprice and wit than by international law and discipline.

I spoke for us, giving the same correct answer regardless of the question. The other women did not attempt to reply to the French questions, remaining as politely aloof as possible with empty stomachs and the itching of a day's dust.

"*Oui, nous sommes américaines. Oui, touristes.* No, we have no weapons."

As it grew dark, the Voltains, who had, with a very low-key vigilance, attempted to treat it as an ordinary event, also became anxious about the delay. We waited, held our thirsty tongues, and relied on their effort to maneuver us through. As a last resort we showed our Peace Corps identification cards. The customs agents did not show recognition of the Peace Corps, but the cards bore the seal of the United States Government. After a brief consultation among themselves, they stamped our passports and released us.

Only fifty kilometers more to Niamey. It was dark, but not too late to find a place to stay. We had heard there was a Peace Corps hostel. Niamey was only half the size of Ougadougou, a place we could expect white foreigners to be conspicuous. This would be a help to us.

"We may make it," said Jean-Marie, but Mustafa silently shook his head.

"What's the problem?" asked Victoria, "we'll be to Niamey in less than an hour, won't we?"

"Niamey is on the Niger River. We will certainly be to the Niger within the hour."

"Well, then?"

"We will be on this side of the Niger. Niamey is on the other side."

No one had ever mentioned this bit of geography before.

"And to cross?"

"A ferry, which is not permitted to operate after sunset."

"Impossible! No bridge? No ferry at night? What does one do if one arrives after sunset?"

"I'm afraid one waits until morning."

Which is precisely what we did.

After a lengthy palaver with a fisherman, who in the end could not be persuaded to take us across because he feared being reported by his tribesmen, who stood nearby saying that is what they would do, we had no recourse but to wait.

We broke out the can of corned beef, the water bottles, part of Darlene's cache of cigarettes, and some chewing gum. The radio—until all the stations were off the air—and the car lights helped cheer us, but did nothing to relieve the growing cold or the assault by mosquitoes.

Throughout the night I could look over to a nearby building where Victoria lay stretched out on a narrow porch wall. Arms folded serenely across her chest, as if she were in her bed, she slept, unmolested by a single mosquito.

At dawn the first sound on the radio was the recitation of the national farm report brought to us in solid midwestern English by the Voice of America. Surely, we were the only people in that part of the world awake at that hour able to understand it. And we really didn't give a damn about the egg production of Rhode Island Reds.

Approaching a place by ferry is a definitive act. You don't accidentally find yourself on a ferry. You don't unexpectedly arrive having lost track of the time. There is no slinking up on a place by ferry. No. A ferry is an act of choice. A ferry requires a stop, a wait, a schedule. A pause in which persons and vehicles alike become passengers. Arrival by ferry is just that, an arrival, a moment of high drama. A hyphen, instead of a line, in the life of travel.

The romance of the ferry was displaced as we loaded onto the barge that morning. Tired and dirty, huddled in blankets against the cool morning air, we faced Niamey and surveyed the banks of the river from the deck. Even approaching its winter flood level, the Niger did not seem much of a river. I knew rivers. I had grown up entwined with them. But even the Youghagheny and Monongahela of my childhood were wider, deeper and faster flowing than this. I did not understand why there was no bridge. The rivers I knew had so many bridges we could forget they were rivers. Here was the capital city of a nation with one river for water, for transport, for irrigation, for electric power, for fishing—and no bridge. You could not live in Niamey and forget the Niger.

The Voltains, as hungry and tired as we, unloaded us on the doorstep of the American Embassy and went off to find their friends. At a little after 7 a.m. on a Sunday our chances of getting help or information seemed slim. There wasn't a person in sight. Down the street to the right an awning protruding over the sidewalk led us to hope the corner shop might be a cafe. Victoria and I walked in that direction, leaving the others to guard our belongings and rattle the Embassy windows to perhaps rouse a *gardien*. At the very least, one could expect an American Embassy to have a bathroom.

Wrapped to our chins in blankets, we shivered down the block.

A remarkably dapper man strolled toward us. "Can you believe this?" I whispered to Victoria. "In Niamey?" Pointy Italian shoes, grey pin-striped trousers, white silk shirt open at the neck to reveal a striped cravat, fine-combed silver tipped hair, morning paper and walking stick under one arm, cigarette in long holder—he seemed a caricature, a model for a European fashion magazine.

We giggled into our blankets and tried to continue as if it were perfectly normal for us to be there in our present attire.

"I'll bet he's Italian," she said. "I wish we could ask him about a bathroom."

"We can try. He'll probably understand some French."

But as we came nearer, he seemed so immaculate and aloof, and we even more scruffy by comparison. I couldn't get the words together to interrupt him. At the moment we would have silently passed each other, he spoke with the faintest smile.

"Good morning, Peace Corps."

Not only did he speak English, he was an officer of our legation. Assessing our circumstances, he offered us an apartment over the Embassy. He gave us a key, showed us the direct access to the apartment by the stairs at the back of the building, and introduced us to the *gardien*, who had been hiding under the stairs.

Everything we could have asked for was contained in the sweet oasis above the Embassy; a good sit-on-it toilet in a very

American white bathroom and a large clean airy room with screens on the windows and half a dozen mattresses on the floor. We did not know how long we would have this haven and did not ask. Within minutes of moving in we all fell fast asleep.

There were many things to arrange if we were to cross the desert in the time we had left. School would resume in a few weeks and we had to be back to Liberia by then. I still needed a visa for Mali. We had to find a way to get to Gao. Everywhere we went, we accumulated information. Everyone we spoke to advised us—most often to lessen our ambition, to give up the desert. Their greater knowledge and experience in the region warranted respect, but none of them had actually crossed the Sahara.

While doing everything we could to move onward, we were drawn to be with many different people. The time we shared with them was all we had to exchange for being advised, fed, befriended, and helped in hundreds of ways.

The Voltains were leaving later in the afternoon to return to Ouagadougou. They invited us to join them and their Nigerien friends for a last party. In the meantime we had shopping to do and letters to mail. I spent the rest of the morning walking to the Malian Embassy, only to learn they issued visas (or rather, would consider issuing visas) on Wednesdays only. That meant, even if we found transportation, we could not leave Niamey for two more days.

We gathered that afternoon at the home of someone's cousin, who happened to be the inspector of police, to say good-bye to the Voltains. The house was filled with young Nigerien women and men.

Amid dancing and rounds of Fanta, we filled them with stories of the America we had left, which, unbeknownst to us, would not be the America to which we would return. They lamented the murder of our president and had a great curiosity about the processes by which our government and our people recovered from such a blow.

They told of changes taking place in their governments, the

juggling of personalities, the expectation that some of that power would one day be theirs. It was a politics of realism they debated, made up of the hopes and shortcomings of corruptible humans. While one pounded the table to make a point, another speculated about behind-the-scenes intrigues.

Our heads were full of all the energy and intensity of the afternoon when we arrived for dinner at the home of George Klein, director of the small Peace Corps contingent in Niger.

The old part of Niamey is made up of narrow arteries, unmarked troughs of sun-baked earth. Like the ancient neighborhoods of Kano, Katsina, Kaduna, or any other town of the savannah where people have used the earth to shelter themselves, it is an architectural expression of limits: the structural limits of unreinforced mud and straw, the design limits of imaginations never stimulated by a yearning for change, the social limits that define and enclose the space of the clan. The result is a labyrinth of public troughs through which to pass from one private space to another. Channels flow into each other, their earthen walls unrelieved save for an occasional, anonymous gate.

Inside the gate is another world, a sight that calls for a pause, a sigh of wonder. The private courtyard of tile paths and gardens, with perhaps an aging acacia or the sweet scent of jasmine, is stunning in its intimacy, its welcoming caress. To the sedentary people of the Sahel, home is not a vantage place for watching the activity of the street or keeping an eye on neighbors. It is a shelter, a refuge focused on its inner life.

George Klein's inner life was sustained by classical music. He chose to live as the people did, in a traditional house in a traditional sector with an earthen wall and an inner garden. But he would have his Bach and his Verdi. In a few moments we passed from the void of the street to a richness embellished with plants, music and food. We had left behind an afternoon of lively dancing and heated discussion, the rhythm of Hi-Life and the breezy songs of Françoise Hardy, and entered an evening of symphony and opera, of quiet conversation, sipping wine and thinking distant thoughts.

We adapted.

In a few days we would have to break away from all the comforts and social life of Niamey and try for Gao. So many grave faces as we talked of crossing the desert.

In the letters I sent that afternoon I promised to write from Gao and to cable the embassy in Algiers to expect us. I hoped my friends paid attention to the dates. I hoped they'd notice if they didn't hear again in a reasonable time. But I didn't say that.

We heard of other Peace Corps Volunteers who had tried to cross the desert, from our side and from the north, but there were no stories of anyone making it. From Niamey they said the crossing was nine or ten days instead of the five we had anticipated. We also learned that the system of check points across the desert and the bush plane that provided travelers a bit of security or an emergency rescue had gone out of service as each country became independent from France.

That night I dreamt one of the variations of a recurring dream. It always involved a difficult parting. Someone left and someone stayed behind. No matter how perilous the journey, how fraught with unknowns, it was always frighteningly more easy to leave than to be left behind. I would always choose to go, to act instead of wait. My secret terror was in being acted upon, left behind, left out, set aside. I awakened more determined than ever.

Darlene accompanied me to the Malian Embassy for one more try for a visa. With that, the last obstacle had been overcome. We could be off for Gao on the late Friday afternoon bus.

We came around to the back of the Embassy, looking forward to an afternoon rest.

"There you are!" said a bright-eyed woman who was coming down our stairs toward us. "I'm Barbara, here with USIS (United States Information Service). I just heard you were in town. I'd really like to get together with you. How long will you be in Niamey?"

"Leaving on Friday afternoon."

"Darn! How about dinner tomorrow night? It will be tight because I have an adult class, but I'll make curry."

"Sure. Sounds great."
"I'll pick you up at four-thirty. How many are you?"
"Five."
"I hope you can all make it. Got to run."

Living in the Embassy apartment, "over the store," stirred our imaginations. While the employees in the offices on the ground floor took care of our country's business with Teletypes and typewriters and diplomatic pouches during regular business hours, we lived upstairs. Our underwear was washed in the same bathroom that would have been used by a visiting VIP, if any VIPs ever came to Niamey. We looked out across the town to the orange, white, and green flag atop the Nigerien National Assembly or glanced down from the balcony to a turbaned old man trotting his donkey on the road below. It was the same view a political refugee given asylum might have seen, if anyone had ever cared about asylum in the Embassy in Niamey. Since we were neither VIPs nor refugees, we were largely ignored by the people who worked downstairs.

"They hate it here," said the USIS Barbara, as she filled us in on the kind of official community our government had in Niger. She spoke and worked quickly, checking the rice and chopping curry toppings.

"They think it's a dead-end assignment, the end of their careers. They don't get much traffic through here, so there isn't the chance to meet people who are influential, who will remember you when the time comes for a promotion. Also, it's such a small community, social life is pretty limited."

"How do you feel?" asked Victoria.

"Well, I've been here six months and when I first got the assignment I didn't know what to think. I knew nothing about the area. I guess I looked at it as an adventure. Now I'm fascinated! You can step back in time and feel you're seeing life as it was lived here five hundred years ago." She caught herself becoming more animated and smiled. "I guess that's the anthropologist in me."

She was like us—curious, energetic, open to the experience

and willing to share it. We liked her a lot.

"Anyhow, it's turned out to be great for me here," she continued. "I might not feel that way if I were older, or had a family—you know, kids and their schools to think of. Professionally, it's wonderful. I get to do a lot on my own, to try out a lot of my ideas for programs. That would never happen in a larger mission with more levels of supervision, more people looking out for their best moves."

The anthropologist in her came out again when she spoke of the people of the desert and the ancient city of Agadez, about 850 road miles northeast of Niamey. In the six months since she had arrived, she had devoted all her free time to learning about the region, to traveling to remote or historic sites. Her little house was filled with the artifacts she had collected. She spoke of Gao, Timbuctu, and Mopti. But above all, she was enthralled with Agadez.

"Why did you choose to enter the desert through Gao?" she asked.

Whatever reasons we might have had faded with her stories of Agadez. It was possibly the oldest continuously inhabited place in the desert, the capital of the southern Tuareg, an important trading center throughout its history. It had a renowned mosque, built of mud, dating from the time of Mohammed.

"Can we get there on the bus?"

"Yes. But from there on you're on your own. Getting into the desert is not easy. But you can always take the bus back and would have had a far more unique experience."

Agadez was it. The information we had gathered about Gao, the anticipation of leaving for there the next afternoon, the effort to get my visa for Mali were all set aside.

It had seemed so easy to change our minds and turn to Agadez. But the next morning we had to act. The Agadez bus, we learned, would leave sometime in the morning. No exact schedule.

We had to exchange the Gao tickets.

Fill all the water bottles at the Embassy cooler, finish packing boxes of excess baggage to be mailed to Liberia.

We needed film, flash bulbs, emery boards, batteries, food for the bus, hand cream.

Who will go to the post office?

The *chargé d'affaires* says we must vacate by noon so they can get the rooms ready for people from Washington.

Who will stay with the baggage?

How will we get the bus tickets?

Lines, information, lines, misinformation, short tempers, confusion.

Everything must be handled in person. No telephones. No schedules. The bus depot is in one direction, the post office in another.

The depot is crowded and dusty. The bus is sold out.

"I insist. See, here we are with all our baggage. We must leave today."

He hesitated.

"I must speak to your supervisor."

"How far?"

"Agadez."

"How many?"

"Five."

Trans-Africain will not take travelers' checks. Someone must go to the bank to change money. 4686f each, times five is 23,430f, almost a hundred dollars.

"Stay with the baggage."

"When does the bus leave?"

"When the driver is ready."

"See to it that it doesn't leave without us."

In the end, it didn't. After all the anxiety and the rushing about and being separated and not knowing, we stood by the bus and waited. We boarded and waited. We were finally off by noon.

After an argument with a hot-tempered woman over seats, we secured our territory and settled in. The bus was comfortable except for my facing backwards for the first hours.

We made friends with our eyes with two well-robed and jeweled ladies, like sisters, fat, bouncing with the bus, effortless, spreading to fill the seat. One threw candy wrappers out the window for us. I gave her an empty biscuit box to spit in. We smiled and shook hands and were delighted with each other.

Victoria and I spent the time to Dosso talking and joking with an Englishman, Malcolm, who'd been in Niger for three months with International Voluntary Service (IVS). He was a little discouraged with the place, the apathy he found.

"I hadn't been prepared...to...deal with the weight of such...inertia," he said. He struggled to consciously speak to us in his language, which was our language.

He was still fresh with observations, notes on differences, awareness of losing his skill in English. It was something we all felt. Vocabulary was replaced by gesture and inflection. Complex grammar by simple patterns. It worked well enough for day to day business. But when we really wanted to say something, we found ourselves frustrated in the search for words and structures we knew we'd once had.

At a rest stop we saw an odd mound in the distance. It was not a dune, though it was the color of the earth. It was not a wall though the parts lay together like overlapping bricks. Without any tree or building as a reference, it was impossible to tell how large it was or how far away. I asked the driver.

"*Ils sont arrichives.*"

"I don't recognize that word."

"Here, look it up."

I asked the driver again and pronounced what I thought he was saying.

"*Oui,*" he said, "*arrichives.*"

I asked him to write it down. In my little book of accounts and shopping lists, he printed: *arichives.*

"Sure enough, that's what I thought he was saying. It's not in the dictionary."

The only way to be satisfied was to walk to the mound and see. The bus hadn't been turned off, so I hurried across the field. The mound turned out to be the start of a pyramid more than 150 feet long and already twice as tall as I was. It was built of burlap sacks filled with peanuts. That explained the peanuts and shells strewn across the field. Peanuts were the chief export crop of Niger, and almost all of them went to France. I looked up peanuts and added *arachides,* correctly spelled at last, to my French vocabulary to make up for some of the English I was losing.

Despite the steady jostling of the bus, I tried to make notes. I wanted to remember the fat ladies, Malcolm, the food we carried and the cooked meat, bananas, and bread we bought along the way, the lingering nausea of riding backwards, the dust, the antics of the driver, his long robe and turban, his playful good humor—he could have driven a tour bus anywhere.

We learned it was Ramadan, the Moslem holy month. And this was definitely Moslem country. Along the way, men prayed to Allah, washing feet and hands, spreading their mats wherever they found themselves. To observe the fast, they did not eat or drink from sunrise to sunset. Neither did they swallow their saliva—thus the ladies spitting into our cast-off box. In this dry hot land day-long fasting was truly a personal physical sacrifice.

We were something of a sensation, we five white women, Americans and Peace Corps. I was sure there was nothing finer to be. Everywhere we received kindly curiosity, attention, and smiling approval. Lovely gifts. How should we repay them? I would start by recording and remembering. Even as I did, I knew no journal would be complete enough and I was sad about the parts being lost.

Before he got off, Malcolm gave us the names of two of his British co-workers who lived in Zinder, which we expected to pass through sometime the next day on our way to Agadez.

After dark the bus came to the village of Birni-n-Konni and we were shown to a room in a mud building. A *campement*, the driver said. Another word to take from French and add to our everyday vocabulary. It was literally an encampment, a minimal shelter built by the French as temporary quarters for troops in transit, now providing very cheap lodging for travelers.

We were uneasy about leaving the suitcases in the rack atop the bus, but the driver secured a tarp over everything, and only those passengers leaving the bus for good took their things. We were too tired to press the matter.

There was no electric light, and after a whiff of the stale odor in the room, it was probably just as well. We carried blankets, food, and hand bags inside, found the beds with our flashlight, and fell to sleep as we were, in all our clothes.

From the depth of a sound sleep, I was awakened by a bright light inches from my eyes.

"What...what is it?" I tried to remember where I was.

"It's OK, it's OK, Jer. I just wanted to be sure you were still here." It was Gruber. She leaned over me, looking for all the world as if this were a normal and honest investigation to conduct in the middle of the night.

"Where did you think I might be?" I sunk back into that abyss of a bed, breathing deeply to quiet my racing heart. "You can go back to bed now."

"I am in bed."

"Then why do I see light flashing around this room?"

"I'm just checking for spiders. That's how you find them. Start with complete dark, then suddenly flash a light before they get a chance to hide."

"Gruber, what time is it?"

"Three-fifteen. No, wait. It's three-eighteen."

"Please put out the light."

I slept instantly, transported to a heavy, dreamless state without effort. But when I heard my name called, I knew it could not be day.

"Jer! Jer! Darlene! Hey, you guys...did you hear that?" Gruber whispered loudly.

"Why are you shining that light over there?" asked Darlene.

"I thought I heard something. It must be a rat. I'll try to get it in the light and you guys catch it." Gruber directed from a crouched position on her bed. The light flashed off and on, darting about the room.

"Quiet."

We held our breaths for a moment and heard nothing.

"Gruber, put that damn light away!"

"I was just checking, just checking. What if there are rats? Somebody ought to be awake to warn the others."

Once again I fell off to a sleep where neither spiders nor rats could reach me. Only the persistent voice of Gruber in a hushed, anxious call.

"Hey you guys. It's time to get up. Come on, you guys, we don't want to miss the bus."

"What time is it?"

"Four-thirty."

"We have three more hours before the bus leaves."

"Well, I think we should be ready. We don't want them to have to wait for us."

"Gruber, you're crazy. Go to sleep," said Darlene, at once begging and demanding.

"I don't want to believe we're even having this discussion."

Moments later a faint flicker of light forced me to turn toward Gruber's bed.

"Oh for Chrissake, Gruber, what are you doing?"

"Well, you guys told me to put the flashlight away," she explained, lying on her back, striking one match after another and watching them slowly burn out.

With the weight of the day's heat upon us, we came to another town fixed in a drifting haze of dust. Undaunted by the glare or the squared mud buildings set tight against each other, the driver accelerated through a narrow street and swung into the bus yard. In the final seconds he stood and pulled to a stop as if reining in a stubborn monster.

The passengers moved slowly, stretching and lingering over daydreams of drowsy half-sleep, not sure the effort and disruption were worth a few minutes in the cool station house. I longed for a drink other than warm metallic water. With a slow drop of Murine in each eye, I was ready to stand. Pat sat unmoved in her glassy stare of a smile, while Darlene adjusted her orange head scarf and looked this way and that to see what was happening. Victoria awoke, cranky that the bus had stopped and the people were moving. Gruber took refreshment orders and began to organize the ten yards to the station house.

Neither heat of day, nor distance traveled, nor moments shared, changed any of us from her central self. Well, almost. An odd little thing happened as we shook off sleep. I noticed it, as I'm sure the others did. Gruber reached into her pack and slowly pulled out a long, long piece of white cloth. She knew we were watching.

"It's OK, you guys, no big thing."

"What is that?"

"It's my new turban. See...really long and soft, just right for a turban."

"Where did you get it?"

"No min' ya," she brushed off the question. "It's too late to change anything now."

"Gruber! Is that what I think it is?" The long cloth looked a lot like a bed sheet.

"It's not just for me, you know. I'm going to share it with you guys." She held up the cloth, picked a point and tore it lengthwise.

"You actually stole a sheet?"

"Where did you get it?"

"It's not a sheet anymore. And it's just from that horrid campement."

"Horrid or not, why did you take it?"

"It wasn't really stealing, more like taking a souvenir. Here, who wants this piece?" Gruber held up half the sheet.

Now we did look at each other. Who would become an accomplice? After a long moment, Pat shrugged and put out her hand.

"Well it's already here and I wasn't the one who stole it. There's no point in having it go to waste," she rationalized. But she kept her eyes cast to the side as she said it.

One of the nagging frustrations of trying to function in a foreign language or a foreign culture is the difficulty one has understanding the small, everyday things a native takes for granted. While the big concepts are discussed in wonderful long, detailed sentences, everyday business is often conducted with a grunt or a nod. The short-cuts, the gestures, the subtleties that would tell us about a person's intentions or character make up the missing signal, the static-garbled message. There is the lingering discomfort of not completely understanding. Perhaps this is why many people think of travel as tiring, why there is such a relief to come home.

We faced one of many such moments at the rest stop. How long would we be there? How far to the next one?

We had very little water remaining in our bottles. I asked the driver if there was a place where I could get some drinking water. His face did not show great comprehension.

"Eau potable?" I repeated, holding up an empty bottle. He nodded and signaled in a vague way to a house in a junkyard outside the courtyard, out of sight but not too far. Our driver was amiable, even rather flamboyant. But when it came to specifics, I never felt I really understood.

I was uneasy about losing sight of the bus. We took our cues from the other passengers, who had relaxed in pockets of shade with no sign of concern about a sudden departure. Victoria and I would go for the water, while the others would see to it that we were not left behind.

"Aloo! Personne ici?" Among the odds and ends of machinery in a miniature junk yard we came across a small building that looked not at all like a house, not even the low mud types to which we had become accustomed. It was very small. An average-sized person could put her hand on the roof. It had sloping mud walls and a low narrow doorway. Even among mud buildings, it was crudely built. Across the doorway, flapping aimlessly, a faded striped cloth stretched to cover the opening. Close to the entrance, it smelled like a house.

"Personne ici?" Anybody here? I tried again, pleased that I had done it with such a convincing French lilt. *"Personne..."*

"Bonjour, bonjour," called an excited voice from far inside. In a moment the curtain was pulled back by a very short French woman who smiled a lot. With a sweep of her arm and a small bow, she welcomed us inside. She was more than fifty years old, with graying dark hair of tight curls as from an unset permanent. She didn't say a word until she had seated us on a

dusty pale green mohair sofa and pulled up a straight-backed wooden chair for herself. She folded her rough plump hands over an apron that covered an indefinite waist and finally addressed us in a mixture of kindness and anxiety.

"*Ah, oui, mademoiselles?*"

With that great encompassing question/statement she treated our sudden appearance as nothing out of the ordinary.

"*Ah...oui...bonjour, madame. Ah...*" My first words broke to a small nervous laugh.

"*Nous sommes américaines.*"

"Aah. But you speak French."

"A little."

"We are traveling on the bus to Agadez."

"*Oui.*" She nodded.

"And, please, we need water to drink," I said, holding up two empty bottles.

"*Ah! Oui, oui, oui,* of course." She took the bottles and bolted out behind another faded door cloth into another room.

Victoria and I sat silently on the mohair sofa, feeling like giants in a doll house.

"Fifteen years we have been here," *madame* began when she returned with a tray of drinks, but without our bottles. "Not always in this house. My husband is Spanish. At first we moved often. *Monsieur* is an engineer, of roads. And roads do not stay in one place so people can live civilized."

"*Vraiment* (truly)," I nodded. My responses weren't always appropriate, just the sound that slipped out.

"I tried to keep my children. For a few years it was not bad, moving and teaching them myself. But children must go to school. They must know their own country and civilized ways."

Victoria smiled and looked at her watch.

"Are these your children?" I asked, pointing to the many pictures in lacy gilt frames.

"This one, and that. The others are my grandchildren. Already I have three."

"*Madame,* we are *en route* to Zinder and then to Agadez, we cannot be late for the bus."

"God willing, we will see them in the summer." She was not ready to release us.

"Is your husband working far from here?"

"I believe it is quite far. He has been gone for four months this time. I used to go with him everywhere but I am too old now." Her constant smile turned sad and distant. "It is for women to wait and worry, is it not?"

"Perhaps, I don't know," I said, but I didn't mean it. To myself I said, not for me. Not this giving up. I could not bear it.

"Of course, you don't know. You are young. Your life has not been written."

"*Madame*, please, our bottles..." We had to go.

I saw the melancholy that passed over her eyes, the flash of long-past times, the terrible sense of loss in the sigh that accompanied her glance at the photographs, the fragility of being forever a foreigner. I understood a little, but it frightened me.

We stood.

"*Ah, oui*, your bottles." She smiled and brought them to us filled with water.

"Many thanks for your generous hospitality."

"*Bon voyage*," she shook each of our hands, "*bon chance*."

"*Merci, madame. Au revoir.*"

3

A Grain of Sand

The only ties now were those among the five of us. We rode for several hours out of Zinder without speaking. Contained in our island *camion*, we savored our independence. We felt vital, whole, strong. We had done it, were doing it. We were crossing the great Sahara Desert because we wanted to. We had come so far, with the help of many others to be sure. But at that moment, on the top of the *camion*, over the infamous, indeterminate *piste*, we felt the great power of having done it ourselves and we relished it.

This was the *piste*, seen and felt, but ever eluding definition. It seemed to be anything as long as it was less than a road. It varied from bone-rattling rocks to frighteningly soft sand. At best it bore the imprint of tires of previous travelers—a lifeline stretching to infinity, before and behind. But when the marks in the dust have been blown off by the wind, the *piste* is a wish, a hope, is nothing.

The other passengers were two men; one an Arab the color of sand, the other black, but Arabic-speaking. Both were turbaned and bare-footed. The dark one, never without his worn brown overcoat, was the driver's assistant, the "greaser," as they were called. Whenever the *camion* began to slow down he was over the side, running along to see to any problem. When a wheel spun in sand, it was he who dashed forward to shovel a slope in which to wedge an iron grate.

These grates hung from both sides of the *camion*. Each was about two feet wide and ten feet long, heavy enough to support the weight of the vehicle while providing traction. The greaser laid several grates in a row. Once the tire caught hold of one grate and passed over it, he picked it up, ran in front of the slowly moving *camion*, and threw it down again to extend the track. Where the earth was soft for a long distance and the driver could not find a space firm enough to stop, the greaser collected driven-over grates, ran to catch up with the *camion*, and hung the grates on their racks while the *camion* continued to move slowly ahead. The other passenger, although he did not handle the iron grates, shared in other chores and in the maintenance of the vehicle.

The *camion* lumbered on, guided by the watchful driver. We knew about the danger of soft spots. They could appear anywhere along the ever-changing and uncharted *piste*. A slight miscalculation or mishandling could overturn the truck. Decisions had to be quick, maneuvers deft. Both the driver and the greaser respected the perils of the desert.

It did occur to me that we ought to have been frightened by the looks of these tough, leathered truckers. At home, in a similar situation, we could have easily expected to be propositioned and embarrassed by a lot of macho posturing. But at home there would not have been a similar situation. We would never have felt as free and as safe. Despite their rough looks, the men on the *camion* were restrained and gentle, facing serious and frustrating work with patience and quiet voices. We didn't understand a lot of what they said, nor did we know what they thought of us. But they treated us as equal adults, and we countered by taking care of ourselves.

The bubble of invincibility which had enveloped us on our bumpy perch at the top of the world thinned with the falling sun and burst on a rising wind. Pat tied the hood of her yellow sweatshirt tightly under her chin. I rewrapped my turban to leave only my eyes exposed. We divided the blankets and snuggled down below the sides of the load. The wind would curl over our little cavity, we thought, and we would weather the chill.

Instead, the temperature dropped even more. The wind swelled without a pause. We huddled together and stacked the blankets over us. It was not enough. The *camion* seemed to be moving faster. The wind whipped from every side and from beneath, through the cargo. My feet grew numb. The tarp, stiff from cold, emphasized the angular shapes under it. Its texture turned abrasive. Night fell. We raced onward. The speed of the truck and the bombardment of wind and sand took our breath away.

Why did the driver not stop? Didn't he know what was happening to us? Didn't he care? When would we eat? It was madness to charge on headlong like this. The world swirled out of control as we burrowed under the blankets, unable to talk, unable to move, unable to see.

The *camion* stopped, abruptly, mercifully. It was over. We had not been catapulted off the edge of the earth after all. We staggered into the *campement* at Tanout, dragging our stiffened selves, blankets and baskets. The shelter was basic, iron beds, mud walls, crumbling whitewash. It didn't matter. After a drink of water and a little food, we slept, as we were, unchanged, unwashed, soundly, where the wind could not reach us.

In the morning sun we warmed ourselves slowly. The old *gardien* brought a pitcher of washing water and hot coffee. Eighty cents each for the bed and breakfast. Gruber was the first on top of the truck. The rest of us made a few trips, hauling and arranging things and just for the fun of going up and down.

A crowd of children danced about. Beggars, the blind and crippled, reached out for alms. Through it all Gruber did not budge. She was securing her territory, not giving anyone a chance to do her out of it. I finally realized what was happening, but not until the *camion* was about to pull away and I found myself the last one standing on the ground, left to ride in the cab.

The cab was stuffy and confining, boring after riding on top. But the windshield made it possible to look directly toward the horizon. I could follow the gas gauge or watch the speedometer. Now and then I converted kilometers-per-hour to miles-per-hour in my head. I chatted a little with the driver in French, though it meant shouting to be heard over the roar of the vehicle. Throughout the day we moved steadily at 35-45 kilometers per hour (22-28 MPH).

The route from Zinder to Agadez was well known and regularly traveled, as flat and constant and fascinating a landscape as any 300 miles can be. This is the great wonder of the desert. At first it appears empty, fixed, lifeless. Nothing more. Hour after rumbling hour the horizon holds firm. We will never reach that line at the edge of the earth which is as far away as it has been. But closer there are rocks which we do reach and pass. And twisted acacia, brittle bushes of wild thyme and mint. Scattered across the land, these seem of no consequence to us, but the desert people know them and how to feed them to their animals or cook them in their tea.

At one particularly long stretch I sat back in the cab and allowed a lovely lake mirage full play. Only my mind knew it was a mirage. My eyes saw glistening water, the hint of a forest on its far right bank and a black post the size of a road marker on the left. When I tired of staring at this rippling scene out of that window, I closed my eyes to wipe it away and started anew to fix my attention to a place on the other side of the truck.

It only took a moment for the water to sparkle on the horizon. This time the background took the shape of clouds instead of trees, but the black post was unquestionably a black post. With the mirage shifted to the left, the post now stood at its right.

I watched that post for perhaps half an hour until the bottom of it appeared wider than the top. I even imagined that it moved. It did move! A teen-aged boy, wrapped and turbaned in blue-black cloth, walked steadily on until his path met ours.

He brought a skin of goat's milk to trade for a bag of salt. With an exchange of friendly greetings and gentle joking, he and the driver completed the trade. We drove off and the boy turned to walk in the direction from which he had come. In all the time I watched him on the horizon, he was alone. There was no camp, no animal, no other person in sight.

Our colors atop the *camion* announced our coming. At Tuareg camps the women and children, unrestrained in their curiosity, climbed the sides of the truck, peered and laughed. We looked them over in return and commented openly in English.

"Look at her hands and neck. They're blue from the dye of their cloth."

"Just like the magazine said."

They admired our jewelry, pointed to a ring or watch and asked for it. The women touched our hair, freely talking about us in their language as we did about them in ours.

"What a great face!"

"They do have marvelous fine bones."

We smiled broadly at each other. Later we would be advised that it was important to smile and laugh a lot when dealing with the Tuareg. But we did it then because we couldn't resist.

"I don't see any fat ones."

"Hey, what is she doing!" Darlene cried as a young woman pulled at her arm, nodding and grinning with approval.

"She likes you."

"I think she wants to take you."

"What do you think we can get if we trade Darlene?"

"At least a camel."

Darlene didn't think any of this was funny.

"I knew it was a mistake to ride up here," she said as she shrank back into our canvas pit. She never voluntarily rode on top again.

One might expect hours and days of such a journey to be tedious, but the opposite is the case. A dun-colored fluttering in the distance becomes a herd of bounding gazelle. I watch a line far to the left grow to a caravan as we gain on it. The camels bob and sway against the western horizon. We run parallel for a few minutes before leaving the caravan to its pace and time. I later learn that a pack camel in caravan travels at about two miles per hour. The lumbering *camion*, by comparison, travels ten times as fast—a blinding speed.

The sweep of sun itself is compelling, passing over the earth from grey dawn to rose to gold to blinding white to apricot to burnt orange to beige of evening. The earth, the rocks, the thorny shrubs lie low and monotonous, gradations of a mass, prostrate under the power of the sun. Thus, neither the light nor the land can be called the name of one shade, moving as they do in endless mutation from one to another. Only Victoria's red blanket poncho, Pat's yellow sweatshirt, Gruber's blue and gold Mandingo robe, Darlene's orange scarf, and the flutter of dazzling white, pink and blue turbans punctuated the monochromatic pallet of the desert.

In the morning, before the world had passed from rose to gold, we discovered a wreck by the side of the road. An oil tanker had broken from its cab and overturned. It was a clean break, no oil spill, no fire, no mangled metal. We saw nothing in this bare, flat space to account for the force that had jack-knifed and flipped it. Such was the treachery of soft sand.

We passed with care. The cab of the oil rig innocently faced the road, a large plain "D" painted on its roof. This was the rig Stanley had hoped to ride. We took a picture to show him.

By and by we came to the wells of Takoukout, *l'eau douce* (sweet water) of Eliki and Tchin-Garargen, *l'eau bonne* (good water) of Tadelaka, Aderbissinat, and Timboulaga. The Michelin map told us which wells had sweet water, good water, or water that was not potable. Those that had been improved by the French had concrete rims and pumps. Water could be drawn out of them most of the year. They attracted many more people and animals than could have been supported by hand-dug wells subject to long periodic dry seasons.

The French wells changed the patterns of migration and the ecology of fragile scrub grasslands around them. Some wells welcomed travelers, some marked the seasonal camps of the Tuareg, others nurtured small settlements. In every case, the place was the well, and the name of the place was the name of the well.

At one especially fine well, walled with a broad concrete platform, we counted more than a hundred head of blue-black longhorn cattle drinking from a concrete trough. A score of white goats nudged for places among them. The driver sat for a while on the rim of the well visiting with the owner of the animals.

What did they talk about? The price of goats? The water level? The five white women staring at them from the *camion*? They smiled amiably and nodded, neither of them ever looking at a watch.

The sun moved to gold, warmed us, and reddened our faces, feet, and hands. We passed around the *crème* and eye drops. With Gruber having had her turn at the top of the truck, we rotated without much to-do. Despite a steep rise in the temperature, we kept on the many layers of clothes which protected us against sunburn and dehydration. Throughout the day the wind never rested. It varied from gentle to forceful but never stopped, never let us forget the experience of the previous night.

This is where it begins, I thought, as the sandy haze enveloped us on the second day atop M. Joyce's *camion*. The Harmattan rose out of the desert with a force that carried sand and dust more than a thousand miles south to the Atlantic. This was the season—the months of winter—of Harmattan. Days of unrelenting wind, of unabated discomfort. The noise of wind and *camion* grew oppressive. We could not read, or write, or have a conversation. We tried to protect ourselves with a low tent made by tying a blanket to the guy wires. The tent helped to shield us from blown sand, but it was only about two feet high, and, in addition to turning the little pocket underneath into an oven, it required us to lie flat and still so as not to dislodge it. I felt so confined and uncomfortable under the tent, I preferred to take my chances outside, with the wind.

As I settled myself in the open, a sudden dust-devil churned a spout of sand into my face, straight into my eyes, nostrils, mouth, and hair. I spit out what I could and lowered my head to try to shake it out of my hair so that it would not blow back. Impossible. My eyes closed and filled with water. I felt my way back under the tent.

The little pocket of air in which we huddled grew stale and heavy. There was something in my eye. I couldn't pinpoint it. The whole eye and the underside of the lid were sharply painful. As luck would have it, Victoria was next to me in the tent— Victoria, who froze at the thought of pain and was repulsed by any bodily wounds or imperfections. Nevertheless, she agreed to look at my eye, but could not see well enough in the dim light under the blanket. I tried to lie very still, to avoid moving my eye, to not touch. It did not get better. I needed to sit upright, if not to directly relieve my eye, at least to give myself a sense of greater control. This meant going down into the cab.

At the first lull in the wind, we instituted the system we had devised for communicating with the driver. Soon after leaving Zinder, we had discovered that shouting or pounding on the roof of the cab was ineffective. Any racket we could make was lost in the rumbling of the *camion* and carried off in the wind. The only way to get the driver's attention was to catch his eye. While the truck roared ahead into the wind, I climbed out onto the baggage at the front and hung head-down so my arms reached to the side window of the cab. It was my method, and I did it even now because Victoria and Gruber were afraid. They did, however, hold my feet.

I took Pat's place in the cab. In the rear view mirror I saw that a large grain of sand was embedded in my left eye, in the exact center of the pupil. This one white speck, implanted as if on target in the center of the blackest part of the eye, now loomed larger than all the rest of the desert.

We reached Agadez late in the day. The driver cruised the streets slowly, so that by the time we pulled up at M. Joyce's store, quite a crowd had formed.

"Can you believe this?"

"Where did they all come from?"

The people smiled and cheered as we alighted, greatly amused by our arrival. They approved of Victoria's blue eyes and the bright colors of our clothing.

"Hang on to your stuff."

"Is this how Tecumsah felt when they put him on display in London?" Pat wryly observed through her green tinted glasses. But she continued to smile, as we all did.

There were murmurs and nods of astonishment when we carried our own baggage. The people congratulated the driver, who beamed as if he were the father of the bride.

By this time my left eye was swollen shut. I worried about communicating. The bulk of translation had fallen to me, and I simply did not hear French well enough. Lip reading and eye contact would be impaired with only one useful eye. All of this was on my mind as we met the edge of evening in front of M. Joyce's store.

The young woman who managed the store turned out to be M. Joyce's daughter. With her help, word of our arrival was sent to the priest, who, her father had assured us, had guest rooms we might use. We paid the driver as arranged, $10 each in West African *francs*.

The *camion* drove off, the store closed. As night fell, the crowd dispersed until we were left nearly alone, sitting on our heap of belongings, growing cold.

With a flash of headlights and dust across the square, a small open Jeep sped to a stop before us. A fiftyish man of stocky build and wiry grey hair stomped out. He paced back and forth between the Jeep and us, and again around the Jeep and around us. He gruffly mumbled in a harsh-sounding French something about a mistake. A terrible mistake, and what was he to do?

"There are no rooms," he said.

"But M. Joyce told us! Here is his letter to you," I protested.

"Ach!" He brushed the letter away. He did not need letters.

It was always hard for me to communicate in French with someone who was impatient. And as the priest paced about, muttering and angry, I found it even harder to understand him, or to respond quickly enough.

Victoria sat very still on the edge of her suitcase, staring straight ahead, rocking ever so slightly, as she did when she was very tired.

"Do you speak English?" I tried. No answer.

Two days of being jostled on the truck and battered by the wind had drained even the reserve of excitement we were usually able to draw upon when coming to a new place.

I explained to the others what I thought I had understood him to say. We were too weary to be upset. Even Darlene rallied and put aside hysteria to discuss this latest predicament in a quiet voice.

The priest scratched his head and paced in frustration.

"*Sprichen sie Deutsch?*" he sputtered, his eyes darting from one of us to the other.

What was that? We were caught off guard.

"*Sprechen sie Deutsch?*" he asked again.

"*Ja, ja,*" popped up Pat with awakened enthusiasm. But after realizing how misleading her enthusiasm might be, she added "a little."

From then on he spoke only to Pat, though never looking directly at her or at any of us. He used an impossible mix of hard-edged French and lightning-fast German, disregarding the fact that she hardly understood him. It was just the way he talked.

"There is a terrible mistake. I don't know what's to be done," he said, throwing up his arms and turning to his Jeep.

"No, no, don't let him go!" Gruber hopped about excitedly.

"*Monsieur, monsieur,* wait! Somebody tell him about Jerrie's eye. Look, look," she shouted over the sound of the unmuffled Jeep, pulling him toward me and pointing to the inflamed, swollen-shut left lid. The word for eye was not easy for us to say in French, and the more excited Gruber got, the less clear was her pronunciation.

"*Sic hat etwas in die augen!*" Pat blurted out.

"What did she say?" asked Darlene.

"Beats me."

The priest glared at her.

"Oh God, I hope I said it right." Pat planted herself firmly in the path of the priest. "I said," she explained without flinching, "'she has something in her eye.' At least I hope I said that."

He looked closer and nodded that he got the idea. He would keep us for the night, and we would go to a doctor.

"But it is only for this one night," making the point sternly with his finger in the air.

"What about the doctor?" Gruber continued.

"*Demain, mademoiselles,*" he said.

"When, when?" Gruber persisted.

"Tomorrow morning," he assured her.

"OK you guys, you heard him, tomorrow morning," she repeated.

With the wave of his arm, we picked up our things and moved toward his vehicle like robots. There were too many things. Too many of us. He'll realize that. We should split up, I thought, make two trips. But my thought was slow and never made it to words. He meant us all to go at once. So, sitting on each other, standing, holding onto suitcases slung over the side, and altogether clinging to that Jeep for our lives, we raced through the dusty night of Agadez to...to wherever it was we were going.

We sped through town and out the other side a short distance to a cluster of low buildings. We called it a mission, but the priest insisted it was not. He opened the door to a small dark room and said he would return.

He drove away, taking the light and noise of his Jeep with him. We were left enveloped in sudden darkness and welcome silence.

Even in the dark, we could sense the room had not been used in a long time. The essence of dust that pervaded the stale air warned us to move carefully so as to not stir it. With Gruber's flashlight we saw a small room divided in half by a post and rail partition about three feet high which ran from the far wall about three-fourths of the way across the room. On the near side of the rail was a low narrow bed, strung with a sagging wire spring and no mattress. A small bedside table stood near the door.

Pat and Darlene pulled back a part of an old gate that leaned against another narrow steel bed. This one had a pad, too thin to be called a mattress. They tried to be careful, but every move stirred more dust. In no time the room became hazy. They took the pad off the second bed so that someone could have it on the floor.

"I think Jer ought to get a bed tonight," Gruber said. "She's the one with the problem."

Even though we shared the obvious things, there was still plenty of jockeying for small advantages. Gruber had followed each one's movements and spoke up to avert what she antici-pated would be selfish positions. I appreciated her looking after me.

"Thanks," I answered. "I don't want a bed. Those springs make me seasick." It was true. My eye ached and my ears rang from the day-long howling of the wind. I longed to sleep on something firm and unmoving. I dragged a straw mat to an empty spot between the bed Darlene would use and the door and slowly unfolded my blankets. In the yellow glow of the flashlight, I watched the others arrange themselves. We were hungry. But were we more hungry than tired? That was the question. Everyone seemed to move so slowly, even to think slowly.

"Shh. Do you guys hear anything?"

We listened.

"I can't tell if it's anything more than the wind."

"Should we open the door?"

"Are you kidding!"

The knock was gentle, but clear and repeated. As Pat went to answer it, Gruber focused her light on the opening. A small dark man holding a large box tentatively stepped inside.

"With the compliments of M. Joyce," he said, handing the box to Pat and leaving.

We were stunned. The box contained oranges, *pâté*, canned foods, cartons of English cookies, a long *baguette* of fresh bread, and two bottles of red wine.

"How really thoughtful," Victoria managed to say as we examined our gift.

Within minutes there was another knock at the door. This time a single thud pushed it open. The priest stood with a lantern and a steaming bowl of food. He handed the bowl to

Pat, who was about to protest that it was far too much for her when he swept his arm out to indicate the food was for all of us.

"Do you think that's all we're going to get?" asked Darlene, as if the priest were not standing a few feet from her.

"*Merci*," Pat remembered to tell him, ignoring Darlene. Then she repeated herself in German until it finally sounded sincere.

"*Oui, merci*," the rest of us added.

The priest continued to stand in the doorway after we had run out of thanks and nods. How could we talk to him, catch his darting eyes? His French was too difficult for us. It was up to Pat.

He handed her a small bottle, nodded toward my eye, and rattled on in German. Pat had a bookish knowledge of German, which she hadn't used in years. She was lost.

"I think it's weird the way he's so brusque," noted Darlene.

"He looks so uncomfortable."

"Oh man, you guys, we're the weird ones. Five of us, dropping in from nowhere."

"What's in the bottle?" I asked.

"Eyedrops."

"I know that," I sighed. "What kind of eyedrops?"

"Ah, come on, Jer, what difference does it make?"

"I just like to know what I'm using." It was not a protest, only words to assure myself that I was awake and not dreaming. I managed to get a few drops into my eye, and many more down my cheek.

"*Merci beaucoup, monsieur*." I did not know what to call this priest in French, since he acted so unlike a traditional "father." He did not seem to care what we called him, but abruptly took his eyedrops, wished us good sleep, and left.

"What's the food?"

"Seems to be a stew. I think I see some big chunks, like potatoes," Pat reported. She was guessing. She looked closely and stirred the bowl. The kerosene lantern provided barely a flicker of light.

"Would you believe a lamp could be so dim?"

It was not a question, just another groggy sigh, much like

inquiring about the taste of the food, or the contents of the bottle.

"I don't see any meat, but it tastes a little like ham or bacon."

"Pass it over here."

"What I'd give for a pressure lamp."

"There's some rice in it, too."

"That's not rice, it's couscous."

And so it went, each of us setting forth an expert opinion, like the blindfolded wise women called upon to identify the elephant, each on precious little evidence.

"I swear, I can't see a thing." My space by the door was farthest from the lamp. When the bowl came to me, a little sauce ran off the spoon and down the outside of the bowl.

"Oh damn." I blamed that one on impaired depth perception. But really, I was just tired. And hungry. But more tired than hungry. I allowed myself only a few sips of orange sweetened water to wash down two APCs to cut the pain of my eye. I did not want to think of searching for a toilet before morning.

The conversation drifted on, becoming more sparse, less coherent. I don't know when it ceased, or who put out the lantern. I closed my good eye as Gruber prepared a place on the floor, curled in the corner with her beloved pack as a pillow. Victoria lay straight on her back on the thin bed pad. Carolyn's wool blanket, in which I wrapped myself, protected my legs from the concrete floor. The wind shifted. The draft from under the door stopped.

I awoke confused about where I was, but did not move or open my eyes. The blanket cocoon in which I'd gone to sleep was still wrapped tight. I concentrated on the sounds in the room to orient me. I knew them well. The voices. The flopping of Darlene's slippers as she shuffled about.

Our room at Lott Carey appeared whole in my mind.

Too dry and cold for there.

The sound of a little water poured into a basin.

The Buffet Hôtel?

No mosquitoes. Without them it could not be Ouagadougou.

I should open my eyes. Too hard. Must wait.

Pat began, or was she in the midst of telling a story. I listened carefully.

"I was so intrigued by his German and his mysterious manner," she said, "I had to find out more about him and what he's doing here."

She had gone out to find the priest before anyone else was awake. He took breakfast at a small table outdoors behind his room. She had spent part of the night preparing for the meeting, dusting off the back rooms of her memory in search of what she had once known of German.

He had been more kindly disposed to Pat, knowing she spoke his language. He offered coffee and hot milk and spoke of the old days. It was a vague remembrance, of a time "before the war" without dates or names. For Pat, as for all of us born in the forties, the war was World War II. Before that, we had heard from our parents, was the Depression, and before that the Dark Ages of our parents' childhood. Their childhood was also his, and it was of that time he told, of the blissful distant time when he was young and his world was whole and German.

He was born in Alsace, that place we casually hyphenated with Lorraine and knew to be contested and traded repeatedly over the centuries between France and Germany. He corrected Pat when she used the combined name. For him it was quite specifically and solely Alsace. As to whether it was French or German, he was not as sure.

"We had both been staring out over our coffee cups into the desert," Pat continued, "when I realized that he would begin to repeat himself and glance at me as if to say 'now where was I?' or 'who are you?'"

Someone poured more water. Darlene picked up her restless pace. I knew where I was—on the concrete floor of a dusty room in Agadez. Why were my knees warm while the rest of me felt so cold? I couldn't open my eyes. I wanted to sleep and be warm. Instead, I was stiff and cold. I concentrated on Pat's story.

Alsace went to France in 1919, Pat reminded us, before the priest was grown, but well after his language and identity were clearly and immutably German. With the political change, he became an alien in his own land. Later there was an occupation, by the German enemy, who were his ancient cousins returned to restore their language and their power. It confused this boy, growing up not sure who he was. Years of hiding and testing his identity, of surviving by not revealing anything which might compromise him took their toll.

He came to his middle age with a studied craftiness metamorphosed to a sad and frightening disorientation. His eyes darted in search of friend or foe. But now he could not tell one from the other, could not trust himself to distinguish, could not trust.

How much of this was his telling and how much Pat's interpretation, we did not know. It was an intriguing story, and everything she said rang true enough to be an "explanation" of his odd manner.

"Do you think he was a Nazi?"

"How did he get to be a priest, if that's what he really is?"

"How long has he been in Agadez?"

"I don't know any of that," Pat admitted. "As soon as I asked how long he'd been here, he said 'a while' and ended the discussion."

"Just like that?"

"That was it." She sighed. "Just when I thought he was a little more relaxed, he shut up completely, stuck this pot of tea in my hands and waved me away."

My right eye slowly opened to a hot shaft of light cutting across the room from the little window. The left would not budge. It had oozed in the night and now was sealed shut and adhered to a stiff blotch on my sleeve. I carefully pried it free and lightly touched it with my finger. It was swollen and encrusted.

"Let's go, Markos," Pat pulled at my shoes, "last call for breakfast."

I propped up on one elbow. The beam of sun passing over my legs saturated the dark grey wool blanket and explained my warm knees. The rest of me shivered in the shadows, and I did not want to move.

"How's your eye?" Darlene inquired.

"How does it look?" I asked.

"Red. Swollen," interrupted Gruber. "Does it hurt?"

"Sure."

"Gee, maybe you won't be able to go on."

Darlene said it. The thought had just occurred to her. The rest of us had understood that possibility for nearly a day.

"And then there were four," Pat added, taking advantage of the opportunity Darlene had opened.

It was not an idea I wanted to become established. I ate what was left of the bread from M. Joyce's surprise package —a quarter of a loaf spread with jam, now so dry it crunched when I bit it.

"Gee, Jer, you're really a sight." Darlene had her way with words.

"Hey, you guys, I don't think it's fair to pick on Jerrie." Gruber stepped in again to my defense. "Think of all the good she's done for us. All those times she has to translate. That's a big responsibility."

"Oh stop! I'm not dead yet."

My right eye watched Victoria methodically washing herself. She had filled a basin from a pitcher of water. While the rest of us felt and looked as if we had been in the desert for two days, Victoria's skin gleamed fresh and rosy. Her fair hair, dampened and combed down, began to spring into its soft curls.

"You better get moving," Pat said. "The priest will take you to a doctor this morning."

"Do you know what kind of a doctor it is?" I asked.

"French. He has a clinic," she replied.

"Has anybody found the bathroom yet?" I asked, unwinding my blankets.

"It's a flush and run, out back."

I rewrapped my turban and reached for my dark glasses.

"It's just around the building, not across town," Pat commented.

"I don't want to scare anyone."

When I returned, there was less than half a cup of water left in the pitcher. The price of Victoria's cleanliness. I rinsed my eye, brushed my teeth and carefully wrapped the turban across my face.

The priest drove like a madman. We heard the Jeep well before it screeched to a stop at our door. It had no muffler and made a great racket even over the wind. I got in behind Pat and, squinting through swirling sand, held on as we careened through a maze of nameless narrow streets.

On the outskirts of town, the long low earthen French clinic rose out of the haze on a knoll above the road. We ascended a series of wind-swept terraces, making our way among others who waited. Dozens of patients filled the broad steps and landings, waiting to be touched by healing hands.

How could they stand it? I'd had enough of the damn wind that scratched my skin, tore at my clothes, stole my breath, and blew a grain of sand in my eye.

Yet they waited. A leg wrapped in a wooden splint, a spastic cough, an open sore, faces that neither smiled nor scowled. Only an infant squealed its misery and was put quiet at a breast. The young men leaned against a low wall, the old squatted beside their baskets. The women stood or sat, as ever with their perfectly straight backs, their heads up. They wrapped themselves and their young against the wind but did not cower from it.

I walked on through an illusion bathed in dusty rose haze, two-dimensional and filtered through the tearing of one eye. Apparitions lined the terraces, weightless sentinels, their edges blurred. So many people exposed to the dust-stirring tempest which engulfed us. So many poised with patience in this surreal still-life. Was I an apparition, too?

I hesitated, rewrapping my turban, clutching the lapa around my shoulders to break the wind.

Seen through only one eye, the world was flat. I stumbled along not sure how deep the steps were, or how far it was across a terrace. I hesitated and began to turn back.

"Pat," I shouted, "I've only got a piece of sand in my eye."

"Sure, sure. And you don't really want to cross the desert, do you?" Pat turned me toward the clinic.

A film of bleached dust, like rose-colored snowfall, covered everything. Flies harassed without mercy and drank at every eye, nostril and mouth. Those who could see stared at us. How could any place on earth be so desolate?

"Shouldn't we at least wait our turn?" I held back.

Pat was as uncomfortable as I about going to the front of the line. Risking the wrath of the priest, she told him in German that we would not mind waiting.

Even as she said it, I knew I would mind. I would mind very much being lashed for hours by the sand-ladened air. I would mind.

Her words and our feelings were of as much consequence as the wind. The priest stormed forward, ignoring everyone. He charged up toward the clinic, leaving us to make our way through the crowd of waiting patients. I clung to Pat, whose two eyes guided us.

Before we reached the second level, the priest returned with the French doctor. Wind whipped at his khaki shirt and deepened the furrows in his face. Our introduction was brief, wordless, a nod of the head, a quick handshake.

The doctor led us up to the clinic, to an inner room which was cold but miraculously quiet. How I was growing to hate the wind!

The doctor was a small thin man, fortyish, a major in the army. His manner was curt, expressionless, but not unkind. He moved with his head down, not catching anyone's eye. His angular gestures had an air of formality about them. Was that the military influence, or uncertainty? We had enough time to ask a lot of questions to ourselves. Why was he in Agadez? Was it a punishment, a reflection of his competence, or merely an unlucky draw of duty?

"*Voilà, mademoiselle.*" He held open my eye so that I could see it in a mirror.

There was no speck of sand. It had washed away in the night, leaving the pupil black and smooth. I was deeply embarrassed. I had taken his time away from those who were truly sick for a non-existent speck. I wanted to run.

Instead, he took more time to give me a bottle of eyedrops,

instructions to stay out of the wind, and to assure me that the swelling would go down in a day. It was not the importance of my ailment, but my self that merited this attention. I stumbled out past the scores of silent, waiting faces, not catching anyone's eye.

4

Agadez Welcomes You

It was time to choose whom we were to trust, in whose protection would we put ourselves so we would have the greatest probability of continuing across the desert.

As we packed our bags in the room the German priest had lent us, we knew the decision could not be put off. During our life and travels in Africa we had learned a little about how things were done. We had come to Agadez as any native person might, overland, mile after grueling mile. In the process, our bodies grew accustomed to dry air, dust, and the extreme changes in temperature that occurred each day. We acquired the pace, the gestures, of ordinary life.

Agadez was a tough place, people had told us, not known for coddling inhabitants or travelers. An ancient trade center and link in the trans-Saharan caravan routes, it was populated by diverse peoples who tolerated each other but never abandoned their historic rivalries and suspicions.

Nigerien nationals, mostly Blacks, held positions in the civil service and police. The Tuareg, whose capital Agadez had been throughout the collective memory of their oral history, recognized no national boundaries. It was in Agadez, their songs and poems recall, that they besieged the French garrison in their short-lived, last triumph as warrior-bandits of the southern desert. They used this oasis to rest and trade, a periodic homing on their nomadic circuit. The Arabs kept shops, and, more importantly for us, drove the *camions*. The French military kept a garrison in a conspicuous but low-keyed presence. A number of French civilians remained after independence to continue operating their shops, restaurants, and two hotels.

We could not afford to alienate any upon whom we might come to depend for our lives or well-being. Yet we had to choose. Each of them, except the Tuareg, who had no particular interest in us beyond the curiosity we had for them, would have a part to play and a unique importance. But only one person controlled the traffic between oases.

"I would not go to him if I were you," the priest had said without further explanation when we asked for the directions to the office of the commissioner of police. "Are you sure you would not prefer to go to a hotel?"

The commissioner of police was Aboubakar, cousin of the chief of police in Niamey, from whom we carried a personal letter of introduction.

He received us in a cavernous office that dwarfed his desk and the few chairs set in a perfect row along one side. A detailed topographical map of the vast territory under his jurisdiction covered almost all of the once whitewashed wall behind him. The volume of space, the sparse furnishings, the uniformed guards framing each door gave our reception the aura of a state event.

Aboubakar himself was an average-sized black man in pressed khaki. He had a pleasant face, watchful yet confident. He stood and shook each of our hands.

"*Nous sommes cinq,*" I began, knowing very well that he could see that for himself. I introduced each of us, giving my prepared correct sentences that told we were Americans, Peace Corps teachers in Liberia, on a journey to Algiers. I watched his face as I spoke, looking for clues. I prayed that he would respond in simple, clear phrases that I would understand.

Would he laugh at the sight of us, weary and dirty, so obviously without resources or friends? Would he be angry that we had come unannounced to disturb his day with our problems?

Would he be indifferent or mislead us?

We five were not nervous about the encounter. Perhaps we were too tired or too confident ourselves. But a flood of questions flowed through my mind, reminding me how much depended upon the moment we had to assess one another.

"We are on our way to Algiers. We need to arrange a ride on a truck to Tamanrasset," I continued. "We also need a place to stay until we leave Agadez. We prefer a *campement*, if there is one. We understand you will know of such things."

Pat gave him the crumpled, sealed letter she had carried from Niamey. He reciprocated with a printed business card which read:

> MAHAMANE Aboubakar
> officier de police
>
> BP 34 Agadez   République du Niger

Was his first name Mahamane or Aboubakar? We referred to him as the commissioner or Aboubakar because we liked the sound of those syllables. But we called him *monsieur*.

"*Monsieur*, is it possible?"

"*Oui, oui, mademoiselle*. I will certainly help you. All vehicles coming and going report to me. I will find you a ride." He did not smile easily, yet his voice sounded sincere. He would arrange for rooms at the *campement* and send his driver for the things we had left in the priest's care.

"And," he added, "I would be pleased if you would all be my guests for supper this evening."

"It will be our pleasure. You are very kind, *monsieur*." Astonishing, I thought, all the help we need and supper, too.

Agadez rose out of the earth and was of it. All the buildings were of the same color and the same material—earth. There was no stone, steel, plastic, concrete, or glass save for a few small window panes. Precious wood planks were reserved for doors.

We couldn't see a single plant. Even the tenacious acacia, scattered throughout the dry open country, had not set down a root among the streets and squares of the town. Nothing grew in Agadez.

The composite profile of the buildings from a distance—straight lines and smooth surfaces—softened close-by to rounded corners, gradually sloping walls, and the unique "woolly" texture created by straw mixed into the mud for strength. Human hands had shaped every surface. Despite the severe limitations mud imposed on the builders, no two structures were alike. Each bore the imaginative hand of its craftsperson—a pointed turret, a square one, slits in the parapet, or the diamond-shaped lattice design of a veranda wall. Each building conveyed a sense of tremendous weight, of earth-rootedness, which perfectly suited its function as a refuge from a relentlessly hostile world.

The *campement* was such a place. Its massive walls stood 24 inches thick at shoulder height, rising from an even broader base, and tapering to the roof. The walls sealed out the heat of day and the frost of night. It had not been designed to flatter the whims of its inhabitants or publicly proclaim their status. Its purpose was to protect them. In that, the *campement* was like every other building in Agadez, making shelter more egalitarian than we had ever known. Surely there were class, sect, and political differences. But they were not expressed in architecture.

Stepping in under a low front door, away from the rising Harmattan, we knew at once that the *campement* would shelter but not pamper us. Four steps down into a broad, unlit hall we paused to allow our eyes to adjust to the sudden darkness. The only light came from thin bright shafts escaping under a few of the doors that lined both sides and from the open door behind us. Before we had focused, a Frenchman dashed by from the shadows of the far end of the hall.

"Help yourselves. The only one that's taken right now is the last room on the right."

That was the one and only time we saw him.

Of the seven remaining rooms, two were padlocked. The

rest had no locks at all, not even inside hooks. Having the run of the place, we dashed from room to room, calling out our discoveries to each other. We tested the beds, searched for plumbing, and noted the amount of light and the view from each window. At 60f ($0.24) per day per person, the *campement* would do very well.

I chose the first room to the right of the entrance. The flies followed. Or were they waiting for me? A single window faced the veranda, allowing me to keep an eye on comings and goings. As it turned out, most of the comings and goings were our own. Had I known this, I might have chosen another room. Every choice was conspicuous, every step into new territory advanced from an effort to evaluate.

I whisked away the flies and hauled my things to the bed under the window. This was a lucky choice, for it was a sturdy iron bed with a reasonably good mattress.

Darlene shuffled about, unable to decide where to alight. Directly across the hall, Pat and Victoria took a room with one large sagging bed and lots of sunlight. Meanwhile, Gruber, in the room next to theirs, discovered some plumbing from which she coaxed a trickle of water. We found that a strip four or five feet wide across the back of each room had been dug out a few inches deeper than the rest of the floor. Dust-clogged drains marked the center of each of these depressions. Two or three pipes with spigots hung high out of the walls above them. We surmised they had been used as showers in the time of occupation by French troops for whom the *campements* had been built. Now, except for a few drops tapped out of one pipe in my room and the trickle from Gruber's, they were all dry.

Gruber appealed for someone to share the view and the treasure of water in her room. Darlene wavered several times before she finally unloaded her things on the bed across from mine. Gruber was unhappy about being alone, but we persuaded her to stay there so that we might have access to the water.

We had talked about how much we looked forward to beds and a safe place to sleep. Until we moved into the *campement*, we felt the weight of accumulated tiredness, the battle against the cold, the stress of having to be "on" every minute, to think faster than unfolding events. Now in the *campement*, we could sleep as we had hoped. But we also knew we could sleep later. The simple assurance of having a place wondrously refreshed us.

In a few moments, our concerns shifted. Our clothing was inadequate for the cold desert nights. We needed to send messages to let people know where we were if we became missing. We did not know when a ride would be available.

Before going out to market, we made a list and brought our accounts up to date. We had developed an accounting system in which each of us kept notes on what she had spent. Whenever the expense was for a group item—food, fares, hotel fees— the amount was divided by five and added to or subtracted from the accounts of each of the others. This simplified paying for things and kept us aware of balancing costs among us. The method suited everyone but Victoria, who refused to keep any account because she felt it was nit-picking. Reckoning with her depended on tallies the rest of us kept. These usually showed that she owed more than she thought she ought to owe.

We had lost track of the days and thought it was Friday. That meant we had to get to the PTT (*poste, téléphone, télégraphe*) before it closed if we were to send any messages from Agadez. I started a letter to Tom Quimby, our Peace Corps Director in Liberia, on behalf of all of us, to let him know where we were and the approximate timing of our plans to reach Algiers.

While I wrote to him, Gruber and Darlene went in search of a toilet or its equivalent. Knowing the French had used this building, we expected it would have a satisfactory facility.

"There isn't any," Gruber reported.

"Not an outhouse?"

"Or a flush and run?" we asked.

"I'm telling you, Gruber," Darlene interrupted, "that place on the side of the *campement* is it."

"But it's right out in the open!" Gruber protested.

This was a serious matter. Out in the desert it was different. But to not have a toilet facility while living in a building in town would be awful. Four of us tromped out to investigate, leaving

Victoria lying straight on her back, gazing at the ceiling, as she often did.

We worried about Victoria, increasingly tired and withdrawn. With exhaustion her smile became weak, her eye distant. The rest of us, with a little sleep and food, could be refreshed. And while a crisis or a new place usually summoned that extra spurt of adrenalin that allowed us to rally, Victoria's fatigue accumulated. Each decision, every question asked of her, added to the burden of all the ones before until it seemed she would be crushed to dust. So while the rest of us checked on toilets, made lists, kept track of our accounts and struggled with French, Victoria stared ahead and lay abed, never resting.

Along the side of the *campement*, toward the back, a wall extended out and wrapped itself into three sides of a closet-sized out-building. The opening, on the far side, was out of view of the main road. Sand sloped against the base of the wall and filled the floor of the tiny room. Piles of partially buried turds dotted the space, clung to the sand slide flowing from its doorless entry, and blemished the smooth golden sand, wind swept against the wall.

"I don't believe it!"

"Christ, there has to be some other place."

"Really, you guys, Darlene and I looked everywhere. I don't want to believe this is it either. But there isn't any place else."

We each took another look into the little room only to be driven off by the odor.

"Maybe this is where the animals go?"

"Sure, all the little old ladies come out in their veils to walk their dogs at sundown."

"Let's get back to reality. This is Agadez, not New York City."

"That isn't very funny. We could get in a lot of trouble by using the wrong place."

"Oh, right. This might be a shrine for secret ritual movements."

"I think this is getting silly."

"Well, how do we know they're human? There's no toilet paper."

"They don't use toilet paper."

"But they always wash their hands."

"Who?"

We broke into laughter at the absurdity of our standing in this wind-swept courtyard, strewn with not-so-old turds, trying to understand the cultural context and hoping against all the evidence that we would find a more suitable toilet. How were we to know? We could not ask the commissioner. This was one of the real handicaps in traveling in a Moslem land and rarely encountering a local woman. At times it seemed the last straw. In the midst of great physical discomfort, we were always in danger of committing a grievous insult.

We dealt with it as best we could, with a spree of raunchy jokes and side-splitting laughter that momentarily eased the tension.

The accounting we completed that afternoon straightened out which day it was—it was Thursday, not Friday—and confirmed our poor financial situation. Our money would see us through only thirteen more days. It took ten to cross from Agadez to Algiers. We set the day after next, Saturday, the 8th of February, as the day we must depart and drafted a telegram to the Embassy in Algiers to expect us on the 18th.

The *campement* was a creation of the French, one of a loose cluster of buildings on the plain north of the city from which they had attempted to subdue the tribes and control the desert. The original garrison at Agadez had been largely destroyed in a siege by the Tuareg in 1916, the subject of the legendary book and movie *Beau Geste*. The siege of Agadez proved a temporary setback for the French. They regrouped with greater vengeance and within a year carried out a series of massacres which pacified the Tuareg by decimating them.

Since independence in 1960, Niger had continued to rely heavily on France for economic and military assistance. The continued physical presence of the French, however, served as a reminder of that dependence, and of the ongoing influence of the French in a society trying to sort out its own form of self-determination.

Even in Agadez, a deeply Moslem, tradition-bound city, the long French habitation left its imprint. At the entrance to the city close to the *campement* there was an arch, in the French tradition of processional boulevards and triumphal arches.

As we trudged toward town to take care of business, we passed wooden bleachers constructed to face the road.

"The better to watch parades by," noted Pat with only a faint smirk.

Two identical earth and straw obelisks rose on either side of the road, their smoothed sides adorned with large golden emblems precisely placed above the middle of each. The symbol was known as the Cross of Agadez, or the Tuareg Cross. It was said to have been taken from the constellation of stars in the Southern Cross, which rises along the southern edge of the desert sky. Four points of a diamond were connected by concave curves. The bottom was elongated, and each point was finished in the shape of a bulb. The Cross of Agadez was the dominant design motif throughout the desert. Jewelry, camel saddles, chair backs, leather goods, and parapets were designed with variations of this motif. It was as pervasive throughout the Western and Central Sahara as the Christian cross in Medieval Europe.

Hung high between the obelisks, high enough so that the tallest *camion* could pass under, was a sign of straightforward black block letters on a white background. With the wind to our backs, we read:

(Agadez
welcomes you)

Such a glorious sign, straddling the road, alone on this austere plain, welcoming all who entered Agadez. Without it there may not have been a "road" to town from the flat unmarked hinterland. As if to confirm the road and the entrance, someone had valiantly attempted to plant trees to line the way. Circles of stones, spaced at regular intervals marked the effort, although all that remained of any trees were a few twigs staked against the wind, some still protected from animals by chicken-wire fences set inside the stones.

Down the processional road and under the triumphal arch, we marched, bracing ourselves with fragile smiles for our first expedition into Agadez.

We learned from Aboubakar that there was no bank in Agadez, but we might cash travelers' checks at a certain small French hotel.

"In the vicinity of the roundabout," he described it.

Indeed there was a painted blue roundabout marking the French quarter. A pathetic landmark it seemed, more an obstacle than an aid to traffic, so worn and blue and out of place.

We stopped just inside the door of the hotel to let our eyes adjust to the dim interior. The manager and several of his cronies leaned against the registration desk, drinking beer. They continued their conversation, their only gesture toward us a cold stare. I would have liked to leave, but we needed the cash.

"So, you're the Americans?" he said in French, to let us know he'd heard of us.

I did my best to politely explain that we wished to exchange travelers' checks for West African *francs* (WAF).

"This is not a bank," he puffed.

"These are good checks, American dollars," I tried.

"We normally only take checks as a service to our own guests."

So that was it—a bit of pique.

"The commissioner of police suggested we come here."

"Ach!" He waved the thought away with his hand the way the ticket vendor in Abidjan had when confronted with a reality that did not suit him. "How much do you want?"

We needed enough for our stay in Agadez, but weren't sure how long that would be. Once we crossed into Algeria we would need New French *francs* (NFF) and might have trouble trading a lot of WAF. As we conferred, the manager added that the service charge for handling travelers' checks was 10%. We were outraged, called it robbery, usury, illegal.

Worse, although we did not tell him, it pointed up our vulnerability.

"I have to take them south myself. In the meantime I have nothing. It takes time. It's risky," he shrugged.

We decided to exchange as little as possible, hoping to find a better deal elsewhere if we needed more.

"$60.00."

The next stop was the PTT to send our letters and cable. Fortunately, we were the only customers.

"No problem," the operator said when I asked about sending a cable to Algiers. He carefully studied the words I'd printed. He conferred with his colleague. Several men came into the office. The operator showed them our message.

"Wait a minute," I protested, "this is a private message. It's not for all the world to read."

Several more men came in and pressed around the counter. They smiled, nodded and shook their heads.

"It is impossible to send this," said the operator.

"Why?"

"We do not understand it."

"You don't have to understand it. It's in English. The recipients will understand it."

"Our Teletype does not know English."

"This is absurd. Just copy the letters. Here, just as I have written them. The letters and the spaces."

"*Je regrette, mademoiselle,*" he smiled and shrugged, "*c'est impossible.*"

While I conferred with the others, I motioned to him to go ahead with customers who'd come in after us. They smiled and continued to watch. Apparently, their only business was to pass the time amused by us. When the operator agreed to send the cable in French, we made a careful translation:

107

L'Ambassade des États-Unis, Algier
5PCV LIBERIA PARTANT AGADEZ
8FEV. CAMION ARABE
ATTENDREZ 18FEV.
Marksafpoldahlgrub

(To the Embassy of the United States of America. Leaving Agadez Feb.8 Arab truck. You will expect Feb.18—one long name was all we could afford.)

It was not an accurate use of the future tense, but the best we could do in few words. As an after-thought, we also sent a copy of the cable to Tom Quimby in Liberia to make up for any delay in the regular mail. We trusted those messages to cover us from both ends, having no idea of the confusion and trouble they triggered.

Stung by what the check cashing service charge meant to our meager resources, we consoled ourselves by focusing on our good luck to arrive in Agadez in time for Thursday market. On the most important African market day of the week we would have plenty of vendors to choose from and get the best prices for the things we needed.

The square, which had been empty when we drove into Agadez the evening before, hummed with shoppers, vendors, goats, sewing machines, and flies. Most stalls were simple lean-tos of spindly unsawn branches lashed together into frames over which were thrown skins and blankets. Moving among clusters of stalls, shoulder to shoulder with the Tuareg, dodging goats and donkeys and carts, was both exciting and tortuous. Walking in the dust of ancient and legendary Agadez, like the Tuaregs, the Arabs, and the Nigeriens, we carried out our ordinary business.

The wind made hats impossible. The sand swirled against our bare legs. In the open spaces, the sun penetrated our heads and strained our eyes. We leaned into a stall to examine a piece of cloth or an enamel pot, ever on the lookout for socks, lingering, seeking the shade. But moving back and forth between the extremes of sun and shade left me with sun spots before my eyes and the start of a headache. Every step was a reminder of how badly we needed more than cotton skirts and thin sweaters.

We were looking for pantaloons in the style we had seen many people wearing. There did not seem to be any ready-made, so we placed an order with a friendly black tailor who happened to be sewing exactly what we wanted on his Singer treadle. Five pairs in white muslin at $1.50 each, and we could pick them up tomorrow.

Finding something warm was more difficult. We had been impressed with the robes worn by some of the passengers on the *camion* from Zinder. Each time we described them to someone in the market, we were told, "aha, *djellaba*", but no one knew where to find any. Victoria insisted that we keep at it, convinced that only a *djellaba* would do. At last we received directions to a building on a side street. The door which was supposed to be that of the merchant stood two high, narrow steps up from the road. There was no sign or window, just a closed door flush in a long solid wall.

We hesitated, knocked. The door opened. Three Arab men leaned against a counter in a tiny dark room. We saw no merchandise. We crowded into the doorway to conduct our business, but kept the door ajar. They had *djellabas*.

"He wants 2500 WAF for each one. That's ten dollars," I reported in English. "Shake your heads and look shocked at such an outrageous price." Darlene was particularly good at this.

"What should we do?"

"I think it really is too much."

"I'll try to get him down."

We held up the sample he had taken from beneath the counter.

"And is it made of wool?" I asked.

"One hundred percent," he assured me.

"It's not as heavy as the one the guy had on the *camion*," Victoria noted.

"*Monsieur*, this robe is not bad. We wish to buy five. How much will it be for five?" I returned to examining the seams of the black wool in the dim interior light. He discussed it with the other men. We all knew what we were up to. Now it was a question of how far each of us would go.

"Eleven thousand WAF for five," he said firmly. He folded the robe and placed it on the shelf behind him.

"That's still almost $9 each. I'll give it one more try."

"*Monsieur*, as I said, these robes are not bad. But have you any others, similar to these, which are not so expensive." If he was willing to bargain further, he could do so now without losing face. He would go into the back room to find a robe identical to the first. We would examine it and all would exclaim over its inferiority. We would agree to take this lesser product at a lower price. He would have a sale without admitting he had been bargained down.

It didn't work. This fellow didn't respond in the manner of any Lebanese or Syrian trader we knew, or even like an outdoor vendor. Perhaps he knew he had the only *djellabas* for sale in Agadez. We five deliberated among ourselves. The Arabs did the same. We wanted the robes, but could not appear eager. I made my final offer—to pay in American dollars. Surely travelers checks were worth some discount. Wrong again. Not only would he not lower the price, but he insisted on cash in WAF. We gave up, although not without a great deal of face-saving ourselves, carried out by examining each robe for workmanship and size and finding a flaw that allowed us to reject one and request a suitable substitute.

We walked off from the robe merchant disheartened, heavily weighted with our new woolen robes, our old purses and cameras, and the additional evidence of our ever more frightening vulnerability.

"How much cash do we have left?"

"A dollar fifty."

The sun pierced my left temple. My head, preoccupied with its own pain, could do nothing for the leaden body dragging beneath it. I felt feverish and cold at the same time.

"I've got to get out of the sun."

"Somebody has to go back to the hotel for more *francs*," Victoria pointedly reminded me.

"I can do it," Gruber offered.

"Here," I said, "I'll carry your robe back to the *campement* if you get the money."

The room was an icebox. Although it was past noon, the massive walls had not warmed through to the air inside. After the long walk back along sun-scorched roads, I was dazed by the sudden drop in temperature. I pressed my forehead against a cold wall to steady myself and took slow, deep breaths to control the nausea.

The flies were so mean in the afternoons. They seemed to take out their dislike of the cold on us, ceaselessly buzzing and dive-bombing.

The thermometer confirmed my fever. My feet and hands were icy. I trembled, taking off my shoes and spreading my new robe over the blankets on my bed. I wished only for a pair of socks as I shuddered under the heap of covers. In a metal canteen hung on the bedpost was enough water to wash down a few pills. I damned the flies and pulled a raw muslin sheet up over my head. Thick warm socks faded in and out of my mind's eye as I alternately tossed and slept, my body confused by cold and fever.

By the time Gruber awoke me with a Coke and food, the battle was over. The temperatures of the room and my self had achieved a tolerable balance. I ate and fell exhausted into a sound sleep.

At supper Aboubakar looked older and less comfortable than he had in his office that morning. Though we chatted over a long meal, telling of our work and he of his, interrupting each other, asking many and difficult questions, he seemed uneasy.

He seemed more keenly alert than necessary to the other people in the restaurant and to the attention and service accorded. Was this simply the by-product of his occupation, a ceaseless attention to every whisper, to every change, to the slightest nuance out of the ordinary? Or was it racism? Did he glance about in expectation of some slight from the French patrons? With tables arranged among several rooms, we could not see all of the restaurant. But during that meal, Aboubakar was the only black person in sight. Could that have been mere chance? Or had he come this evening only because of us?

On the one hand, Aboubakar indulged us kindly, like the children of a friend one feels obliged to look after. On the other, he found it hard to believe we had come this far, and for that fact alone, he admitted, we deserved a certain amount of admiration. While remaining discreet and perfectly correct, he seemed pleased to talk about his work and its intriguing political overtones.

He spoke as a serious individual understanding the hostility of the land and the volatile jealousies of its people. This was not a typical officious civil servant, but a man committed to maintaining himself as an element of peace and order. It was a burden he did not take lightly.

"I have not the men nor the arms of the French, nor the mobility of the Arabs, nor do I know the desert as the nomads. I simply have authority," he said.

He saw the remoteness of Agadez as both his greatest threat and his greatest asset.

"In a place so remote, I must rely on myself. I cannot call in reserves," he smiled, as if the very image of calling upon reserves were the most amusing thing he had thought of in a long while.

"In such a place the law could become the tool of the powerful, in which case we would be doomed to great violence or anarchy. I prefer to remain separate from all the old interests, to not fall under the control of one group, to not offend another. I try to keep the balance, which is to say the peace, by pointing out our interdependence, by setting an example of tolerance, and," he smiled again, "by not telling too many tales."

Hardly a soulful outpouring of his personal prejudices—he remained too disciplined and cautious for that. Yet, there were tales to be told, problems solved, intelligence gathered, insights, victories, which he had carefully accumulated. We were the perfect listeners. Outsiders, travelers, never to become one of the elements of his community. Americans, there were no Americans living in Agadez. And women. It was a questionable compliment, but in that time and place, women could not have been expected to be a part of any power structure or represent any competition. It may have also helped that we found it terribly interesting.

Despite hours of talk, there was no mention of his personal life. We learned nothing of his family or friends. Unlike his cousin in Niamey, Aboubakar would not take us to his home, or regale us with parties and dancing. He was not angry or morose, but gaiety simply did not suit him.

He had not ordered wine, and as the evening passed we grew tired without becoming mellow. Since he did not seem a person of wealth, we felt it an imposition, even a hardship, for him to pay for all of our meals. We did not know how to bring this up without offending him. We wrestled with a solution and ate modestly. In the end we were not able to intercept the check.

On the drive back to the *campement*, he reminded us that it was not wise to walk about in the mid-day sun. He would send his driver to take us to market the next day.

I settled in bed, sweater, blankets, and robe tucked about me and tried to write in my journal:

> It is late and all the others have gone straight to sleep. I want to record as much as possible of this full and incredible day. Someone has left us a lamp. I wear more clothes to bed each night. The room is finally warm and it is so wonderful to stretch out in a real bed of my own. I will try to write tomorrow.

The promise was all I managed as I turned down the lamp and snuggled under my heap.

In the morning we were awakened abruptly by the *gardien*, who marched into our room without knocking and very forthrightly shook my hand and then Darlene's. We had expected the *campement* to have a *gardien* and this one proved to be a classic, a frail old fellow who charmed us by the way he popped in

113

to declare he was master of this domain.

We were immediately disarmed by his good humor and knew he was amused by us. He admitted to having filled and set out the lamps and to have brought the water the evening before. He assured us he would continue to do so, *trés bien et avec plaisir* (very well and with pleasure).

We got on our new black robes, the folds not yet fallen out, and had our picture taken with the *gardien* on the veranda. What a picture! We, draped in black from our hoods to our ankles, only our very white faces catching the sun. He, with the blackest skin, grandly turbaned and robed in blinding white cloth. We stood him in the middle of our row and all of us stared at the camera balanced on the veranda wall, waiting, still, until fourteen seconds passed and the self-timer clicked. If the old man thought we'd lost our marbles, he never showed it.

My eye improved, the swelling went down and the drainage became sporadic.

The commissioner's driver arrived, as promised, and took us to market. We picked up the pantaloons we had ordered and bought more *crème*. Still no socks. Riding was certainly more comfortable than the long walk from the *campement* to the town, but it was awkward to have the driver standing by while we fooled around, following our whims for as long as we could stand the sun and wind.

In truth, Agadez was bleak, not a place for strolling. Soon after we finished our business, we let ourselves be taken back to the *campement*.

I was beginning to feel the *campement* a refuge and a prison. There would be no trucks leaving that day. And so with boundless horizons surrounding us, we had no other place but our rooms to spend the time.

During the afternoon, while the unremitting sun baked and blinded outdoors, my room was cold and dim. I bundled in every warm thing I owned and stayed there to write letters and journal notes, avoiding the other room, full and noisy with talk.

We set the next day for our departure, though we had no

control over it whatsoever. If we didn't leave soon, we wouldn't make it across in time. In time for what? I kept finding myself writing that. I had known my hour of terror at being left behind with the grain of sand in my eye. Now it no longer mattered, whatever it was we had in mind to be on time for. We were here and from now on there was only one direction. Grace had let me stay in the desert, and I would not squander the gift.

At mid-day, heat radiated from the sand so that we could never be sure whether a distant wavering image was matter or mirage. To step away from the ponderous walls of the *campement* across the bright baked plate of space that separated it from the town was an act of faith. I knew the town was there. Yet my eyes stared through dry intense light to feed me vibrating forms the exact color of the earth from which they had risen, or were rising. The brain does not easily accept vibrating buildings.

Until the desert, my environment had been one of close-ups, river valleys and hollows, the deciduous forests of Pennsylvania; the dense cities and cozy towns of the eastern United States; the rain forest of Liberia, so close, green and intertwining, the width of a road or clearing of a village was the only open space. Anything seen could be reached in a walk. The Sahara was my first unreachable, unfathomable horizon.

Our touchstones had changed so often that it was hard to say with confidence what was reality and what was not. Thus in crossing the plain from the *campement* to the town, I always felt a conscious relief to have my wind-whipped legs bring me into the shadow of the first building.

During our first full day in Agadez we had scurried about in a frenzy to complete all of our business so that we would be prepared to leave on a moment's notice. That done, we were left with conspicuous and unexpected idleness. We had hours for reading and writing, for washing our clothes, for carefully sorting and packing our things. We had long leisurely meals and vast pockets of time in which our thoughts wandered and incubated.

After weeks of constant activity, of pivotal and trivial decisions, of continuous movement, making arrangements, meeting new people, assessing, choosing, listening, struggling to understand outside our own language, we had come to this utterly empty time.

We became quieter, careful not to intrude on each other's time. Darlene at last stopped talking about turning back. We read for, I cannot say hours, but as long as we needed, and knew that the books we carried had been worth their weight.

From time to time we had brief visits from Aboubakar, asking about our comfort and reporting, yet again, that he had not located a ride for us to Tamanrasset. We continued to be the only inhabitants of the *campement*. The *gardien* appeared and disappeared at will, his, not ours. Otherwise, we were alone. To counter the weight of such profound isolation, we regularly walked to town, passing under the welcoming arches, following the route of painted white stone circles, until we reached the shelter of the shadow of that first building.

We moved freely about the town, stopping at M. Joyce's store to buy cold drinks, or at the hotel to change ever smaller amounts of travelers' checks for *francs*. Not knowing how long our wait would be, we gave up eating at the restaurant to save money. There were no cinemas or other amusements. Agadez itself was our diversion.

Beyond the shadow of the first building, we explored various routes and wandered through new quarters, absorbing and photographing until the sun and wind drove us back to the *campement*. In a lane off the main market we found a fascinating row of attached buildings of different lengths and heights. They were of the standard red earth and straw, but they had been profusely painted in lovely designs. A white chalky border outlined the base and roof line, rising to the tips of tall pointed turrets. The solid walls had been divided into sections. Moons, arches, abstracted flowers, and the Cross of Agadez were repeated again and again in panels, bands and borders. Large blooms of poinsettia, daisy, clustered petals of mums, beautifully drawn in red, purple, orange, and ochre stood tall in their geometric blue and white painted pots, or bent gracefully from thin green stems, embellished with delicate leaves.

There were no gnarled branches, no black-green brittle twigs scattered randomly across the landscape as there might have been if the artist had taken the desert as his model. Instead, lush, cultivated blooms, watered abundantly and never knowing more than a gentle breeze filled this painted garden.

No such plants had ever grown in Agadez. Where had the artist seen them? To us the paintings represented a visual oasis in an otherwise barren aesthetic. What did they represent to the artist? To the owner of the buildings? Perhaps he was a rich man wishing to distinguish his home from the unrelieved monotony that surrounded it?

While we frequently walked down the lane of the painted garden, we observed the ancient mosque only from afar. We had learned before we arrived in Agadez that it was one of the first mosques built upon the rapid spread of Islam through the desert after the death of the Prophet.

Quite apart from its historic distinction, the Agadez mosque was probably the most unlovely structure in the world. An astonishing tower of more than five stories of mud and sticks, its four sides tapered to a ragged top about a third as wide as its base. The sides were punctuated by rows of run-off poles which, from a distance, made it resemble a giant pin cushion. Angular as they might have been, the poles protected the building from sudden violent rain storms. Its height and mass had varied over the centuries according to the abuse of nature and the industry of the faithful to maintain it. But withal, it was said to have stood continuously on the same spot since the seventh century.

I spent some of my time reading *Clea*, then rereading before I went to the next part. This was my strategy to make the book last. It had become one of my companions, and I didn't want it to end. Durrell's Alexandria swept over me, and I let myself sink into its complexities, the language, the landscape, the disorder, ornate, intertwined. No energy wasted there on coy purities. The characters seemed so adult, unself-conscious in their motivations and desires. Alexandria, Agadez, societies unsanitized (un-American?), the fantasy, the reality. Where was I?

117

We were ready to go. Waiting for the call from the commissioner. We all thought about it.

In the meantime we were summoned to bring our papers to the *gendarmerie*. It was a very civil request, *à la convenance desmoiselles* (at your convenience). I supposed their curiosity got the best of them and we would probably comply. Still, I didn't see that we were any business of the *gendarmes*.

I did learn that there were 2,000 French military nearby to guard the border. It was a secret. I wrote it in my journal in my own code in case it became important later. Was this really what the *gendarmes* wanted to talk to us about?

When it is very quiet, the smallest sound can disturb tranquility. Conversation or the scratch of a pen can be enough. The same is true for visual purity. Our eye goes to the fingerprint on white paper. Against the aesthetic monotony of Agadez, a monochrome palette of red earth and red earth structures, the painted blue traffic round-about of the French played the fingerprint.

In the uncluttered world of Agadez, we became newly sensitive to the harmonies and disharmonies of the physical environment.

The French garrison, despite a sense of grandeur in the use of symmetry and columns, was constructed of earth and straw, and retained the architectural integrity of Agadez. This was especially evident in the *gendarmerie*, the chief public administrative building. Square columns in relief flanked the massive door and marked the corners. The columns continued into turrets above the second story of the roof. The orange, white and green flag of Niger flew above the entrance.

In the morning we walked across the road *en masse* to present our papers to the *capitaine*.

"I have the feeling I've been here before," Gruber commented.

Shielding our eyes from the morning sun, studying the facade, we were suddenly caught in the middle of the road by two soldiers hooting and racing their camels. After a few charges back and forth, they came to a stop right in front of us.

"Help yourself to the animals," they called as they swaggered off.

"Now I remember! You guys, this is just like it was in the movie, just like when Lawrence came back to headquarters in Cairo in his desert clothes."

"Shh," Pat cautioned, as we swept into the cool interior in our desert clothes.

High whitewashed walls enclosed the reception gallery in quiet austerity. Opposite the door the *capitaine* waited at a dark wooden desk. There were no other furnishings. Several other men in uniform stood at attention at the doors leading to other parts of the building.

"I can't believe it!" Gruber whispered. "Wait 'til you guys see the movie."

The meeting was brief and cordial. The *capitaine* advised us to inform our people that we planned to travel north. I assured him that we had taken care of that.

"*Bon voyage*," he nodded.

"*Merci, au revoir, capitaine.*"

We stepped away in a confident pace, but once outside ran to have our pictures taken with the camels.

On the plain outside the walls of Agadez stretched an extensive cemetery with graves encircled by rocks and marked with pottery. At some of the gravesites large slabs had been carved with lengthy inscriptions.

At first the cemetery seemed far too large for a town of a few thousand people. But this was the desert which preserved. To an American, an artifact or a place inhabited for two hundred years is an awesome thing. The ground water of Agadez had refreshed the caravans of more than twenty centuries. I struggled to understand the time known to the desert.

The first Christian to reach the "lost" city of Timbuctu and return to tell about it was the Frenchman René Caillié. He did not accomplish that feat until the early nineteenth century, and then did so only by way of the great deceit of disguising himself as a Moslem. But while Timbuctu may have been lost to the

French, it was very much known to the people of West Africa and the desert. A thousand years before Caillié, lines of camels loaded with salt from Bilma paused in Agadez to prepare for the months it took to reach Timbuctu with their treasure.

While the Normans took England, and the Vikings sailed to the west; while China was united and the Roman empire torn apart; while Caesar and Christ walked their parts of the earth, the Berbers, Arabs, Tuareg, Senufu, and Syrians continuously traded salt, silver, slaves, dates, and camels in the markets of Agadez.

Through times ancient, medieval and modern, kingdoms and empires rose and fell to the north, the west and the south. Their pillaging warriors, their seasonal migrations, their merchants and refugees were the traffic of Agadez. In and out they streamed until they came for the last time and stayed, their bones joining generations of others in this rock-adorned plain outside the walls.

The desert preserved, but the wind destroyed. And these stone slabs, gouged by faithful carvers to record a people who had once been, would succumb as well to the wind which had raged for ten thousand years, erasing names and smoothing stones. This wind would wear down the slab itself, break and bombard it with the grains of other rocks until it, too, was pulverized and blown about like the dust of crumbling clay pots.

How long would it take? I wanted to watch. I wanted to stay still for the next ten thousand years to watch the wind do its work. My skin was raw, my eyes stinging. If only I could suspend the pain and watch without feeling. I would see the change in the desert and its people creep by like a receding ice age.

It appealed like the life of a monastery, simple, uncluttered, focused on an inner search without distractions. At first I did not understand. There was simply the compelling feeling that I was experiencing a wholeness I had not known before. Had not, could not, because such understanding demands time. The time I had grown up to know belonged to others. And when others define and eat our time, they have defined and eaten us.

My spirit was willing, but my head and eyes ached. I took

the sense of wholeness, all the strength and certainty and calm I felt, back to the cool shelter of the *campement*.

Agadez may have nurtured our spiritual life, but it never let us take for granted the physical. The pipes in our rooms turned out to be a great deception. No matter how we coaxed or cursed them, we were only able to collect a few drops from any of them. Victoria was so annoyed about the extreme shortage of water, she was driven to deal with it. She found a way to the roof and discovered our "supply" was merely a barrel with a plugged outlet which she was able to unplug. It was a small gain in terms of water, as the barrel was nearly empty. But as she told of her accomplishment the brightness returned briefly to her face.

As the days passed, our money dwindled, and it seemed we might never find a ride. When we dared talk about our fears, overcome with paranoia, suspecting everyone of plotting to never let us leave, we did it without hysteria. The frenzy of hysteria is an abandonment, a plea for someone else to help, to take over. It is the luxury of those with abundant resources. We had only ourselves, our terror and our strength.

5

Tests

Late one afternoon Gruber stood in the doorway, very still, until we noticed her.

"M. Joyce's daughter was at the store, and she was surprised to see that I was still in town. Listen, you guys," Gruber was almost shivering, "two trucks have left for Tamanrasset since we've been here."

"What!"

"I swear it's what she told me."

The chill passed through each of us.

Why?

Why hadn't we been told?

Had we made a mistake in relying on Aboubakar?

Why had we trusted him?

What did the letter from the chief of police in Niamey actually say? What if it was not just an introduction? But if it wasn't, then what?

I wanted to lock the door. We couldn't lock the door. There was no lock.

"Everyone in town knows we're waiting for a ride."

"They also know we're not spending much money. If we had more, we'd spend more. They must know it won't be long before we're broke. Then what?"

"Why don't they want us to leave?"

"Who?"

"I don't know who!"

"Don't shout!"

"There must be a good explanation."

"Name one."

Nothing we could think of relieved the knot of fear hardening in our stomachs.

"I don't think anyone should go out alone anymore."

"Are we letting our imaginations run away with us?"

"I don't know. At least let's all be back before dark. I'd feel better if we were all inside together after dark."

"Tomorrow we'll ask Aboubakar what's going on. We'll just ask him why he didn't help us get on those trucks."

We gathered in Victoria and Pat's room that night and made an effort to get our minds off our fear by making an event of our supper. We felt well equipped—an enamel pan with a decorated lid in which to mix our tuna, five colored plastic cups, five spoons, a loaf of bread, baked beans, sliced cling peaches in heavy syrup, and four cans of soft drinks.

"Well, don't look at me," Darlene huffed, "I could only carry two cans."

"We didn't know what kind you'd want," Victoria said to me.

We opened a bottle of M. Joyce's red wine. We talked about our pasts. The rituals and tensions of our intensely shared time did not melt away in the sentiment of private memories. But telling each other of some special fun or deep experience which predated *nous cinq* lightened the load of isolation and concern.

Pat remembered her car, a Karmann Ghia, and San Francisco. Water. From the city and the back bay, from every hill, one could see water. Driving across a long bridge at night, towards the lights. And the Telephone Bar where she went with her friends to meet men.

"Every table has a phone. If you see someone you like, you ask the waiter for the number of his phone. You can see what kind of a person he is without having to let him know who you are. It's safe. And when somebody calls your phone, you sort of draw out the conversation while you're looking around, trying to figure out who it is. I've met some neat people there. No commitments, just fun."

I had never been to San Francisco, but whenever I think of that cold whitewashed room in the desert, it is accompanied by an image of a sparkling city of sparkling lights, sparkling water and lightheartedness.

The wind blew harsh against the window, gusts ground sand against the glass. But inside, the blankets in which we huddled slipped away as evening and our bodies warmed the room.

Before we left Liberia, Darlene had started seeing a Dutch bush pilot and hoped he would be there when she returned. She blushed at our little jokes about the flying Dutchman.

Victoria remembered Pennsylvania winters with wet snow weighing down the branches of trees. How could anyone in Agadez ever imagine wet snow?

"This is really neat, you guys," Gruber said. "I'm really glad we're here and that we're having this really neat-o meal." And she meant it.

8 Fev. 64, Agadez
Dear Jim,

We are ready with desert trousers and robes hung on the wall awaiting a call from the commissioner. The Tuaregs, in turbans and blue-black cloth with dirty white pants hanging from beneath, mill about the market among the camels and donkeys, just like us. I don't think the Tuareg notice the weather which is very hard on us. We five move rather easily and well together—a surprise to me that it could happen. So often now, we have eaten bread and jam and passed the same bottle to wash down our vitamin pills. So often sleeping two in a small bed, three in a large, or on the floor. Or to-gether loading our bags and baskets and bottles and

blankets and selves, and again, unfolding and un-
loading. Victoria and I are far apart, due perhaps to
lack of effort. She will not be alone and now it is
Pat who is caught in the dance, mutual tiptoeing.
Scene: dinner of our own making.
Situation: one bottle of Coke and one of Sprite.
Both V & P prefer Coke.
Conflict: Who will win out and drink Sprite????

To maintain anonymity and because I really
don't remember how it started, let us say that
Character A has the Coke before her and Character
B, very obviously, has the Sprite. The set is other-
wise silent.
A: (In a grave manner) Do you want me to drink
the Sprite?
B: No, it's all right.
A: But I know you don't like Sprite.
B: Well, I can drink it tonight. I really don't mind.
A: No, I want you to take the Coke.
B: But you don't like Sprite any more than I do.
A: It's all the same to me. I can drink either.
B: There's no reason for you to drink Sprite if you
don't want to.
A: Really, I do want to. Here, take the Coke.
B: Are you sure you don't mind?
A: No, I don't mind at all.
B: Are you sure?
A: Of course, here's the Coke.
B: (Starting to exchange the bottles, then hesitat-
ing.) No, let it stay. I think you're just saying that
and I don't want you to take it if you don't like it.

A: In case you change your mind, there's still time.
B: No, it's all right.
A: You're sure?
B: Yes.
Curtain. All sigh, take a sip and hand each other the same can of beans.
Scene 2—Who Begins the Beans?
(The above was necessarily condensed as to not prove a postal burden.)

And so it goes, day after day. This in contrast to Darlene's bluntness. She got the worst bed, a hard scratchy straw one. Spent two days thrashing and complaining. Finally, she asked if I would trade for a night. I agreed. Fini!

I will write you more before we leave here.

It is late.

I was beginning to love Agadez. My feelings transcended the heat, the cold, the wind, and the flies. The severity of Agadez, our plain lives and social isolation forced us to rely on ourselves in a way none of us had ever experienced. Stripped of amusements, diversions, even tasks to fill our time, we were left with inner reflection.

I realized why, in the beginning, gods were of nature. The first humans shared the earth with all other forms of life and power. With an inherent sense of their human needs and limitations, of their place in the riddle of interdependence, they granted nature its right to harbor secrets and manifested that respect with a broad allotment of divinity.

This was the earth that the gods had made. An earth of supportive harmonious elements which go on to infinity, regenerating themselves in perfect balance. I reached deeply to understand the awe my ancestors must have felt for the wonders they saw and struggled to understand. I knew that they too had not only the special capacity to nurture a spiritual life, but to doubt and ask questions. What doubt upset the balance? What question tore them from the instinctive repetitious patterns that had always been the way of human life?

Was I losing my mind in Agadez, or finding it?

For those who trusted that the next day would come as it had before, it did come. And they accepted the whole and familiar, neither doubting nor disrupting the harmony watched over by their gods.

For the others, who were not sure, blind trust in a future faltered. Doubt drove them to act, to strive for control, to become creators of their own next days. The time that had been used to savor and understand the wholeness of the given earth began to be used to accumulate, to protect themselves against the possible lean times. Once the hoarding began, what had been sufficient for all became plenty for some and scarcity for others. Only the most isolated people escaped.

Perhaps the fact of some having a little more than others was not of great importance in a material sense. However, its social result was the creation of enemies against whom one had to be protected. This is the tragedy of accumulation. The time we have on the earth to be spiritually fulfilled, a capacity in which we are presumed unique among all the species, is spent in fear and uncertainty, begetting power which is never enough, and securing territory which our souls tell us is never ours. It is spent in fragmenting, labeling, and parceling our life's experiences in so stingy a way that most people get just a few, which they mistake for the whole. Along the way, the more the process accelerates, the less time remains for contemplation. This great gift of the human species atrophies and is cast out like an embarrassing appendage.

Some say the process is driven by the human need to insure immortality. The modern result is a world of variety and richness far surpassing all previous times. But humanity has paid dearly for its comforts. It has sacrificed time in the service of things and the spiritual experience is nothing if it is not time.

I would bring everyone to Agadez. I would bring them to this barren place, free of clutter, to be born again, to see everything anew, to feel strengthened by the force of primordial stillness.

Time hung like that in Agadez. I could not say it passed. While I luxuriated in the freedom of wandering thoughts there was no measure of time, only its uninterrupted being.

"Desmoiselles, desmoiselles!" Aboubakar called, rapping sharply at the door. "I have found you a ride."

A moment of wavering. What if I didn't leave? The thought was at once intriguing and forbidding. To have come so far and learned so much...would leaving betray it? I had leaned into the abyss to see how deep it was, not to tempt fate by seeing how far I could fall. I walked the sun-bleached roads of Agadez, adapted to its pace, tread water in its dusty pool, but I would not deny the main current of my life. However painful, leaving was better than being left. I would be on that truck tomorrow.

Aboubakar took us to meet the owner of the truck. He was a dirty, disheveled fellow with one eye, who could have played the brooding villain in a sinister movie. We were secretly thrilled and outwardly calm. More than anything we wanted the ride.

The deal was arranged for 12,500 nff (Algerian *francs*, about $10) each, to be paid after arrival in Tamanrasset.

For our last night in Agadez, we treated ourselves to a good meal at Mme. Dodet's. Mme. Collette Dodet, who ran the restaurant where we had been eating, was the kindest person. She had surprised us with the first warmth we'd received from a *colon*. We ate early, while there were only a few diners. *Madame* lingered longer each time she came to our table. At the main course we asked her to join us.

She was fascinating, a white woman who had come to Agadez and stayed. Between answers to many things she wished to know about us, and her gentle pampering with extra bread and wine "on the house", we did our best to understand her life. We pieced together the parts she volunteered along with the questions she appeared not to hear.

She had come overland a dozen years before, during the treacherous summer when even the Arabs will not travel. Her car broke down outside one of the oases to the north. For weeks she was manipulated by one group and then another. Each offered to help, demanded her loyalty, then "forgot" her. It was a cruel game, she said, of the fat cats playing with one frail mouse. All the while, she was frustrated by messages from her husband, who had already arrived in Agadez from the south. He had sent letters and telegrams to every place along her route attempting to locate her. His letters indicated he had not received any of her messages and had no idea of her predicament. It was years before she would venture into the desert again.

We were smitten by this romantic, mysterious woman. It never occurred to any of us to ask why she traveled alone, or why her husband came from the opposite direction. Everyone was entitled to a story.

But what of her husband now? There had been no sign of him at the hotel.

"Why did you come? What did you do before you came to the desert?"

To these and questions like them she gave no acknowledgement. But neither did she leave our table. It was not unusual for Europeans in Africa to be vague about their pasts, and as we moved deeper into the desert the replies became even more cryptic. Some people maintained an even stare, never looking directly at anyone. Others looked about restlessly, eyes darting.

I could not like or admire most of them. But I loved knowing them. People who had cut their own paths, they were, in both the harshest and most poetic sense, alone. Whatever their reasons, they had not come lightly. Anyone in exile has touched life. To know such individuals, who expect nothing and offer the same, gives one courage to define one's own self.

They might wonder about us as well. After all, who can believe that five young American women, who claim to be teachers, just happen to be crossing the desert with no vehicle, no friends, no government papers, and most astonishingly for

Americans, almost no money. Perhaps that is why, when we presented our passports at the *gendarmerie* and told the *capitaine* who we were, he nodded politely and replied, "Very well, if you wish."

"It has not been a life I imagined for myself," Madame Dodet continued, saying it to herself as much as to us. "Yet it has become my life. I am not unhappy," she decided after a long thought. "But here, in the desert for so many years, I long for companionship, for other women."

She said that to us, who had far too much of each other. She conveyed a sense of fortitude against an inevitable and tragic fate. She was quintessentially French in the way Piaf and Jeanne d'Arc were French. Yet she was neither of them, or anyone but a fragile-boned woman with dark eyes and a thin, hesitant smile. She seemed to have slipped into her forties without ever having had a prime and so would never have a decline. She endured entirely in the reality of the present, without a nostalgic past nor a hopeful fantasy of the future.

"And tomorrow you shall tell me more of your work," she said.

"*Madame*, we are leaving tomorrow."

"Ah," she said, and after only the slightest pause continued, "of course. You must go. And you have found a suitable ride?"

"*Oui. Camion arabe.* The commissioner has arranged it."

"*Ah, bon.* That is the way to do it these days."

"Perhaps we'll come by for breakfast. Will you be open?"

"*Certainement, certainement!* And I shall have eggs for your journey as well."

"Thank you, *madame*, but I don't think we can manage to carry eggs."

"I will boil them!"

Walking back from her place in the evening we had a glimpse of our low-lit shadows in the last minutes before the sun fell. Five long black shapes shot out from our feet and ended in the elongated points of our hoods. In our shadows we were medieval monks or the Ku Klux Klan. Scary. All in a row, we passed under the arch and, after the last light, dropped into cold darkness. The robes were not as warm as we hoped or needed.

In the *campement* that night I took out my journal to record the day. The oil lamp cast an amber glow over the long pages. The journal had become my companion, my confidant, the ballast of my sanity. Here my thoughts wandered. Here my perceptions, the intake, were translated into the outflow of words. A personal, inward communication. But that night I longed for more. Perhaps it was Mme. Dodet who triggered my longing to break out of the silence of isolation, to touch someone.

Did the others feel as I did? Five alone together. A part of each of us was having a profound experience and the other part was watching the rest have it. This ceaseless surveillance separated and stifled us. I was not close to any of them, but especially far from Victoria. We rarely even said anything directly to each other.

I watched the dance the others did. Victoria and Pat, for instance. They were endlessly bowing and seeking each other's pardon. Like the repressed little ritual with the Coke and Sprite. It shouldn't have mattered, but it irritated the hell out of me. I went to sleep with great phrases to describe it, but by the time I awoke the words were gone.

Victoria was so many people. She required someone's physical presence at all times. I read a passage in *Clea* which described a unity of mind and body which I could not find in Victoria. I thought I knew the book by heart but when I went back to look for it, I'd lost that passage, too.

By the time we were ready to leave Agadez, Pat had become a quiet shadow figure. She watched more and better than anyone. She became Victoria's buffer and protector.

The presence of the others with whom I did not really share pushed emotions far from the surface.

Yet the group was holding up well. We were bonded by knowing we must cross. We held our tongues and kept demands within what we could handle. As the intensity increased, the limits of our tolerance shrunk. We withdrew into ourselves and withheld.

I took out the letter I had begun two days before and the ball point pen that left random deposits of thick ink among my words.

> Jim —— continued February 9, 1964
> We leave tomorrow. Yesterday, deep in our uncertainty and interpreting the looks of the people around us to be suspicious, we talked ourselves into a drama of intrigue about being captive. Free to move about Agadez, but not permitted to leave. It was all in our heads but completely believable. Then Mme. Dodet, at the hotel where we eat told a real story of that happening to her! Fantasy and reality are one and the same. Today Darlene killed 17 flies before covering her head to take a nap. We tested our open-air toilet with our bloomers and robes. Not an easy job. Must balance all off the ground with the wind and flies to battle.
> The trousers are made like this:

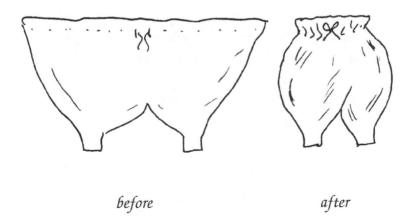

before   after

add a robe (black) and we are a frightening sight.

Otherwise we are fine and I think we will make it across. Within all this nonsense, I'm wanting to say something nice of my own. But a day of reading Clea makes my words pale and awkward. There is especially Arnauti's line 'However near we would wish to be, so far exactly do we remain from each other.' Wondering about your film?

A thought on this night before departure. All warnings and advice culminate into the sobriety of the step. The desert men are rugged and weathered. And we, all too white and fragile beside them. If all goes well, our first station is four days away. It is not the time, but cold nights in the sand which seem most awful. I hope you will not have to go back to Sinoe before we return.

Be well,

J.

I wrote on both sides of the small thin paper with the ball point pen and folded the brittle sheets in half to fit the thin air mail envelope. Such a fragile object, such a fragile link. It would be my last letter from the desert.

6

The Garden of Allah

Like an overloaded parade float, the *camion* glided away from the marketplace. Our bright-colored turbans and blankets festooned the top of the drab vehicle, and the late afternoon sun lit our faces. We sat tall to better see and be seen. We cruised through the narrow streets, slowing to exchange greetings, stopping once to take on an additional passenger and again for a package an old man asked the driver to carry to Tamanrasset.

All the while, the engine hummed, the gears performed what was asked of them and the tires ground evenly onward. We drove down the street of the painted garden. Passersby waved and wished us safe journey, Allah willing. Standing, we were taller than most buildings in Agadez. Along the roundabout, a boy threw us a present of hard candies in a cellophane bag.

The *camion* gained speed. We steadied ourselves around corners. After the last bend we headed straightaway to the arches, under them, and then, free at last, forward to the great empty horizon in a joyous lunge of the hungry toward a tempting feast. We threw off the town and shelter to ride away on the wind.

Au revoir, Agadez.

Each of us wore a woolen robe with many layers of pants,

pantaloons, shirts, sweaters and other robes underneath. Only Pat did not wear the baggy white desert pants that had become indispensable to the rest of us. Day after day she wore a pale green cotton knit skirt. She drew no attention to it. At first we didn't notice, but once we did she admitted that in Zinder she had decided to make it her desert-crossing skirt and since then had stuck by her vow to wear it every day.

We felt a chill with the drop of the sun, but stayed comfortable, nestled among the baggage with our blankets. We were tougher now, we said, used to it, not about to disintegrate in the face of a cool breeze. There would be plenty of opportunities later for eating those words, but for the time we reveled in our heartiness, our sense of belonging as much to our end of the *camion* as the desert men did to theirs.

With the five other passengers, all Arab men, was a child of about five. She wore only a cotton dress and sandals. Her dark curly hair whipped about wildly in the wind until the man who looked after her (and who was heavily clothed himself) wrapped her in a blanket and made a space for her to snuggle beside him.

At sunset the driver stopped for supper. Out came our enamel pan, cups, spoons, and some of Mme. Dodet's eggs. The bread had dried to a hard stick. We dipped it in tuna oil to soften it. How well prepared we were. How resourceful, we thought.

The driver and other passengers were all Moslems and for them it was the first meal since sunrise. Nevertheless, they did not hurry. They knew what needed to be done, and each went to his task. None appeared to either take command or look to another for direction. Tradition and grace had as much a part in eating as did hunger. The Arabs did not let empty stomachs deprive them of the pleasure of the process. We watched carefully to learn the protocol.

However much we wished to be participants, we remained observers. Present, yet apart. For us it was a unique event, a picnic, camping out. For them it was a way of life, refined and ritualized.

The younger, darker man dug a hole and over it laid an iron

grate which at another time would be used as a track to get the *camion* out of soft sand. Another gathered twigs and small branches from the dead parts of nearby trees. (And we thought they had chosen this site because of the discreet distance and relative privacy the low bushy trees would give us!) They set a meal of gazelle meat in soup to simmer upon the fire. The driver clamped a battery-operated lamp to the *camion* and adjusted the reception of a portable radio. Light, music, food. We had everything.

An old man, settled by the fire, carefully lined up tea glasses. He unwrapped a conical chunk of sugar about ten inches long and three at the base. To the water and tea leaves that had begun to brew in a graceful blue enamel tea pot he added a chunk of sugar. In over three thousand miles of desert I never saw anything but blue enamel pots used for tea. He poured a foaming, steaming stream of tea into the glasses from high above them and back into the pot, again and again.

The driver measured his medicine, exactly twenty drops of belladonna. For his stomach, or was that his heart as he gestured with the sweep of his wide-spread hand across his chest. He carefully counted out twenty drops before eating every morning and evening.

How comfortable we were in the quiet of the camp; the warmth of lamp, full stomachs, the blue pot raised through three rounds of tea, each sweeter than the one before.

Each sound stood pure against the stillness. In those moments when the wind rested, there was no ambient noise, simply the hiss of tea boiling over, the murmur of human speech, a footstep on the sand, the *Star Spangled Banner* on a Voice of America relay.

"It was near here that I heard of the death of your president," the driver said. "We were very sad when the BBC came on that night."

"Ah yes," the man with the child agreed. The others nodded their heads, looked down for a long moment, and sighed.

One of the others said something to the driver in Arabic, which he relayed to us in French.

"He said it was a dark day for the peace of the world.

137

Kennedy alone seemed to care about other people, about the understanding of one people for another. We do not know if that is true, but that is what we feel, what we hoped."

"*Merci*," I said, "that is our hope as well. That is our work."

The camp fell silent. I pulled my knees up tight and stared into a glass of beautiful amber tea, recalling the days after the assassination.

We lived those days in our household like stones, each in her own silence. Dissected from each other, our other parts, yet always present together. Together listening over the static for some words. Together wearing black to the ill-draped capitol. Covering our eyes with black glasses to close out the disrespect of the incessant Liberian sun. Sitting on black chairs. Numb to President Tubman's recitation.

Then out across the night, to the Catholic Mission, through black cloth doors to the Requiem Mass. Step to the front, seats reserved for Americans.

The first to come and fill most of the section were Peace Corps.

By and by others, ordinary Americans, came. Across the aisle reserved for "foreigners" sat Liberians with suits and black dresses and the Europeans. Native people to the rear. No seats left for the nuns from the Convent School. Over an hour and still more came until the faces of all Monrovia seemed to crowd in the open windows and doors and smother us.

"*In nomine Patris, et Filii, et Spiritus Sancti*," it began as usual. But this time one priest translated into English.

The Bishop spoke. It was tight and hot and he drained us. He knew us, we young ones, so pale and still. He brought every eye upon us.

"Behold the living monuments. Behold the spirit that lives while his body is dead. The Kennedy Peace Corps." He said it too loudly, too directly. We were packed too closely. The pain, the heat, candles and incense swirled and I was consumed. My stone body stood but tears simmering inside boiled over. They burned my face. They burned until I could not see and still he called on us, on all to see us. What right had we to be watched!

We knelt on the floor, stood, and knelt again. Puffs and plumes of incense choked the little mission church. Candles struggled for life as we did. At last there were prayers over the flag over the black cloth covering the empty box in the center aisle.

Outside, the steamy night was almost a relief. Victoria, Pat and I walked to a cab in silence. Home to more silence and more listening to words from the air.

How many nights to sit still and listen!

The next day a black sign on our door and drawn curtains closed us in our silence, and we slept.

There would be one month of "official" mourning. We would wear a black ribbon on our black and white dress, in the Liberian tradition.

How unprepared we were to mourn. The Liberians, even the children, had mourning in reserve, close by, for death is here, just past or soon to come.

We didn't know death. We had not even a single whole black outfit among us. Can this have happened? Be happening?

Had I not just taught my students that such does not happen in my country? We have a system. People vote and choose and agree to wait and try again. Our "system" deserves their skepticism.

Quietly we returned to school. The children tried to please, but as we talked of the assassination we seemed to be losing touch. The cynicism of their political experience demanded a Machiavellian explanation. They may have loved the pure and perfect theories I brought to them from the philosophers, but they had no expectation that human behavior could be pure and perfect. Reality was reality.

"Ah truly sorry, ya?" one boy came to say. "But for true, Ah know it' dat man Johnson to blame. Ain't i' so Mi' Mar? Ain't i' so?"

"For myself, Ah would say, who can gain da most from such a ting," an older girl nodded with confidence.

"Mi' Marke, the one who wears his shoes is the cause."

"Some people say his brother is behind his wife and she one fine woman-o."

Words. Nods. Sighs. Words. Tears.

The distance across the field from the classrooms to our house grew longer. The dry season bore down without mercy. I was tired. I felt as if I had always been tired. Tired from the nightmare of the preceding week. Tired from the distance my mind had to travel with my students.

"I say Mi' Ma', Ah too too sorry about President Kennedy. De children all feelin plenty sorry, for true."

"Myself, Emmette."

"Dey say President Kennedy die because he di'n have good med'cin. Dey say no man can kill President Tubman. He have strongest med'cin of all. If President Kennedy had such med'cin, he would live too. What you tink, Mi' Ma'? You tink it can be so?"

"You believe it, Emmette?"

"I don' know. It' jus' what I hear people say."

"One day you told me how juju couldn't hurt us because we don't believe it. So, if President Kennedy didn't believe in African medicine, how could it save him?"

"It jus' how some people talk."

"African science is for Africans."

I turned away, unable to break through the limits of my past time or theirs so that we could touch each other and understand.

I am the teacher. Yet it is I who learn. I who am ever aware of the dark chasm between us. Can't you see? I am not of Africa. I am of another place. It is different for me. My mind sifts in other ways.

"Oh people..." I tried to explain. But I could not reconcile madness with the democratic process.

America was not all that civilized. Our suffering showed us to be frail humans, like other people. It provided a common condition—vulnerability—to share. Softly, softly, I eased myself into this new awareness. We had inadvertently, yet assuredly come to what I had hoped for from all my teaching, to a moment in which we touched.

Pat broke the reverie. I glanced about and knew each of the others had recalled what we would never forget. She began to say something and found herself fumbling for the words in French.

"Oh damn! I don't think I could even say anything meaningful in English. Do you realize how incredible it is to think that the BBC and VOA reach into the center of the damn desert? And that these guys listen to them?"

"I think the incredible part," said Victoria upon hearing the translation, "is that they care."

"Tell them that wherever the world turns, and whenever they meet other Americans, we hope they will remember us, for we will not forget them."

"I don't think I can say all of that." But I did the best I could.

The fire burned down, and the temperature fell. The driver recommended that we sleep on one side of the *camion*. The old man would stay with us while all the rest went to the other side. Victoria followed his suggestion and made a nice hollow in the sand with blankets tucked in all around her. Pat was about to join her when she discovered the cab was empty and that she fit very well across the seat. The sand was cold. I was sure it could not be the best place and convinced Gruber and Darlene that we would be warmer and away from the wind huddled together in the hollow atop the *camion*. It was a logic rooted in ignorance.

The wind raged. And to our amazement, it reached all the way to the top of the *camion*.

"Who has all the covers?" Darlene shouted. It was necessary to shout to be heard even inches away.

The wind drove sand into every crevice and sucked our breath away. We thought we couldn't stand it another second. The Harmattan blew over and around us and up through the tons of cargo turning the heavy canvas tarp into cheesecloth. By the time we realized that it was impossible to stay on the *camion*, the force of wind made it impossible to get down. We were trapped.

I felt my body getting stiff. I envisioned the headline: *Peace Corps Women Frozen to Death in Sahara.*

"My toes are purple," screamed Gruber.

"It's dark. You can't see your toes."

"My toes are purple," she insisted.

We spent the night burrowing under the blankets, clutching them so the wind would not steal them, and hiding our faces from the grinding sand. By and by, the night faded to grey and the wind rested. Only when it stopped did I feel free to relax and sleep. But then the aroma of coffee wafting up from a small lively fire and the compelling presence of sunrise lured me off the truck.

It was worth it. I savored the precious quiet. The sky, which had inhaled the light and held it through the night, could not hold it any longer. It exhaled steadily, from grey to ash to pink to rose. At this latitude, and unobstructed by trees, or hills, or...anything, the desert day unfolds more quickly than it ends. Where evening is a lingering, morning is a burst of excitement, of anticipation in which all the forms and fears of night are exposed. The giant self, which is our overwhelming perception and preoccupation in the dark, shrinks to a speck as the vast plate of earth is revealed. We can immediately forget what it was like to not see.

Before the sky became full rose, the edge of sun creeping up on the horizon was enough to pick up a sparkle, as if minute crystals were laid upon the sand. Investigating, I found it was frost, formed from cooking water thrown away the night before.

A strange sound broke in the distance, shaking us out of a comfortable doze. We had been bouncing along without incident, warming in the late morning sun. In that fuzzy-minded state between sleep and wakefulness, I was not sure whether I heard or imagined the sound. I listened. It was shrill, heavier than the wind, even rhythmic.

"Jerrie, get up! Something's happening. Look out there, far on the right."

I saw nothing but a grey cloud on the horizon. We were all up, agitated by the strange sound. In a minute we realized that the sound was produced by the grey cloud which moved rapidly toward us, growing larger and louder.

Confused and frightened by this bizarre unknown, I turned to the Arabs just in time to see them curl up in terror and cover their heads.

"*Les sauterelles, les sauterelles!*" they cried.

"What did they say?"

"I don't know. I don't recognize the word. Give me the dictionary."

But there was no time to use it. In an instant we were engulfed by a swarm of locusts. We burrowed under blankets as they beat their wings against us in a frenzied cacophony. The attack lasted only a few seconds before millions of locusts clacked off to again become a grey cloud. The broken bodies of dozens of their swarm were left to writhe to death in the crevices of the *camion*.

That was it. A moment of intense confusion and excitement interrupting the ordinariness of mile after mile of desert. Afterward, we settled ourselves, prepared again to pass the time watching the movement of the sun.

Cantilevered over the roof of the cab of the *camion* was a shallow wire rack which held baggage and a tool box. Gruber amused herself by perching precariously on top of a suitcase, on top of the rack that hung over the cab.

"It's Gruber Washington crossing the Delaware," Pat heckled after Gruber ignored warnings about the danger.

"No, no. It's Gruber, Maid of Orleans."

"Haven't we got a flag we can give her?"

"That's my suitcase you're sitting on," Victoria pointed out.

"Kate Gruber, you're crazy. You'll fly right off there when we hit a bump."

"I'd rather you didn't sit on my suitcase," Victoria repeated very exactly. "It isn't meant to be sat on."

But Gruber ignored us all. She continued steadfast and cross-legged on her perch. With the rhythm of the *camion* and the warming sun her grip on the rack slackened and her head bobbed drowsily. By and by, of course, we hit an enormous pothole, just as the rest of us expected and just as our glances told each other. Gruber flew into the air and crashed down on Victoria's suitcase, cracking open a jagged scar across the pale blue container.

Gruber gathered herself up and matter-of-factly apologized for the damage. "No min' ya?" she offered in the Liberian manner. And, as only Gruber among us truly believed, she added, "we can't let material things be that important." Gruber's sore back and shoulder healed, but Victoria never let her forget the wound she had inflicted on a treasured possession.

At our midday rest stop we separated ourselves from the Arabs so we could eat without offending them. As they napped and tinkered with the truck, we used the time to read and write, activities we could not accomplish while being jostled on the truck or after dark.

During my turn in the cab, I asked the driver how he knew where to go. I saw no route and was not able to make out any system for the twists and turns he took. I hoped there was something more to it than following the sun.

It seems the barrels we occasionally passed were not just throwaways, but were weighted and placed by the French to mark the *piste*. The land was too soft to bear repeated traffic over the same place and so changeable as to make it impossible to improve a section for road bed. The barrels were situated a kilometer from each other in two lines a kilometer apart. These lines mark the eastern and western limits of the *piste*. Keeping within this guide then, one had a kilometer's width within which to choose the best surface and not get lost.

Our driver had been over the *piste* sixty times and read the sand. The shape of certain depressions, a subtle change of tone, the configuration of rocks told him what would support the *camion* and what to avoid. His skill was formidable, but there were times when there were no good choices and despite every effort, the *camion* would simply sink to a stop.

Even with the barrels and remnant rock piles that marked ancient caravan trails, there were long stretches over which the only tracks were ours and some places with many clear tire tracks going in every direction. We passed barrels on the left or right and then went for a long while without seeing any at all. Lumbering around a dune to suddenly confront a small tree, or swerving to avoid large rocks, I lost all sense of direction. The driver's instincts and reflexes alone—his modest explanation about barrels notwithstanding—would get us to Tamanrasset.

Late afternoon of the second day out of Agadez, we approached a long sand bank resembling the side of an immense basin that walled our path for as far as we could see to the left or right. Without hesitation, the driver veered the *camion* to the left, lunging up, up and over the rocky dune. Just beyond the crest, a few minutes away down the far slope to our right, a few black-green trees blotted the sand. We bore down rapidly and saw that these were not the gnarled dwarfs which appeared from place to place along the *piste*. They were tall, heavy with fronds, trees that water nurtured. They rose directly from the sand swept against their trunks and seemed as unreal as the paper trees stuck into the clay model of a child's classroom village. Beneath them, rose-beige sand sloped and mounded against the outer walls of a small compound, tapering to an abrupt end at the flat roofs. Only the long shadows of a low sun distinguished this angular earth from its surroundings.

We had found the tiny fortress oasis which they called In Guezzem. The Algerian flag, boldly flapping above the beige monochrome, told us we had crossed the border.

A lone man waited by the flagpole at the entrance. His skin was desert weathered, though otherwise he was not young nor old. Neither from his features nor his mix of desert/western clothes could we tell whether he was French or Arab. I saw no vehicle nor camel. Was his presence here by preference or punishment? This keeper of the oasis and our driver seemed happy to see each other. Indeed, they talked and laughed with the comfort of old friends.

The other passengers alighted and settled on sand banks at the entrance to the compound. Here they chatted and enjoyed the last rays of a slow sunset. Would we spend the night? Were we to unload and eat?

The driver had a great deal of news to tell the keeper. We waited.

"It looks like he's telling him about the locusts."

He gestured toward us and nodded when he caught us watching.

"I guess he's telling about us."

"I wish he'd tell us if we're staying here. When the sun goes down, it will be cold again. I'd like to prepare a little better than last night."

"For true."

We wandered into the compound and quietly and separately explored its shadows. The rectangular space had once been a fort and border checkpoint. Now it slept, blankets of sand covering its outer walls and creeping around the unguarded entrance to fill inner corners and unused rooms. In the center, the shade of a sprawling acacia protected a well and enveloped the courtyard in an early dusk. We spoke little, and then only in hushed whispers. For a few moments we saw no other people, only the quiet, the unadorned buildings, the still-life quality of darkening forms against a fading sky.

Two long rows of mud rooms joined by a shorter one at the far end surrounded the courtyard. Each room was exactly like the others with a low doorway and one window. Those on the left had been haphazardly boarded closed. To the right, kerosene lanterns in two of the rooms revealed a table and sleeping mats. Our eyes swept about the compound to learn more, but by then it was too dark. Even the curb-high rim of the well blurred at our feet.

Outside, the men were unloading and preparing a hole in the sand between the truck and the building for the fire.

I asked the driver if we would stay the night.

He said yes.

Then to make sure we had understood each other, I asked if we were to eat and sleep here.

"Yes."

"What time are we leaving?"

"Seven o'clock."

"This evening?"

"No, tomorrow morning."

"Good, we sleep here and leave tomorrow morning at seven. That's quite early."

"Yes."

I climbed onto the *camion* for our food and the enamel pan with lid. Five cups and spoons were still nestled inside as we had carefully arranged them.

The others lingered at the well, Victoria sitting on the edge of the concrete rim, her chin between her knees, gazing at her feet. How different were the inner and outer spaces. Outside the compound, with the help of the light of the truck, energy and movement prevailed, unloading and preparing. A few feet away, beyond the invisible curtain of the entrance, the mood was subdued. A spell of solemnity lay over the courtyard like a viscous membrane. Light and sound offended it.

I mixed a can of tuna with pickles and the last of the hard-boiled eggs in the pan lid and stuffed the mixture into the crevices of pried-open chunks of dried bread.

My friends were hungry but not anxious. The enamel pan squeaked as I placed it on the concrete surface of the well rim. Pat's glare told me that I was intruding. Passing out the cups was disruptive.

A woman appeared, drew water and disappeared into the darkness without a word. Things like that happened. There was no explanation. She was real, but she might as well have been a ghost. We could not talk to her or touch her or even ask about her. We did not see her again.

I lowered the bucket as I had watched the woman do, and listened for it to make contact with the water. Coil after coil of heavy rope followed it down, but so deep was the well and so low the water that at the end of the line I heard nothing and drew only half a bucket.

"I'm going to sit by the fire and make tea."

They did not respond.

I stood with my shallow pan of water outside the ring of men until the driver's assistant made a place for it on the grate. The old man indicated that I could sit. I took a place beside him against the wall as near the fire as I could and pulled my feet under my robe.

Their tea had already brewed and been tasted. By offering me the first foaming glass, the old man included me in the social ritual.

In its broad open pan, my water was slow to boil. From time to time one of the group came to stand by the truck. Pat even sat a few minutes. But for the most part they stayed in the cold dark of the compound.

Enclosed by the great desert, we encircled the fire and watched the old man hold high the tea pot and pour glistening amber fluid to fill a glass. Then another. Flames ate bits of wood. My turban slackened about my shoulders. Individual sounds lived their moment in utter clarity before they were consumed by the greater silence. Smoke stung my eyes and burned the quiet upon my memory.

The driver led us, loaded with suitcases and bedding, along the inhabited side of the courtyard to a damp square room just large enough for the five of us to sleep in. It was not actually a damp room. This was still the desert. But it felt damp as only a tiny space with mud walls and a concrete floor can. I didn't like it. I preferred to stay near the truck. The vermin attracted to a dark vault seemed far more threatening to me than any danger one might meet in open air. The driver insisted the wind and sand would be less. He inspected the entire space with a lantern to assure us there were no other living creatures and placed the lantern on the empty floor. Before leaving he showed us how to lift the not-quite-solid door into place.

Nothing to do but pick a section of floor and sleep. Victoria and Pat, who put their blankets together, chose to be under the window, their feet stretching nearly to the door. Gruber, Darlene and I marked our thirds of what remained and laid our blankets so that we could see across Victoria and Pat to the outside. Already feeling the chill, we determined not to suffer as we had the night before and quickly began to insulate ourselves against the cold.

Taking my arms out of the sleeves of both robes and working under them, I covered my cotton shirt with a sweater and thin jacket, then the brown robe, finally the black woolen one. Under the pantaloons I pulled snug jeans, replaced my sneakers and finished with a thorough rewinding of my turban. I stretched out on my blankets and rolled into them, snug as a sausage. My arms would be a pillow.

As I lay on my stomach, struggling to lift the hood of the black robe over the turban and pin it closed at my throat, smug in the satisfaction of my thorough preparations, I noticed that Pat and Victoria were smoothing out two blankets and unfolding a sheet over them. They continued with another sheet and two more blankets. The top half was folded back neatly as a guest bed. I waited for them to get into their warm clothes. Instead, Victoria very carefully undressed, slipped on a sleeveless yellow batiste nightgown and put out the lamp.

"Hehehehee." Darlene giggled next to me.

"Darlene!"

"Guess what?"

"What?"

"I have to go to the bathroom."

"I swear! In the next oasis, I'm going to buy you the biggest cork…"

So, others were awakened as well.

"Hehehehee."

"Are you going to giggle all night?"

"Who said that?"

"I have to go to the bathroom."

"Why didn't you think of it before we all got settled?"

"Oh man, you guys, do you have to talk?"

"Darlene's bladder calls."

"Well, I can't help it if I have a problem."

"How far is it to the place?"

"Just next to this room, a sandy space with no roof. There's a goat tied up at the back of it."

"Please come with me?"

"Bring the paper."

We unrolled from our blankets, dragged the barrier away from the entrance and scurried around the side of the building.

Back in our room we rubbed *crème* on our faces and hands and wrapped ourselves in our bedrolls for sleep.

"Jer, are you sleeping?"

"If I'm talking to you how can I be sleeping?"

"Hehehehee."

"What is it now?"

"Look outside."

"What?"

"Oh man, you guys…"

"But Gruber, this is serious. Hehehehee. Anything can come through the holes in the door."

"You're right. Anything smaller than a camel, like a Tuareg looking for a nice chubby wife!"

"That's not funny, Jer." (Gruber really was awake.)

"What can we do?"

"You can keep guard if you like. I'm closing my eyes. Good night."

"I just won't be able to sleep."

"Good Night, Darlene!"

Early the next morning, a very old man whom we had not seen before made a ruckus outside our room and gestured with his white robe toward the truck.

"Are they leaving?"

We rose (even Darlene who, to her surprise, hadn't been stolen in the night) without many words and began folding our blankets.

"Who has the paper?" Victoria asked.

"There's a roll in the basket."

"Doesn't anybody have soft paper?"

I continued to fold my blankets, determined to save the little I had for my runny nose. Did Victoria think soft toilet paper just rolled after us across the desert! It was because she refused to be burdened with carrying her own and couldn't be bothered with reasonable economy that our supplies were so low.

The very old man was still at our door, now joined by several others. Their voices sounded more angry than urgent.

"What are they saying?"

"Quiet, I can't tell."

"If people want to shout at us, they could at least do it in some language we understand."

"Get your stuff together, and we'll all go out at the same time."

We dragged the barricade away from the entrance and stepped under the door jamb. One of the men had a goat on a rope. All of them shouted and gestured wildly with their arms.

"What is going on?"

"*Monsieur...que'est ce que...?*" I asked in earnest.

"Just keep on walking fast to the truck."

Before we were able to get past them, the one with the goat pointed angrily to the area behind our room. Apparently this was not the bathroom.

It was a sour note on which to start the day. I was stiff from having slept on the cold concrete floor, bound all night in my blanket cocoon. The dark hovel of a room had prevented us from seeing the sunrise. Now we argued over toilet paper and pecked at each other about the way the baskets were being packed.

We were tired of the confinement of the truck, of crowded rooms, of sharing every move, every meal. We needed to have private moments. We could not part company. Yet we would escape. And we did. We moved away from each other by moving inward. We spoke less and sustained ourselves on private thoughts.

The Sahara was the first desert of my conscious life, but it had stirred a dormant sense of intense familiarity. Once I felt it, it was as if I had always known it. This morning, the third day from Agadez, my body responded with a physical understanding. I moved methodically. I did everything that was required, but no longer felt like bouncing. I no longer lavished energy on talk or superfluous gestures. I still drove the flies away from my skin but now let them set wherever else they pleased. (How could there be so many flies so far from any people or animals? What did they feed on while they waited for our coming? Or did so many hundreds of them stow away on the *camion*? What a hideous creature is the fly, its whole existence signaling disease and harassment.)

In the hollow atop the *camion*, blown sand quickly, quietly, filled the folds of our clothing. Exposed skin grew taut and cracked. I gave my hands and face another coat of *crème* and arranged myself for a morning nap. Gruber once tried to tell me of a change in the landscape, but I did not rally.

When I awoke, we had joined the mountains. The occasional trees and larger shrubs of the northern savannah had been left behind nearly a day before. Only the small dry "kicking" bushes remained; those which the old man had shown us, with a kick, could be snapped and crushed, wild thyme for the stew.

Far to the east, long flat-topped buttes, no more than a dark crayon mark on the horizon, separated the earth from the sky. The driver claimed we were headed toward them, but throughout the day they never grew larger, never more detailed, never closer. My eyes had watched a speck in the distance become a tree or person. They had played with mirage and reality. But for the extraordinary distance from which these buttes were visible, I had no comprehension. It was only the driver's word that let me leap beyond evidence to trust they were real.

By late morning the *camion* pulled up beside a deserted rest house. Sand had swept through the open doors and windows of both its rooms, partially burying them. There was no well. There did not appear to be any problem with the *camion*. We disembarked, expecting a brief stop to stretch and be refreshed.

The Arabs moved as usual, easily, knowingly, not given to lengthy discussion or grand gestures that we might interpret. It had become laborious to continually ask what we were doing, where we were, how long the stop would be, or any of a number of simple pieces of information that satisfied our need to be oriented. This time we asked nothing, but waited and watched.

Without turning off the engine, the driver and greaser gathered large rocks to block all the tires. They carefully jacked up the tons of cargo, each movement in defiance of the wind, which did its best to hamper but could not stop them. Before they were done, they would have rotated five tires. I thought of my father and what a lot of words and irritation would accompany the changing of a tire in the midst of a trip. There would be none of that here. The tone was set by the calm nature of the driver, who never angered or became impatient. Crisis and the unexpected were the ordinary stuff of his work. The belladonna he regularly took must have helped.

We five hoped to pass the time inside the resthouse, safe from the wind. Previous travelers had left their names and dates carved in the walls and their turds in the sandy floor. The thick mud walls kept out the wind, but held the cold and stale air. We ate quickly and returned to our mother, the *camion*. We shared sweets with the child who always looked to her guardian for permission. It would have been interesting to speak with her, but we had no common language and so were each left to our separate amusements. To the steel guy wires we tied Victoria's blanket to make a low tent under which a few of us at a time could comfortably read or write. Midday sun filtering through the red fabric bathed our pocket of shelter in a rosy glow.

We gave a great deal of attention to the processes and rituals by which we carried out our daily activities. The making of food, wrapping a turban, toileting, washing, packing for easy access. We tested and recorded each successful effort in our journals or our conversation. We cherished the satisfaction of coping well.

Here was Gruber addressing the physical assault of nature by herself. She wrapped her turban so that only the slits of her eyes peeked through. The brim of her *djellaba* hood was pulled over this down to her nose, allowing her to sit in the open tanning her legs while protecting her face from sand and flies. Gruber was pleased and offered to show the rest of us how she did it.

These little triumphs filled the moment but soon faded to boredom. We had had enough of this rest stop. Our companions thought differently. When they were finally satisfied with the rearrangement of the tires, the men said their prayers, washing their feet, hands and faces with water from the drum we carried. They spread mats under the *camion*, in the only shade, and slept.

By the end of the day we entered rocky terrain across which the *piste* became more defined. Gravel, rocks, small boulders, the ever larger and more abundant debris of the Hoggar Massif. The long-dormant volcanic mountains glowed intensely red in the falling sun. We were closer after all.

Our camp that night had none of the charm or relative shelter of the compound at In Guezzem. The site was chosen for no reason we could decipher. To make up for the long afternoon break, the driver had not stopped until after dark. We went directly to our tasks.

Our bread, eggs and pickles were gone. We were left a supper of sardines on crackers and a dehydrated soup cooked to a thick green consistency with water from the truck's tank. It appeared similar to split pea, but with a peculiar flavor, which some tolerated and others thought vile. There was, of course, tea, and a small treat of canned peaches.

We ate without ceremony and prepared to sleep. The top of the *camion* was out of the question. Victoria and Pat cleared an area of rocks and scooped away a shallow space into which they wrapped themselves. Darlene put aside her terror of scorpions (but not her talk of them) to help Gruber prepare a space. Gruber invited me to join them but I remembered the night in Zinder with the three of us in one bed and was sure I could do at least as well on my own.

I knew I should not dally. It would only get colder and the wind more violent. But I was distracted by the sky. During the previous nights it had been earthly sounds that resonated with such uncommon purity. This night it was a white clean-edged sliver of moon against a black velvet mat, unobstructed by clouds, ground lights or pollution. I was simply seduced and could not have enough of it.

The temperature fell, and the wind robbed my breath. I moved here and there under layers of clothing, wrapped in blankets. I curled up and lay flat. The fire died. The *camion* engine was cold. From time to time I heard someone try to warm herself by vigorously moving about, only to burrow back to the little warmth her companion in the hollow provided. My fingers became too raw and numb to clear away rocks for a hollow of my own. I climbed into the empty cab to find the soft vinyl seats of day had become stiff icy lumps. Without refuge, I endured the night, tossing in sleepless misery, longing for a pair of socks.

7

A Scorpion to Ward off Evil

*"T*amanrasset aujourdui!"* the driver declared, throwing the last of the firewood into a roaring breakfast fire. The wood had been collected at our first camp out of Agadez and carefully apportioned each morning and evening. Now there was no need to conserve, for this was the last fire.

We had been up before sunrise, if we had slept at all, doing our best to warm ourselves. The fire helped thaw our stiff bodies and ease our mean spirits.

We made a large pot of oatmeal with powdered milk and brown sugar, brushed our teeth, and loaded up.

The crayon line on the horizon which we had followed all of the day before without seeming to get nearer was indeed a mountain range. Since we had driven until after dark, we had not been aware of our progress. Our rocky camp turned out to be on the edge of the Hoggar Massif, rising now before us, austere and purple in the morning light. Our destination hid in the maze of that forbidding rock pile.

Throughout the day we climbed, imperceptibly at first, then at a steeper grade. As the grade increased, the *piste* became a gravel road, clinging to the side of the rock pile or switching back and forth through barren canyons.

A few hours before we reached Tamanrasset, we noticed

a blue-robed Tuareg on a white horse, watching us. Man and animal were poised so still on the opposite wall of a canyon that I did not notice them until they rode off, reflecting flickers of sunlight on a silver three-pointed saddle horn. Several turns in the road later they reappeared and watched until we drove out of sight.

We stood for our arrival in Tamanrasset. Along narrow streets, lacy-leafed branches of willow and acacia bowed to brush our robes. The sun was almost above us, and we welcomed the light-filtering trees. There were no trumpets or children throwing petals in our path, but there were enough children running alongside, daring each other to touch the wondrous *camion*, to give us the air of a triumphal procession.

The driver stopped once, at the *sous-préfecture* to report our arrival. (All of Algeria had been treated as a department of France administered by a *préfet*. Districts within were headed by assistants to the chief administrator, *sous-préfets*. At the time of our trip, this administrative structure was still in place.)

We waited, tired and dirty in the isolation created by the racket of the engine. We could see Tamanrasset, but not hear or smell it as long as the *camion* engulfed us in its own force and being.

It seemed to be taking a long time. I was tired enough to know I could be asleep in minutes. I concentrated on thinking in French. First we needed a place to stay. I knew I had precious little energy left to carry things, to listen, to translate, to make decisions. I hated watching my strength used in waiting. Perched on the *camion*, I felt captive.

Just before impatience and anxiety drove me to climb down and search for the driver, he appeared with the *sous-préfet*. They stood on the steps a moment, nodding and glancing in our direction. Though the air was still and warm, I checked to be sure that my face was covered by my turban.

"This is where you can get visas," the driver called up to us as he climbed into the cab.

"Now?"

"When you have rested. There is no hurry."

Of course. We were here and could not leave without the

cooperation and knowledge of others. There was no hurry.

Tamanrasset did not have a *campement*. We were driven several blocks to the Amenokal Hôtel and unloaded beside the ever-running engine. We thanked the driver but did not say good-bye, for we would see him again. He would return later to collect his fare. There was no hurry.

The roaring vehicle pulled away and out of sight around the next corner, leaving us in quiet, abruptly and totally alone. Our mother the *camion*, with whom we had been so intimate, from whom we had not parted in four days, who had provided for us and faithfully delivered us, was gone.

We found ourselves on the street side of a tall mud wall on which had been hand-painted the initials, FLN and ALN. The National Liberation Front and the National Liberation Army had led the fight for Algerian independence. It was the closest we had ever come to a revolution.

"Personne ici?" I called as I had practiced. The sound was pleasant, accurate.

A hotel would surely be expensive.

"Personne ici?" floated across the empty lobby, down a darkened hall.

A *campement* would have done just as well.

My heart sank when the burly innkeeper appeared. He stood with his arms crossed, in the middle of the corridor, not inviting us to the tiny registration desk. I began the careful explanation in French of who we were and what we wanted. He seemed to be waiting impatiently for me to finish so he could get rid of us. Victoria kept telling me what to say and Pat suddenly became confident that she could translate as well as I. It was a mess.

Finally, the innkeeper, who had not yet said a word, spoke up in plain English.

"Why don't you just tell me what you want." It did not make him seem any friendlier, but it was our language. That is, it was something like our language with an underlying accent I could not immediately place. It was not British. He had learned English from an American, that was clear, but he was not an American. At least American English was not his first language. We would pick over it for hours later. But in that first moment alarms of surprise and confusion rang in my head. What did it mean to have someone outside the five of us know our language? It had been stressful, sometimes terribly frustrating, and certainly limiting to communicate in French. Yet it left us with a private language which we could use at will. We had been free to say whatever we liked to each other and had become accustomed to commenting in front of anyone without restraint. Now this innkeeper in the middle of the Sahara, in a French and Arabic world, soothed and threatened us with the sound of our own language.

His name was Zoro. He had rooms. We would negotiate the price later. It would depend on how long we stayed, on what was to be included, on what kind of guests we were. Everything was negotiable. Nothing was more unsettling to me than this sort of uncertainty. We all felt it but were far too tired to protest. We desperately needed a bathroom and beds. And so, after days of fitful freezing nights, we dragged our things to our rooms and went soundly to sleep. We would deal with the price and Zoro's mysterious background another time.

In a few hours I awoke abruptly, charged with energy, completely refreshed, and buoyed by a sense of anticipation I had not felt since awaking at the hotel in Zinder. Our room had a tiny sink with running water. I was overcome with the urge to wash. While Darlene slept in the half light of drawn curtains, I filled up the sink with cold soapy water and, one after the other, washed myself, my hair, the enamel pan, five cups and spoons. All the water I wanted to wash and rinse and begin again. In the mirror above the sink, I saw the dim reflection of my scrubbed face. Hair that had been flattened under a turban for four days sprang into shiny soft waves. I snipped a bit here and there from the front and was pleased to see it fall into place.

We had only been in Tamanrasset a few hours, but I felt compelled not to waste a moment. I worked feverishly, sorting, piling up dirty clothes, taking an inventory of supplies we needed, mentally noting all the details of finding a ride and preparing to leave. It seemed especially important to call on the *sous-préfet* immediately. It was quite all right for him to say there was no hurry. He had all the time in the world. We had to keep moving, to get to Algiers before our money ran out. To get back to Liberia in time for the beginning of the next school term. I searched for something clean to wear, clean and... business-like. I ought not appear looking like a desert rat. Everything in my suitcase was full of sand. I shook out the black wrap-around skirt and cocoa linen blouse, not worn since I arrived in Abidjan. Seeing them now reminded me of the assurance I had felt crossing the airfield and entering the terminal in my high heels. The heels had metal tips which let everyone hear my firm step. They would do for my call on the *sous-préfet*.

Each of us was required to have an Algerian visa stamped in our passports. The others slept soundly. They would not think well of being awakened. No need. I would appear at the *sous-préfecture* myself and establish our position and good faith.

The *sous-préfet* was an Arab and younger than he had appeared from the top of the *camion*. He had black eyes, curly black hair, and a flash of white teeth in a wide mouth.

He introduced himself as Tahir, at our service.

"*Bon.* My friends and I, we are five, have come on the *camion* from Agadez," I told him, knowing he already knew this and probably much more.

"Ah yes."

"We have heard that it is you who issue visas and stamps. And we wish to have our papers in order."

"Of course, it is true. I am in charge of these things." He fumbled through the top drawer of his desk. Unable just then to find the visa forms, he added, "but there is no hurry."

"We wish to comply with the law," I replied.

"How many did you say were with you?" he asked.

"*Nous sommes cinq.*"

"And the husbands?"

"No husbands. Five women."

His eyes grew larger.

I moved ahead with my business. "We will need a ride north, and we wish to leave as soon as possible."

"The visa stamps must be bought at the PTT," he said. "It is too late today, tomorrow is a holiday, then there is the week-end…"

He was quite sure no vehicles would be leaving until Monday at the earliest.

"*Je suis le sous-préfet, je sais tous ces choses-ci,*" (I am the assistant chief administrator, I know all these things) he assured me, as he would many more times before we left Tamanrasset.

"*Oui, monsieur.* We understand your authority and are grateful for your assistance. It is imperative that we leave as soon as possible. We have many responsibilities."

"*D'accord, mademoiselle.* But you must enjoy your stay and not worry about such things as visas and transportation. I, Tahir, will take care of it."

"*D'accord, merci, monsieur.*"

I left with a firm step, accompanied by the entourage of adolescent boys who had appeared outside the hotel and followed me into Tahir's office. Within the hour my every word and gesture would be reported throughout the town.

The one-story hotel was an H-shaped building surrounded by high walls which enclosed private courtyards. Darlene and I had the first room in the corridor to the right of the lobby, Victoria and Pat, the third. They were still asleep when I returned. Both rooms faced the front and allowed us to observe the traffic to the hotel. Half a dozen guest rooms flanked the center corridor where Gruber had, not very happily, taken a single. Since this corridor also led to the innkeepers' family quarters at the rear, Gruber was able to overhear quite a bit, a benefit which only slightly compensated for her being alone.

Immediately off the lobby, the front left wing contained a dining room with a bar at the far end. How we looked forward to having a cooked meal at a table! I waited as long as I could, then woke them all so that we would be ready for supper and to tell them about Tahir.

There were not many guests in the dining room when we arrived. A very pretty French woman, with the assistance of a passive Arab house-man, served the tables. We called her *ma-*

dame and wondered if she was Zoro's wife.

"She's a lot younger than he is."

"Gruber?"

"I haven't been able to find that out, you guys. But I do know she lives here. And she, or they, have a daughter, about nine years old. Her name is Catharine."

"Imagine being a 9-year old and living here!"

As we ate, *madame* brought us greetings from three men who had taken a table near the bar.

"They're all really short," Darlene noted.

"Who are they?" we asked her.

"Syrians. Teachers," she said as she reached for the plates before hurrying away.

"I think I'll pass on this one," I said. The long day, the great burst of energy that propelled me to the *sous-préfecture,* and the wonderful slow meal left me feeling at ease with no wish but to return to that safe bed for a long sleep.

> 2/14/64 Tamanrasset
>
> Valentine's Day. Finished *Clea* this morning after many rounds of tea and bread with butter and salt and rich, sweet date jam which is very much like apricot.
>
> Today is the end of Ramadan. A great holiday. No Moslem works. I guess we were lucky to have gotten here yesterday. There is much feasting we hear to celebrate the end of the month of fasting. Walked about the streets among closed shops. People out strolling in their festive best. Today's turbans and robes are brilliantly white. Don't know if they have any special greeting for this day, like "Happy New Year" or "Merry Christmas." Two young Arab girls in chartreuse dresses with green and black argyle socks. I was ready to snicker at how garish, even silly, they looked but saw that they were feeling quite pretty and gay–as if it were perfectly right for girls to wear green and black argyle socks with chartreuse dresses. Just a matter of getting used to a different aesthetic.

It's very cold. Much more (if that's possible) here in the mountains than it was in the desert. Do wish we had a thermometer. The cold may be one of the things we remember about this trip, and few people will be able to believe it. Thankful these thick clay walls and many blankets keep us warm at night, though we freeze in the day and move about as much as possible to warm ourselves. One can deal with anything after a good night's sleep.

Tamanrasset is in a high broad valley, like many others we passed on the way here. It is the largest settlement in the Hoggar, and I expect the town is here because of a reliable water supply. It does seem as if the mountains, craggy shades of purple that make the horizon seem hazy, have just been dropped here. Not like mountains which have grown out of the earth with their foothills and gradual changes of vegetation.

During our walk near the market, Tahir tooted by in a pick-up truck. He offered us a ride, but we had no particular place we wanted to go and so pointed out that three of us could not ride in his single spare seat. Tahir, I think, does not like to be teased. Later some teen-aged boys in an old car followed us calling, "Your cigarette is finished," and "My doctor is a good man."

The Arab males here watch a lot of American and French movies. Darlene and I succumbed to "Hey, you want a lift?" and "Hop in, Baby," and went with the boys on a short excursion to photograph the mountains. We had not got far before the car broke down, and we all had to walk back.

The *patron* of the *camion* on which we came has not come for his money. The hotel owner does not press us to fill out forms or pay in advance. The *sous-préfet* is not upset that our passports have no visas or stamps. They all know we cannot leave.

Throughout West Africa the French wounds at having lost the colonies were still tender, but they were nothing like the open sores that ran through Algeria. Colonization, backed by an aggressive military presence, had been well established for several generations. In the Mediterranean region, where the climate was most agreeable, the land and labor cheap, the *colons* (settlers from France) had done very well. During the years preceding independence, the extraction of oil and other minerals, along with an active above-ground atomic testing program, brought French residents deep into the desert, as far as the southernmost district of Tamanrasset, but never so many that it became a truly French place. Nevertheless, the French, being themselves, whether many or few, never questioned what they considered their entitlement.

Long smoldering racial, cultural, and religious antagonisms were vented during the prolonged Algerian war of independence. Well after the outcome was clear to everyone outside, French residents of Algeria chose to be lulled by the rhetoric of de Gaulle and the antics of the Foreign Legion. Having denied the inevitable for so long, the *colons* were genuinely stunned by independence. Those who could left Algeria. The rest remained, embittered by the fatherland's betrayal of them and confused by the losses they suffered.

One of these was Madame Florimound. I am not sure how we met Mme. Florimound. I think she found us—accosted us would be more accurate—as we started on our first walk out of the Amenokal Hôtel. Life had dealt her a cruel turn, she began, squaring herself at the gate so we could not pass. She had worked to secure a good life for her last years, and, now that she had arrived at her maturity, she was abandoned by her country, set adrift in this foreign place.

"Two years ago, those were all in bloom," she said, jabbing for a moment with her umbrella at some weeds along the wall, then stopping mid-jab and glancing about to see if she had been noticed by any but us.

"Flowers everywhere. But now," she shook her head in grief, "what do they care for flowers? To love flowers one must be civilized."

We knew we were in for it, but there was no escape.

"You shouldn't be out without hats on," she scolded. "You

know how these Arabs are. They lock up their own women and then chase after ours. You'll have a lot of trouble here if you go about without a hat."

I wondered if she felt protected by the "Sunday-best" band of navy straw and tulle veil pinned to the top of her head.

"You wish to buy something?" She suddenly leaned closer.

"What, *madame*?"

"Things. I have many things for sale. I am forced by these terrible times to sell my collection."

"I'm not sure, *madame*. We don't have much money."

"Of course, of course. You will come tomorrow at three. I will send someone to bring you. You will see many things of good quality." She began to walk off, then turned back remembering why she had come.

"Are you Catholic?" she demanded.

"Some of us are, *madame*."

Her eyes searched to discover who was and who, God help us, wasn't.

"Well, those who are should not miss Mass. Don't think the Lord doesn't notice. You may think you are on a vacation, but He is watching everything."

"*Oui, madame.*"

"I have come to remind Catharine that I will take her. Someone must look after the spiritual needs of children, you know."

"*Oui, madame.*"

"You may walk with us if you are ready at fifteen to nine on Sunday morning. I like to be a little early to help arrange the altar." She continued into the courtyard, marking her steps with thrusts of her umbrella into the sand.

Tamanrasset, we quickly learned, was a different place, and the difference went beyond the physical environment. Whereas in Agadez we were left alone, free to watch as outsiders, free to find our way, free even to let our minds explore imaginary intrigues, in Tamanrasset we were pursued, and the intrigues were real.

Mme. Florimound was just the beginning. So many men arrived the first day we could not distinguish them even by the uniforms most of them wore. We rarely stepped out into the courtyard without someone waiting to walk with us or to offer us a ride. It was at once flattering, amusing, and oppressive.

There were the Syrian teachers; Tahir, the *sous-préfet*; Brahim of the Algerian Secret Service; Ali Tusi, some sort of supervisor of Tahir. Then there were a few from the Algerian army, the French *gendarmes*, a unit who identified themselves as *génie*, military engineers, from the French regular army, and assorted individuals who wore fatigues or paramilitary clothes but no insignia. In the same breath they introduced themselves and warned us of what scoundrels the others were.

Darlene and I walked through town that afternoon with the Arab boys, who seemed like old friends because we had met them long ago, that morning.

After the austerity of Agadez and the vast emptiness of the desert, Tamanrasset seemed a lovely place. Even though the buildings were built of the same red earth and straw, they were softened by the delicate shadows of acacia and willow. Sidewalks with curbs, street dividers, and a smattering of foreigners reminded us of Europe.

"This is fort of Father de Foucauld, famous Christian martyr," said the one who had identified himself as a Tunisian. He struggled to use his school-book English.

Darlene and I nodded. We had never heard of de Foucauld, but made a note to find out.

"This is the garden," said the one in the camouflage suit. We were touched by their pride in the small intensely green vegetable plot.

The three of them conferred in Arabic and gestured in one direction and then another, apparently discussing which sights to show us. From time to time one of them framed a scene with his hands and positioned us so we got the picture he admired. We walked to the far end of town, across the broad Wadi Tamanrasset, whose bed carried the distinct imprint of rushing water, though it had been years since the last rain. Along its banks, feathery tamarisk caught the wind.

The sun was at late afternoon when we reached the main well. A formidable excavation, it had been dug wider and deeper as the water table fell. Now its terraced levels covered a square more than thirty meters (100 feet) wide. The terraces were coated with concrete to withstand the daily human and animal traffic to the well and to prevent the walls from collapsing in a sudden downpour. The complex of pumps, pulleys, and ropes was more sophisticated than any other piece of engineering in Tamanrasset. We moved cautiously. The boys urged us to step down, to explore the well closely. The machinery groaned and clanked as bursts of water were pumped into open troughs. Adults led camels to drink. Small bare-foot boys with sticks herded goats and kept after strays. A million flies competed for air space and moist human orifices. On the second level dark-skinned, robed women watched us. Slaves of the Tuareg, our Arab hosts told us. By the third terrace the rim of the excavation was above our heads. We could no longer see the camels. The wind rose. I felt cut off. We were buffeted by swirling sand. I was frightened and could not go deeper into the well. Our vision was obscured by sand and flies, our voices lost in the din of bawling goats. We raced back to the hotel.

The Amenokal Hôtel served as the gathering place for French colonial society in Tamanrasset as the Provincial had in Bouaké and the Buffet in Ouagadougou. But the European population of Tamanrasset had dropped from a tiny community to a few remnant individuals. As in all places of small populations, everyone was known and everyone mattered if only as material for gossip. And also as in most small places, people went to a neutral spot for unplanned, expected encounters. In Tamanrasset, the hangout was the Amenokal, the place where we lived. In the normal course of any day or two all the Europeans and most educated Algerians dropped into the restaurant/bar of the Amenokal. Foreign travelers also stayed or ate there, bringing a little novelty and amusement to the regulars.

The dining room was packed that Friday night. The smoke of too many Marlboros and Gitanes and thin brown cigarettes hung over the room, obscuring the light. *Madame* handled the food, dropping tidbits of information about those she recognized as she flew by our table. An influx of Belgians fleeing the Congo would spend the night at the Amenokal while their plane was serviced. A German auto test-driver sat alone, his face rosy and serene in flickering candle light, creating an island of calm for the baby gazelle peeking out from under his jacket. Several French mercenaries sang in a dense cloud of haze at one end of the bar. A Swedish couple whose Land Rover had broken down were planning to leave in the morning.

The Belgians pounded on their tables and shouted to each other and everyone else their good fortune at having escaped from the "savages." Boisterous and red-faced, they called for service, waved their money, and spilled their drinks. Even their women were piggish.

"Why do they have to go out of their way to act the stereotype of arrogant, obnoxious colonials?" Pat observed.

"That's who they really are."

"I think they're stupid."

Madame worked feverishly, brushing damp curls back from her forehead. Course after course, in the French style—soup, meat (mutton, not too different from the night before), green salad imported from France she assured us on one of her flights by our table, soft cheeses and crusty bread, bottles of red wine. She prepared and served the food by herself and washed the dishes between courses because her Moslem workers were off for the Ramadan holiday.

I smiled to the nod of a French soldier we'd seen earlier.

"I can't believe this is real," said Victoria, concentrating, as we all did, on the plates in front of us, hoping to seem casually at home in this exotic gathering.

Zoro was everywhere, filling the glasses of the already drunk Belgians, joining in a chorus at the bar, seating a group of Algerians so that our table buffered them from any hostile gestures or racist remarks from the Belgians. Zoro would do very well this evening if he could keep the alcohol flowing and the sparks from igniting into a brawl.

Victoria was taken with the German and admired his pet gazelle.

"He's so gentle," she said, referring to the man. But he did no more than smile and watch until he disappeared altogether.

We were all foreigners in the hotel that bore the name the Tuareg used for their great chosen leaders. Within this fellowship of common rootlessness, a small familiarity made it all seem quite normal.

Tamanrasset was good for us. After the days of isolation and intense closeness and reliance on each other, we relished having a place where we could sleep without worry and be fed without having to think about preparing the food. In a day and a half we had not had to pack our bags. Best of all, we were free to come and go separately. There were many new people eager for our company. We were, temporarily at least, released from *nous cinq*.

After dinner, Victoria and Pat expected a visit from the Syrian teachers.

Gruber was uneasy about them. "They're too pushy," she said.

"But they speak English," Victoria reminded her. It meant a lot to Victoria not to have to rely on translation.

Darlene and I went to see a movie, "ci-ne-ma" they called it, with the boys of the afternoon. It was an Arab film with French subtitles, a great plotless hodgepodge of soap opera and pantomime, with gangsters, slap-stick comedy, romance, farce, even a belly dancer. As our eyes adjusted to the stuffy, smoke-filled theater, we could make out a rowdy group in military uniforms sitting on an empty bar to one side. The center was crowded with men and boys in disheveled turbans and robes, sitting on folding chairs and benches. A black man in a dark suit, white shirt and tie sat to our right by the door and watched us.

It did not take long to realize that Darlene and I were the only Europeans and the only women in the audience. The black and white film was scratched and dirty, and the action not very interesting despite attempts by our escorts to explain it. The audience smoked, ate and milled about in an agitated way, adding a disquieting tension to my feeling of claustrophobia. Several people noticed us and pointed us out to their friends. As more of them turned around to stare at us, we knew it was time to leave. The boys walked us back to the hotel and invited all five of us for an Arab meal the next day. We still did not know their names or occupations.

Darlene and I went to bed thinking what a full and interesting day we had had.

Hours later we were awakened by Victoria and Pat, who had just had an ugly time beating off the Syrians.

"Can you believe how jealous they are!" Pat said.

"What do you mean?" I tried to wake up enough to understand.

"They said they knew Tahir and the French soldiers and they just wanted what everybody else was getting."

"Oh God," Darlene groaned.

I had been in such a deep sweet sleep, I found it hard to concentrate, much less join the conversation.

"And—get this," Victoria said, incredulous, "they said it was the least we could do for them because they're Christians like us!"

"Where's Gruber?"

"We don't know. Only two Syrians came tonight, and she never did like them. As we were walking out, Tahir drove up and she stopped to talk to him."

We didn't have long to wait to learn what had happened to Gruber. She came in, trembling.

"Oh man, it's good to see you guys. I never thought I'd see you again!"

"Gruber, you look terrible! What happened to you?"

"I'm really sorry, you guys, now we're arrested and in a big mess." Gruber stood as she had come in, shaking as she clutched her elbow in front of her. The left side of her face was red and puffy.

I really did have to wake up.

"What's going on?" Darlene pleaded.

"Here, Gruber, sit down."

"It was so scary, you guys. I was sure he was going to kill me."

"Who?"

"Tahir, who did you think I was talking about?"

"OK, Gruber. Just calm down and tell us from the beginning."

"When Vicky and Pat and I walked out with the Syrian guys, Tahir drove up. I thought everybody was stopping to talk to him, but in a minute, when I turned around, you all were gone. Tahir said you went around the corner and he would drive me to catch up with you. When I got in his truck, he made a U-turn and shot away in the opposite direction. He had this wild look in his eyes. He was shouting, 'I love you, I adore you.' I was scared, but I thought if I just kept calm and talked to him, it would be OK. Then he started grabbing me and trying to feel me. I told him to stop and he got really mad and hit me. All the time he was driving like a crazy man. Speeding, turning on two wheels. I didn't know where we were. He drove in the mountains, up winding roads, over rocks. He said no women were going to make a fool of him. I told him to just let me out. But I was really afraid to be put out in the mountains. I didn't know where I was. Then he pulled out his gun and told me to shut up. He was driving with one hand and waving the gun around with the other. As we came back towards town, he shot it off out the window across the front of me. I don't know what I was thinking. But there was his hairy arm an inch from my face, shooting the gun. I bit him."

"Gruber!"

I knew I had to get out of the car. But we were going so fast. And there weren't any houses or any people around. Man, it was scary, you guys."

"Then what happened?"

"I'm not sure. I had my hand on the door handle. We were racing through town, and we hit a big bump that made the truck swerve. I think I fell against the door and when it started to open, I just fell out. I fell in the dirt, on my arm, and I didn't know whether to move or not, or whether I could move or not. Then I saw Tahir turn around and drive back, zig-zagging, looking for me with his headlights. I got up and started screaming. Another car came. I was so lucky. It was Brahim, the guy we met this afternoon, the one from the secret police. He had recognized Tahir's truck and followed it when he heard the shots. He brought me back here. But before he did, Tahir was shouting, that he was the *sous-préfet*, he was the law, that we were all under arrest. That we were not allowed to leave the hotel. I'm sorry, you guys. It's really a mess."

Early on Saturday morning, Brahim came to tell us his brother in Algiers was the *préfet* and therefore the superior of all the *sous-préfets*. His brother would see to it that Tahir was reprimanded. Another local officer, Ali Tusi, expressed his regrets over "this unfortunate incident." He promised to control Tahir. There were many apologies and prayers that we would not speak poorly of Algeria. When we brought up the matter of house arrest, they were less forthcoming. Brahim and Ali Tusi had a brief, strained conversation in Arabic. We insisted on knowing what our status was. We did not want to be harassed if we went out. They did not seem able to agree completely. In the end they said we must not worry, but we must be prudent.

We came late to breakfast and were the only ones in the dining room.

"One must be very careful here," *madame* said plainly, watching the departing Algerians. Without scolding or meddling, she added, "everything is noticed. How one dresses. How one acts. With whom one associates. One must be very careful."

Madame herself looked wonderful in a stylish sweater and slacks that showed off her marvelous figure, not at all the look of someone who might worry that being an attractive woman gave the wrong signals in a Moslem society. With long wavy hair, loose about her shoulders, and high heeled sandals, she seemed much more a young Parisian ready for a day of shopping and lunch than the proprietress of a remote oasis hotel. No one would have guessed she had fed the crowd of the night before.

Gruber's cheek was puffy and rosy, her arm bruised and stiff. But after some sleep and a good shower, it was clear she was more frightened than hurt. We ate and went over our experiences of the night before, trying to assess what effect the incident with Tahir might have on our finding a ride north.

All the while *madame* worked. She cleared the tables and

mopped the dining room. For two sumptuously indulgent hours, she supplied our table with loaves of fresh crusty *baguettes*, butter, date jam, and pots of hot tea and coffee with milk.

Through the open arch we saw her mop the lobby and carry loads of linens. Each time she brought another round of food to our table, we thanked her profusely and tried to engage her in conversation to understand more of her warning to us. Each time she smiled, said as little as possible, and hurried off.

"*Madame*," I tried with another topic, "We have met Mme. Florimound. She has invited us to see her collections and to go to Mass tomorrow."

"Ah, yes."

"Mme. Florimound takes an active interest in your daughter."

"Mme. Florimound is an old woman," she said. "I know what is good for me and for Catharine." She carried off the cups, signaling the end of our prolonged breakfast.

Once she had gone we realized how diligently she worked with no evidence of any assistance. Tinged with guilt over the comfort of our rooms and the pampered life she provided us, we offered to help.

"It will be good for us to work off a little of this food," we agreed.

Behind the dining room wing of the Amenokal, a private passage led to a kitchen partially opened to a service yard where the cooking and washing were done. We found *madame* there, stirring cauldrons of what would be our supper. She was embarrassed to be discovered working in what should have been the servants' area, and made it clear that the holiday had taken away her staff.

"There are so many Belgians these days," she added.

"We can't cook, but we can sweep and make beds."

She seemed confused at first, then touched, but firmly refused.

We spent the rest of the morning doing our own errands. Even though there was no chance of leaving until Monday, we could not get out of the habit of being totally prepared. In the market, we saw Tahir, subdued. He saw us as well. We walked out of our way to avoid a direct meeting.

To buy film we went to the shop at the home of The Photographer. We were not actually invited into the shop, but inside his courtyard studio. He brought chairs and showed us pictures he had taken and printed of local landscapes, buildings and the Tuareg.

"Tourists buy my pictures of the Tuareg," he broadly hinted. "It is easier than getting them to co-operate yourself."

"Of course." It was clear the purchase of a few of his prints was to be included in our transaction.

We then discussed various types of film and the techniques he used to photograph under the difficult conditions of intense sun, extreme contrasts between light and shadow, haze, blowing sand, and unexpected harsh reflections.

"Can't we just buy the film and get out of here?" Darlene mumbled in English.

The Photographer was not in the least hurry to make a sale. Victoria seemed to be enjoying the discussion more than courtesy required. We looked through the prints again. We made it clear that we wished to purchase film. Finally we took a dozen of his prints and two rolls of film, and ordered more to be picked up on Monday. The price was excellent.

We walked off at a leisurely pace across the courtyard and through the gate. Once in the public street, we felt a great release from the constraint of polite negotiation and burst into an almost-run back to the hotel.

Madame seemed to be looking out for our return as she rushed between rooms, pushing baskets of used linens and cleaning supplies along the corridor. She needed a favor, and, as a result of our earlier offer to help, felt she could approach us. Another planeload of Belgians was expected in a few hours and she was short of rooms. She asked if Gruber, who had a room to herself, would move into one of our other rooms. It was awkward, because, while Gruber hadn't liked being alone again, she liked even less being shunted about. Before we could comment, *madame* shepherded us to the room Darlene and I shared and proudly pointed out the cot she had set up and the tidy stacks of

Gruber's belongings. The deed was done.

Lunch with the Arab boys turned out to be a major meal at the home of Hamid El Bair, the black man in the suit at the movie. Swept sand marked the spare outer courts. Inside, bright striped blankets covered a concrete floor. In the center of the room a low round table with flowers and clear glass dishes waited. We removed our shoes and gathered around the table on large pillows covered in a chintz of white flowers on a red background. The walls were decorated with long mirrors and travel posters. Scant white curtains fluttered at the windows and door.

The three teen-aged boys, Hamid, and the five of us ate, talked, ate, sang, ate, and drank. After each course, one of our hosts collected the dishes and carried them out of the room. Another served bottled water and soft drinks. Wine bottles were added to the center of the table for our benefit, but they were not at home in this Moslem house. After a while the washed and dried plates were returned, accompanied by serving dishes laden with more wonderful food.

We never saw any women in the household. I don't know why it didn't occur to us to ask about them. We were usually reticent to bring up sensitive matters and preferred to observe and learn from what people volunteered. But we also knew we could ask and be forgiven as naive or ignorant foreigners. Most people were indulgent with our blunders. And so I know it was not a conscious decision to not ask about the women of the house or of the town. Perhaps it was because their absence was subtle and there was so much new and present we were too distracted to look beyond. Perhaps we were just having too much fun with the excessive attention of so many men. Whatever the case, it was not until well afterwards that we realized that we had not seen a single adult Arab woman in our entire time in Tamanrasset.

We did not understand Arab hospitality and had not realized how many courses there would be. The food was wonderful. Early during the meal we showed how much we enjoyed it by taking generous helpings. No matter how much we ate or how earnestly we protested that we had had enough, the courses kept coming. We became full. Then stuffed. Then bloated. Then nearly delirious with overeating and drinking. My leg fell asleep. It was astonishing. At last the tea was set out. We drank very slowly. There could be no way to show our gratitude. We only prayed to be able to stand and walk out without an accident.

Four hours after the lunch had begun, we arrived late for our visit with Mme. Florimound and her artifacts. She was not pleased. In the midst of a stern scolding about the virtue of promptness, she sighed as if she had lost track of what she was doing. She tapped her forehead very rapidly with the tips of her fingers and turned back to us, a confused old woman. In another moment she recovered and led us from one small room to the next through low doorways draped in blankets she said had been woven by the Tuareg. In each room the *mélange* of items she had displayed wore a fine coat of sand. They were her life's possessions, really, all for sale.

Among silver-trimmed Tuareg saddles, leather amulets, swords, and silver jewelry were remnants of the china she had brought from France, picture frames, cloth napkins, her long-dead husband's clothing, and several stiff Sunday hats with matching tulle veils.

In the same breath she demanded appreciation for her valuable collection and reminded us that we had kept her waiting. We could redeem ourselves for being so disrespectful by buying her things.

"You owe me something for my time. How shall I survive if you do not buy my collection?" She wavered between anger and desperation. Indeed, we would have gladly bought her Tuareg treasures if we had been able. She would never believe how little money we had.

Rescue came in the form of the Syrian teachers who arrived, much subdued, and persuaded *madame* that we had to hurry if we were to visit the Catholic Mission before Vespers. We chose a few small rings and silver Tuareg crosses—the limit of what we could afford—and left Mme. Florimound feeling she had been deceived.

In the middle of Tamanrasset, in the middle of the Hoggar, in the middle of the Sahara, the *bordj* (fortress) of Father de Foucauld houses the activities of the Catholic Mission. It is what remains of the efforts of an ascetic hermit to establish a Christian presence among the Tuareg.

Charles de Foucauld was born in the 1850s into an old aristocratic French family and was generally remembered as a bratty boy and self-centered youth with no greater purpose in life than indulging in the pleasures of the dandyism of the time. He followed family tradition by becoming a naval officer and volunteered for dangerous missions, including a stint in fervently Moslem North Africa.

Despite years of grand adventures and travel, he felt his life to be without focus or meaning. With the same inner intensity that drove him into ever more dangerous assignments as a spy, he turned to the ultimate in intense experiences—that of religious abnegation. He became a Trappist, the most severe Catholic order of the time. But after three years he found the Trappist life soft and set out to form the Little Brothers of Jesus, according to the rigors of his self-imposed standards. He longed for the isolation of the desert, the purity of a life without material distractions. Only the physical austerity of the Hoggar satisfied the personal austerity of his private spiritual life.

He established himself in Tamanrasset and carried out his mission largely alone, as few were attracted to join him. To his study of Arabic and Berber, he added Tamahaq in order to understand the Tuareg poems and to translate the Bible into their language. In thirteen years he made friends but not a single convert. The Tuareg regarded him as a respected *marabout* (holy man), but always a foreigner and infidel. The story of his conversion and hermetic life are well-known in France, where a movement has been established to have de Foucauld declared a martyr and saint of the Catholic Church.

Rising thirty feet to its parapet without a single window, the massive red earth and straw *bordj* casts the profile of a medieval fortress. One can neither look in nor out. The fortress rejects the influence of the Moslem world outside its walls and focuses on a life within. There, the present followers of the Little Brothers of Jesus and the Little Sisters of the Sacred Heart, devoted to prayer, contemplation, and the nursing of the sick and oppressed, maintain a patient presence.

Within, the stillness calls for hushed voices and a reverence only evoked by places extraordinarily centered upon themselves. Inside the great entry doors a simple frame surrounds a gouge in the wall. We see the gouge because the frame surrounds it and because it is pointed out to us. There are no words or other markings. We are told it was made in 1916 by the bullet that passed through Father de Foucauld, killing him as he responded to familiar voices at his gate. The gouge is nearly as it was in 1916, the desert preserving such things. De Foucauld died at the hand of a Tuareg he knew, who knew him as a Christian ascetic, holy man...and agent of French army intelligence.

The Little Sisters (the "Blue Nuns" from their plain blue headdresses) float across the inner courtyard in white habits emblazoned with red crosses, their eyes cast down, the gentle smiles of their white faces fixed on some mystical distance. It is one of their quiet times, and they move to the chapel, as if anticipating the rapture of contemplation.

"You shall return in the morning for Mass? You are welcome, of course," Père Jean-Marie confirms.

"Of course," we nod.

Moments later at the Protestant Mission where the Syrians had arranged for us to be invited for tea, there was no aura of mysticism. We found plain-dressed white people living a hard life, following "the call." These were the Baggots.

He was English, she was from Altoona. Altoona, Pennsylvania. With them were two single women, both Britons, like before and after, one of them young, recently arrived, the other middle-aged, at the end of her tour, about to return to her home on the Island of Guernsey. We talked a little about Guernsey and Jersey. I was intrigued by people who came from such exotic places.

The Baggots had a daughter on the edge of puberty and the anguish of their concern for her in this male Moslem world was great.

"How long can we stay," they asked, "when she is in greater peril each day? How much longer can we be her only teachers, her only friends, her universe?"

They were serious questions. They didn't acknowledge Catharine at the Amenokal.

The tea turned out to be orange juice and cookies. Theirs was a fundamentalist mission, they told us, which rejected caffeine, meat, dancing, and alcoholic spirits—unlike the degenerate Papists down the road.

We were silenced by their narrowness, their meanness, their fear.

The house was roughly built and drearily furnished. They depended on support from their Mission Board and had to make meager offerings go a long way. The Protestants were more isolated than any others we had met. They were not French and didn't share the cultural bonds of the other European residents. They knew a little of all the languages of Tamanrasset—French, Arabic, Tamahaq—but struggled to be English. There were only the five of them, living a suspicious, intolerant life.

Friendly, in a reserved way, they seemed to speak openly to us, though there was a tension within and among them. In fourteen years they had not been in an Arab home. Or inside the *bordj*. Or perhaps even in the bar of the Amenokal. He, not the women, had been to a Tuareg camp. Did the Tuareg really seem more primitive, more susceptible to proselytizing because they did not live in houses?

All five of them, I thought, were sacrificial lambs in this barren field where they would be shepherds. After fourteen years their flock had "perhaps" ten members. Moslems are steadfast believers in their own faith and are not easily converted.

To atone for their bad behavior of the night before, the Syrians escorted us on these religious rounds and asked us out to dinner at the other hotel. After a day of continual eating, I swooned at the thought of more food.

2/15/64 Saturday, Tamanrasset
It is very late and I am overcome by the fullness
of this day. Just enough energy to put down
these quotes: 'The richest love is that which sub-
mits to the arbitration of time.' 'However near
we would wish to be, so far exactly do we remain
from each other.' ...again, both from *Clea,* where
else? And both recorded here to help me when I
think of Jim. How many realities can a person
live in at the same time? How many worlds can
one move among and not be lost?

By Sunday our breakfast routine had solidified into a tradition. We gathered at our table, set, as we expected, with blue
and white checked napkins and the cups turned bottoms up on
the saucers.

The dining room was restored to its simple tranquil order
after another onslaught of Belgians the night before. We had
seen them, red-faced and pot-bellied (even the younger ones
seemed to have more belly than shoulder), as we passed
through the lobby on our return from dinner at the other hotel.
They pounded for service and more beer even as bottles spilled
on the floor. Zoro managed the loudest ones by engaging them
in cheers at the bar and diverting arguments with his long-
winded stories. Dull as the evening with the Syrian teachers
had been, I was glad we had not spent it at the Amenokal.

We broke apart crusty French loaves and added salt to the
butter, as usual, to protect ourselves from dehydration. We
mixed our powdered Tang with *madame's potable* brackish water
and used it to wash down our vitamins. On this morning, as we
had on every Sunday since the summer of 1962, we each took
two Aralen tablets to protect against malaria.

As was my new custom, I ate half a *baguette* with butter and
salt only. I was giving up jam. Lent had begun and the strong
example of fasting and abstinence set by the Moslems during
Ramadan nagged at me. I was used to giving up something for
the six weeks preceding Easter, something peripheral, something not good for me anyhow candy, soft drinks, movies—
pleasures I hardly noticed until they were named as my sacri-

fice. I started each breakfast at the Amenokal by not eating *madame's* fantastic date jam. I did not need jam.

But I was weak. I began to feel righteous for having already eaten half a loaf without. I added a thin layer of date jam to the next quarter loaf. I had earned this small amount. It tasted so good and who knew when we would have it again. A Lenten offering should be meaningful, penitential, a test of self-discipline, a total abstinence. If date jam was to be my offering, it was too late. I piled a thick layer of jam full of chunks of fruit on the rest of the loaf.

This mental trial became as much a part of my breakfast as the blue and white checked napkins. It was a self-conscious pattern of deprivation and reward which in the end led me to eat at least twice as much as anyone else.

Choosing between pots of hot milk and coffee or strong black tea, we loaded our cups with sugar. I turned away from Lent and savored the security and fullness of breakfast at the Amenokal.

Darlene shuffled about our room, dissatisfied with her hair, complaining about petty things. She was uncomfortable attending a Catholic service, even as a non-participating observer. I understood her apprehension—a little. My grandmother felt the same way about Protestants. And Jews. Even Orthodox Catholics. (I don't know if she'd ever heard of Moslems.) In fact, my grandmother felt her eternal soul was in such peril of being lost to corruption, she was alienated from just about anybody who wasn't a blood relative. She cautioned me as a child to not skate in front of the Assembly of God property (and they had the most perfectly banked sidewalk) lest I be led astray. So I understood, or I should say, I recognized Darlene's anxiety at being contaminated. I could dismiss my grandmother's fears as old-fashioned, but it was curious and unsettling to see them in someone younger than I.

Gruber offered to wait until Darlene was ready and to catch up with us.

Mme. Florimound arrived at exactly a quarter to nine to escort us to Mass. Pat, Victoria, and I fell in behind her and Catharine for the short walk to the fortress of Father de

Foucauld.

"You have something to cover your heads?" She was about to scold us.

"In our bags, *madame.*"

"It is the house of God, you know." The second sentence was out before she had a chance to hear our reply.

We crossed the street to avoid the calls of the men who always loitered at the outdoor tables of the other hotel. Mme. Florimound marched on, staunchly placing herself between Catharine and the spectators.

We chatted with Catharine about her studies, and she replied politely. She was a plump, plain child. Growing up alone, without siblings or playmates, had not left her lonely, but self-possessed. Our attention was not important to her. We were temporary people.

Thick mud walls and buttresses left the spaces they enclosed unexpectedly small. From outside, the fortress of the Catholic Mission loomed as a great forbidding mass, its solid walls relieved only by narrow slits cut high in the parapet. The interior, however, was reduced to an intimate, if austere courtyard. A low wall surrounded the well in the center of the yard. Narrow rooms and solid mud stairs had been built against the outer walls. The roofs of the rooms formed a walkway from which we could look through the slits of the parapet over every part of Tamanrasset. There were no plants, trees, or any embellishments inside the *bordj.*

The chapel was one of the narrow rooms, about 8 feet wide and 20 feet long, with a ceiling of at least 12 feet. Its only furnishings were a dozen low wooden stools set two each in six rows, and a small altar dressed with a white cloth, crucifix, and candle. Père Jean-Marie, assisted by Mme. Florimound, carried in the Mass book and basic implements of the service.

The priest conducted a simple Mass in Latin and French, and we mumbled our way through the responses, following the two Blue Nuns who sat in front of us. Light and warmth streamed in through the open door, accompanied by flies and the voices of other visitors in the courtyard. There was not a speck of sanctimony in Jean-Marie's voice, nor in the merry blue eyes that smiled above his white goatee. He had been, the Syrians told us, a French naval officer like de Foucauld, a wild young man who had a calling that changed his life. He welcomed the American Peace Corps teachers and prayed for their safe journey. He briefly reminded us of God's blessings and His mysterious ways.

We participated as if we belonged with them in this mud chapel in the desert. How easily we fell into being "at home." How easy it might have been to romanticize their quiet spiritual life. How many flies there were.

The Little Brother of Jesus and the Blue Nuns lived in poverty, however dignified. Their words and deeds, the seeds with which they were to bring a harvest of souls to their God, fell on rock. Each day their faith and purpose were tested anew. The miracle seemed to be that they did not despair. They could count no more converts than the Protestants, yet they went about their days as if it were the most ordinary thing.

I walked out into the blinding sun of the courtyard, reflecting on how, how…happy they seemed. Of all the words I could think of—serene, content, fulfilled—just plain happy seemed best. I could not think of anyone else I knew who was simply happy.

"It was good to have you join us," the priest smiled. "Have you had an interesting time here?"

"Very interesting, thank you."

"And now, what are your plans for the day?"

"We go to the Protestants next."

"Ah yes, we must all share our visitors. Have you been to Asekrem, to the hermitage of Père de Foucauld?" he asked.

"No, but we have heard of it. Is it far?"

"You can go and come in half a day. But the trip is over difficult terrain. Some young men will surely be glad to take you. You should not miss it. You will know it is a holy place. *C'est formidable!*"

More than twenty years later I would read that Père Jean-Marie had remained in the Hoggar, living most of his time in the holy place of Asekrem.

We had waited as long as we could for Gruber and Darlene, but just as we started off for the Protestants we were caught by Mme. Florimound, who insisted that we see her garden.

"It is on your way," she pleaded.

We stood outside a small plot of watered but overgrown flowers and vegetables, surrounded by a wire fence meant to keep animals out.

"At independence the garden was confiscated by *e-u-x*." She spelled "them" with a side glance down the lane. "It was my joy."

"Yes, *madame*. I see that it is very difficult for you."

"What do they know of having their own gardens?"

"We must go, *madame*. We are late."

The side trip to Mme. Florimound's garden was not on our way to the Baggots, but along a maze of narrow streets we did not recognize. It took longer than we hoped to find our way out, and everyone, including Gruber and Darlene, had already assembled by the time we arrived at the Protestant mission.

The chapel was a tiny ante-room off the Baggots' living room. It had a public entrance at the back and a narrow door at the right front, leading to their quarters. People were seated on bench-like rectangles made of the same mud and straw as the building. There were three "pews" large enough for two people each against the left wall and another across the back of the room. Reverend Baggot sat on a straight-backed wooden chair behind a small table at the front, waiting to begin. As we entered, Pat steadied herself on the door jamb. She had not felt well all morning and whispered that she needed to go back to the hotel to lie down. She waved off an offer to accompany her.

Mrs. Baggot blew a pitch pipe to begin the first hymn. We all stood and sang *Onward Christian Soldiers*.

"We have been called to this forsaken place," began Reverend Baggot, "to bring the word of God to the pagans."

He faced us, but his eyes were cast down.

"Our struggle is to show the way to the heavenly kingdom to these heathens, whose lives are full of corruption and debauchery. Most of them don't even know how to eat properly."

I watched the lone African in the front row, a frail black

man. The Syrians said he had been raised as an orphan by the mission, though the Syrians did not believe there were any really orphaned children in the desert, the kinship of the tribes always finding a place for everyone. However he got there, his years at the mission doomed him to a life alone. He was distrusted by his people and had no one to give him camels or goats so that he could marry. The Baggots were his adopted people, and they did not believe in marrying with camels, goats, or silver jewelry as brideprice. He worked for them in exchange for room and board and had no wealth nor tribe to offer a bride.

"They lock away their women to keep them from the Truth. They fall on their faces and worship false gods. But we know paradise awaits the righteous. Our forefathers fought the Crusades, protecting the cross with their blood. Now we face the descendants of the infidels."

After fourteen years, this was what they knew of Islam. Victoria's back stiffened. I gazed at the ceiling and tried to concentrate on the pattern of exposed branches that spanned the walls to support the roof. I recrossed my legs. My mind drifted. The once whitewashed walls bore water marks from the rains of seven years before. When my eyes fell to the Reverend, I realized that the room was silent. He stared at me and waited until he had my attention.

"Our work will be vindicated on Judgment Day," he continued, "for we are the chosen people. Unlike the Papists, we do not give out communion every week and make it common. We do not smell up our churches with incense. We do not trick innocent babes by baptizing them before they understand the meaning of being born in Christ. We don't mumbo-jumbo in a dead language so people don't know what we're saying. We don't dress men in long skirts and kiss rings and worship statues."

It was becoming ridiculous. The two single women of the mission sat together, their heads bowed.

Mrs. Baggot blew the pitch pipe again. I did not stand.

> Mine eyes have seen the glory of the
> coming of the Lord;

He is trampling out the vintage where
    the grapes of wrath are stored;
He has loosed the fateful lightning of his
    terrible swift sword;
His truth is marching on.

They sang it like a dirge until the refrain.

Glory! Glory! Hallelujah! Glory! Glory!
    Hallelujah!
Glory! Glory! Hallelujah! His truth is
    marching on.

He has sounded forth the trumpet that
    shall never call retreat;
He is sifting out the hearts of men before
    his judgement seat;
O be swift, my soul, to answer him; be
    jubilant my feet!
Our God is marching on.

They skipped the verse about the beauty of the lilies where
we live to make men free. Miss Avery, the one on her way back
to Guernsey Island, read a passage from the Bible. The Reverend led the Lord's Prayer. Mrs. Baggot blew the pitch pipe for
the last time.

Faith of our fathers, living still
in spite of dungeon, fire and sword:
O how our hearts beat high with joy,
Whene'er we hear that glorious word:

Faith of our fathers, holy faith!
We will be true to thee till death.

The Baggots caught us off-guard.
"It's a good thing Pat didn't stay."
"For true."
The minute their service was over, we bolted out the back
door and across the desolate little garden, slamming the gate

behind us and running until we rounded a high wall at the corner.

The thin dry air of Tamanrasset and an intense mid-day sun brought us back to reality. I leaned against the wall to catch my breath. I wasn't short of breath from running, but from having held it for longer and longer moments as the tension in the chapel mounted.

"Whew! Free in the nick of time."

All the way back to the hotel we purged ourselves of the Baggots.

"It was hateful."

"Pure theater."

"But it's not theater. It's their life!"

That afternoon we drove more than 10 km into the mountains and hiked over porous volcanic debris with the Arab boys. It was rough going. The road bed of pebble-sized ground rock crunched with each step but did not slide from under us. The slopes were more difficult.

Jagged basalt columns, like cracked and fractured stalagmites, rose out of the rubble at their base. Centuries of freezing and scorching, perpetual exposure to the abrasion of the wind, and the complete absence of any soil or vegetation created the desolation that is the Hoggar.

"*Ahaggar*," the Tunisian carefully pronounced in the aspirated guttural of Arabic.

The Hoggar was not so much a mountain as a rock pile. Chunks broke off under foot. The boys scaled the steep sides of buttes with ease and called us to keep up. We trod carefully, rock to rock, testing each before we shifted weight forward. Darlene twisted her ankle. Back and forth through a maze of rocky mounds, we lost all our bearings. Victoria stepped lightly. The wind rose and the sun sank. Black shadows crept forward from craggy pinnacles.

"We'd never find our way out of here," Darlene shuddered under her breath.

"And nobody'd ever find us either," I agreed.

We had a lesson in how to locate water by reading the

shades of fine-ground rocks and gauging imperceptible depressions in the sand beneath. It would have been useful if we had planned to stay, but the idea of knowing how to survive was tied to needing to know because one lived there. We were impatient. It was dry and cold and the sand which we hadn't even seen among the rocks blew against our bare legs. Any thought of needing to know how to find water was more than unsettling.

The boys led the way back to the car. When we reached the roadway, they moved between us and put their arms around our shoulders. It was an awkward gesture and even more awkward walking six abreast across the loose gravel, three short boys and three tall women.

"How old are you?" I asked.

"Sixteen, seventeen, eighteen," said the one in khaki, pointing to himself first, then to each of his friends.

"How old do you think we are?" I continued.

They conferred with each other and agreed we were also sixteen and seventeen.

I shook my head.

"Less?" guessed the Tunisian.

"More."

"Not more than eighteen each," he said with confidence.

"Twenty-three," I began, pointing to myself, "twenty-two for Darlene and twenty-four for Victoria."

"It is not possible!"

"Oh my friends, truly it is."

The Arab boys did not leave us on the mountain because of this shocking revelation. They remained friendly, but from then on there was a difference, a distance. It was as I had hoped.

On Sunday, the fourth day in Tamanrasset, we returned to our cold room and looked at the calendar and our dwindling money. We had not yet come to terms with Zoro over the price of our stay. We had no leads on transportation.

"We just have to try harder to find a ride, you guys." Gruber stepped in with optimism as she saw our spirits weaken. "Talk to everybody you see."

"You're right," I agreed. "I don't think we can rely on Tahir, especially after the other night."

"OK, you guys, starting now, we talk to everybody we see about a ride. You never know who might help us."

"And tomorrow we get our visa stamps, so we're ready to leave."

Dinner at the hotel was losing its charm. A lingering essence of butter and jam wafted from the blue and white napkins of breakfast.

"*Oui, c'est moutton!*" *Madame* smiled proudly as she had the first time she'd served it.

"Do you have the feeling that mutton is not only the house specialty but the whole menu?"

The chunks of tender meat and vegetables, slow-cooked in a wonderful sauce that had seemed such a precious delicacy just a few days before, had become nothing more than warmed-over stew.

The Belgians were gone, as well as the German with the gazelle. There were a few new faces in the dining room, mostly men in assorted uniforms. Men in uniform were also losing their charm. We ignored them, concentrating inward on our circle, getting each other caught up on the events of the day.

That morning Pat met one of the Syrians on her way to the hotel after feeling ill at the Baggots.

"I just sat down for a minute to let the nausea pass," she said. He bought her tea and pledged, "I love you more than my eyes."

"It's hard to know what to say to that, especially when you feel so shitty you just want to go to bed." She continued, "I talked about everything I could think of. The weather. The Palestinian situation. I even remembered to mention that we needed rides. I asked him who his favorite authors were. It was hard work. I felt if I just walked away we'd have another incident."

Madame returned to tell us a French army officer at another table wanted to send us a bottle of wine. "Red or white?" she asked.

"*Rosé*," I replied.

"OK, Pat, then what happened?"

"Then Tahir showed up. He wanted me to tell you," she pointed to Gruber, "that he loves you."

"He has a great way of showing it."

"At first he was calm. Then he seemed agitated. He wanted to know why I was having tea with the Syrian and you wouldn't go with him. Well, one thing led to another and before I knew it, the two of them walked me back here and Tahir said it was illegal to be in public without a proper visa and 'ordered' me to stay here."

"Tahir seems to make up the law as he goes."

"It was confusing," Pat admitted, "but I just wanted to get away from them and get in bed."

"I wonder if there's any connection between that and Brahim telling me there were irregularities and that none of us could leave the hotel until he had looked into them?" Gruber speculated. "It's a good thing you guys already left on the hike."

"This is getting to be a mess."

"I think it's ridiculous. We haven't done anything. You just can't go around arresting people." But even as I spoke I knew what every face at the table confirmed. In Tamanrasset, Tahir was the law. We had neither power nor protection.

"Sounds like a soap opera to me."

"Whatever it is, it isn't helping to get us a ride."

"We have no *rosé* wine," *madame* informed us.

"Then white."

"They would like to join you," she added.

"Do you know them, *madame*?"

"Oh yes. They are from the *génie* camp outside of town, engineers on the road, pleasant fellows. The handsome one is the *chef* (commander)."

The *chef* and his companion, a young soldier, pulled chairs up to our table.

"He looks like William Holden," Darlene whispered under a great blush.

Indeed, the tidy way his brown hair waved back from his

forehead, with barely a part on the side, strongly resembled the actor. He was in his thirties, we guessed, but his filled-out body, thick arms, and calm demeanor made him seem older.

Once again we introduced ourselves and told of being in the Peace Corps and teaching in Liberia. The *chef* spoke in a low-keyed and idiomatic French, as if we easily understood every word. I listened intently and asked him to repeat only when it seemed I was losing the entire drift of conversation. When the silence of the soldier became apparent, the *chef* explained that he was shy, a Polish boy not comfortable in French. The *chef* had a very kindly and protective manner toward the Polish soldier.

"What a nice man," Victoria said in English.

"Your friend doesn't speak French?" *chef* asked.

"No."

"As I don't speak English. What a pity. If only I were as clever as Zoro there—French, English, a little Arabic."

"Yes, Zoro speaks English with an American accent," I noted. "But he is not an American."

"No, no, no," *chef* explained, "Yugoslav."

"How did he get here? How did he learn these languages?"

Chef glanced about the room and leaned into the table, "Foreign Legion."

Zoro grew more exotic even as I translated.

"Tell him we need a ride," Gruber prodded.

"I don't see what good it will do, he can't help us."

"He may hear of something."

And so the *chef* and the Polish soldier were added to our list of contacts.

On Monday morning we awoke with resolve to pursue every source for a ride. We had our list of business to take care of—picking up the film we had ordered at the photographer's, shopping for a few supplies, getting the visa stamps.

At breakfast *madame* said there was no need to hurry out of Tamanrasset now that the ambassador was coming. The comment went by us as it didn't seem to make any sense, and it was said so casually it didn't seem worth the effort to ask her to repeat so that we could get it right.

Getting the visa stamps assured we were legally in Algeria

and rid us of the worry of a hassle over our papers. While at the PTT we also tried to send telegrams to Monrovia and Algiers to explain our delay. None of us had much faith that the messages would get through. We had barely gotten out the door when the men and boys sitting on the stairs rushed in to read what we had asked to be sent.

The scene at the PTT was not unusual, but the tone was. There seemed to be more polite nods than jeers. We sensed a change throughout the town. Tahir passed us with a smile and a bow. The *patron* of the *camion* on which we'd come to Tam asked when it would be convenient for him to call.

We ran into Brahim, who said he had been looking for us ever since he heard the news.

"It will be a very great honor for Tamanrasset," he said.

"What are you talking about?" We seemed to be the only ones not to know.

"The American ambassador will be here on Thursday. We have heard this morning. He is traveling overland from Algiers."

"So that's what *madame* was referring to." Even she had got the word through the town's amazing flash flood of gossip.

The arrival of the American ambassador was interesting but not especially exciting news for us. Thursday was four days away, and we absolutely had to be gone before then.

In the meantime, Victoria and I took up Brahim's offer to ride camels. We went to a small Tuareg camp just outside of town. It seemed to be there only for the care of the camels and was not a true camp where families lived. Nevertheless, we bought a few pieces of rough leather and silver jewelry and had a turn on the camels, who did not seem at all happy with our handling. The wind rose earlier than usual that day and forced us back to the hotel by early afternoon.

Pat and Darlene had already returned from their errands, and so only Gruber was not around.

Hours later we heard a ruckus in the street. The wind had gotten worse and churned up so much sand as to turn the sky grey. From our window we could see only the courtyard and the small bit of street at the gate. We put on our turbans and

193

robes and went to investigate. Coming down the road was a mob of chanting, shouting men and boys in long robes. Some carried placards, others sticks. They were being led by a pair who ran in front, whipping them up with slogans to which the mob responded. The group filled the width of the street and advanced steadily toward the entrance to the Amenokal. I dashed in front of them, took a quick picture while they were less than a hundred feet away, and ran back into the hotel.

"Politics," said *madame*, shaking her head and closing the door behind us. We watched from the window until they had all passed the gate and the sound of their chants was lost in the wind.

Moments later Gruber returned, breathless over the wonderful day she had had.

"If you guys had been here, you could have gone, too. I wish you had seen it."

Somehow she managed to get the Syrians and Tahir, who had arrived at the hotel at the same time, and who were ready to insist that she choose between them, to all go along on a trip to Asekrem, the hermitage of Father de Foucauld. On the way they stopped at a true Tuareg camp and had a meal over much translation from English to French to Arabic to Tamahaq and back through all the layers. The hermitage itself was a stone shack high in the purple Hoggar. De Foucauld had built it himself, stone by stone, at the end of a steep difficult goat trail.

"It took about half an hour to walk up from the road. They said the word 'Asekrem' means 'the end' in Tamahaq. And it felt like it, the end of the world."

There were a few instruments to record wind and temperature—an interest of Fr. Jean-Marie.

"It was fantastic, absolutely fantastic. The priest was right when he said it was a holy place. A little scary, too. But unbelievable!"

The *chef* from the *génie* camp returned to the Amenokal for an early supper. He was sending a convoy north, he said, and could offer us a ride to Columb-Béchar. His men would be in town for supplies the next day and we could go with them to their camp.

It was a stunning offer. He was a nice man. I didn't like the idea of a military camp as a destination. No town. No authorities except the *chef*. The place he called it—Tit—wasn't on our map. We had no idea where Tit was in relation to the main route.

We discussed it with *madame*.

"Of course," she said, "it is your choice. But everyone will know and they will talk." She was serious. "There is nothing there. A camp. A few Tuareg. No electricity. Nothing. Only men." She cast her eyes down. "It is a great risk. What kind of women could even think of such an offer?"

Madame, who had seemed such a free soul herself, was becoming downright righteous.

"But *madame*, do you think the *chef* is telling the truth about a ride to Columb-Béchar? It is a long way and we have found no others."

"I cannot say. I only know there is nothing there. Once you leave Tam you have no control, no choice. It would even be difficult for you to return to Tam. People have an opinion of you from your good behavior here. If you go with the army, they will say you are that kind of women. It is your decision. It is your reputation."

"She's the only woman we can remotely talk to in this whole damn place."

"Here we are, in the middle of the Sahara Desert, passing through, and she warns us about our reputation!"

"I didn't expect such a strong reaction."

"I thought she sort of liked the *chef*."

"You heard her. Didn't she say something like, dinner, wine and conversation are one thing, moving to his camp is quite another?"

"That's the gist of it."

"What are we going to do!"

"We could wait until the ambassador comes and try to hitch a ride with him."

"Get serious."

"The *chef* is a nice man."

"I think it's too scary."

"We are completely vulnerable if we go with him."

"We can't stay here. The longer we stay, the more likely we are to get dragged into the social quagmire. You know how hard it is to stay out of trouble."

"Shit, shit, shit!"

"So what do we do?"

"The *chef* is sending some guys for supplies tomorrow. They should come by the hotel about noon. We either go with them or we don't. That's it. If we don't, we lose that chance."

"It's not until tomorrow. Maybe something else will turn up."

There was not much more to be said and so, little was. We had not made a decision, but the next morning each of us acted as if we were leaving. That is, we did what needed to be done so that we would be ready when the time and decision came. Doing itself, then, became a part of the process of deciding.

Darlene and I went to the market for a last search for toilet paper. We found only the stiff brown kind and were about to buy it and some jam when we saw the *patron* of the *camion*. It was a lucky meeting, as finding him was next on our list. He nodded to the merchant, who gave us the things we were about to buy for free. When we told him we were ready to pay for the ride to Tam, the *patron* and his friend invited us to his home. We did not have time for a visit.

"We may be leaving today," I said. "We have many things to prepare."

"It is because you are leaving that you must come and accept our hospitality now," he insisted.

Darlene and I sat on cushions on the floor of a plain room with the *patron* and his friend. We paid them for the ride from Agadez in new *francs*, as we had agreed. They served tea and couscous, one bowl, four spoons, in the Arab style. "You are what you eat," I thought. And as we and they ate from the same bowl, a little of us and a little of them would go on being nurtured by the same food. As in other Arab environments we had been in, there were no women evident. We had a quiet, far-ranging conversation, and I was sorry we hadn't talked to them before.

Christians had told us of the Moslem fanaticism we would encounter, which the Moslems had seen no need to impose on us themselves. While there may have been staring and jeering comments from strangers, and here and there, a rare temperamental Tahir, all the individual Moslems we met had been quiet and patient people.

It was noon and the *chef's* men would be coming. The *patron* rose and asked us to wait while he went for something in another room. It seemed to be taking a very long time. We had to leave, but I didn't know how to do it. We felt trapped. We knew little about the etiquette of leaving, but I was sure whatever we did would seem rushed and rude. Darlene squirmed. We didn't know why he had gone out of the room or how long he would be. I began to get up and give my regrets to the friend when the *patron* returned.

"We wish you to take these mementos," he said, offering each of us a silver scorpion embedded in orange plastic and hung from a loop of braided black yarn.

"It would have to be a scorpion," Darlene said, suppressing her dread.

"It's OK. It's dead."

Darlene and I conferred further in English. A wrench had been thrown into our leaving. Should we accept? Should we offer to pay? What could we give in exchange? We admired the medallions. I asked how they were made and if they were real scorpions. We stalled our response, all the while watching the hands of the clock.

"These are very lovely," I said, "but we cannot accept. We have nothing to give you in exchange." We stood up. "We are going now. We will be very late."

"You are our guest. The scorpion keeps away evil and brings good luck to travelers. Take them as a little remembrance."

8

Songs on the Plains of Tit

Despite *madame's* oblique warning, we decided to accept the *chef's* offer. I was nervous. Not afraid or confused. Nervous— yet resolved. We had reviewed the risk. It was high. A nice man had said, come with me, I will take care of you, I will get you to Algiers. There was an edginess to our movements as we packed. And a quickness, too, so we did not have time for second thoughts.

I paid Zoro as we had agreed, $5 each per day for room and meals (a real bargain), for a total of $125 in American travelers' checks. It was an easy transaction. Zoro was a person of few words.

We left Tamanrasset in two small trucks. Traveling separated from each other added to our disquietude. Was our decision a justified trust or folly? Every time the other truck fell briefly out of sight, I felt a wave of anxiety.

The *génie* camp consisted of nine tents, several vehicles, and a flagpole set in a sandy stretch of the plains of Tit, a long hour northeast of Tamanrasset. The tents were made of a heavy grey-green canvas. The five large ones, 15 to 20 feet on a side, were entered through "vestibules," triangular enclosures extending from one end. The vestibules contained a labyrinth of canvas flaps, an ingenious way to keep warmth in the tents and wind and sand out. They also provided a bit of privacy by making it impossible to look directly into a tent from outside.

We were led to the mess tent, moving from side to side through the maze of flaps to a room furnished with two rows of tables. We said our names. The *chef* introduced the men present. All discussion was in French.

The atmosphere was low-key, plain and unadorned like the tent itself. We sat among them tentatively. We were offered refreshments. The cook, pot-bellied and avuncular as a cook should be, set the tone.

"Well then, our American teachers. And how long do you do this teaching?"

"Eighteen months already. And another six months after we return to Liberia."

"Ah, the good fortune of the Liberians."

We smiled.

"How did you choose Liberia?"

"The Peace Corps assigned us, after a request by the Liberian government."

"Then you are Peace Corps, the chosen ones, Kennedy's children." He paused and wiped his brow with his apron. "You are the first Americans I have known personally. But I know America. America has been good to France and to all the world." He spoke slowly, deliberately. "I tell you, and I speak for Frenchmen everywhere, the saddest day of my life was the day Kennedy was shot. It was a terrible thing. Who could do such a thing? My heart bled." He used the apron again to wipe his eyes.

The others at the table nodded their agreement and shifted uncomfortably in silence. We were linked to them by our shared grief and welcomed into their circle.

Throughout the afternoon the cook plied us with tea, soft drinks and snacks. We told stories and asked questions. They told stories and asked questions. There was a lot to translate. The troops came and went, so that it was not until supper that we knew the size of the camp—twelve men; five white Frenchmen, one white Polish-born about to become French, three brown and two black Algerians, and one brown Tunisian. At least half of them were younger than we, but the Polish soldier seemed especially young and timorous. His family had immigrated to France and two years of military service was required of him to gain citizenship. None of them spoke English, though the French ones assured us that every French student studies it for six years.

The day drifted into evening. It was easy to understand why the *chef* took them by turns on the long drive to Tamanrasset for a dinner in town. The tents were cold and drab. There were some cards, a box of dominoes. But for the most part, their only amusement was each other and now, us. By this time we had become competent at amusing. We had grown into it, refining our stories, never tiring of the stories of others. Our stories and our songs traded for the kindness and hospitality we received.

Victoria began the singing. With her clear sweet voice she led us in *Five Hundred Miles*. We knew all the verses to this one, having long been more than five hundred miles from our homes. In the pause between verses, Victoria hummed and I rapidly translated. We were sure with our songs and went directly to the next one.

> I gave my love a cherry without a stone;
> I gave my love a chicken without a bone;
> I gave my love a ring without an end;
> I gave my love a baby with no cryin'.
>
> How can there be a cherry without a stone?
> How can there be a chicken without a bone?
> How can there be a ring without an end?
> How can there be a baby with no cryin'?
>
> A cherry, when it's blooming, it has no stone;
> A chicken, when it's pippin', it has no bone;
> A ring when it's rolling, it has no end;
> A baby when it's sleeping, there's no cryin'.

The songs were plain, but we sang them fully and filled the dingy tent with mellow harmony. The *chef*, whose thoughts had drifted, signaled his men to give us a song in return. M. Libert, the mechanic, with a quick mischievous glance around the tent, launched into a hearty tune. His buddies immediately realized its bawdy message and booed and wrestled him to the ground.

The *chef* began a tragic ballad which he said was his favorite. Called *The White Rose*, it was easy to translate, for it had clear narrative verses and a repetitive refrain. He had not sung it in a long while and searched for words. M. Alain, the cook, was the only one who admitted knowing it. The younger ones were embarrassed by the heavy sentimentality. Despite the struggle to remember all the words and the inevitable pathetic conclusion, he kept at it to the end. *Chef* reminded me of my father, who also was touched by the ironies of sad fate and could be moved to tears by a sentimental song.

The Polish soldier played a harmonica. He kept it in a velvet lined box in a trunk under his bunk. The harmonica gave him solace and helped him survive his profound homesickness. It took on the life and importance of a friend. We admired his playing.

"It's getting to be too sad in here," Gruber noted. "How about something more fun?"

"We could do *The Cat Came Back*," Darlene suggested.

"Or something in French so they can join in," said Pat.

Our repertoire of French songs was limited. I knew a few Edith Piaf numbers, but they would not do much to cheer us. We came up with *Frère Jacques*, which was good for several repetitions, including an attempt to do it as a round. We tried:

> Dites-moi, pourquoi, la vie est belle
> Dites-moi, pourquoi, la vie est gaie?
> Dites-moi, pourquoi, chère mad'moiselle
> Est-ce-que, par-ce-que, vous m'aimez?

Not until we had finished singing it alone did we realize that, despite being in French, this was an American show tune.

The Polish boy reached for his harmonica, then frantically searched the bunk and floor under it. He knew before we did what had happened. While our attention had been on our songs, some of the others stole the harmonica and hid it from him. He was hurt and confused at being the brunt of their teasing. Was it a thoughtless prank or cruel jealousy? The *chef* discreetly comforted him and helped him search for the harmonica, but did not accuse or reprimand anyone. The Polish soldier became even more withdrawn and stoic.

Chef distracted us by calling for something sweet to eat and asking for another song. We did *San Miguel*, a favorite of mine. And then *The Cat Came Back*, with verse after verse of absurd efforts by the master to get rid of his cat. No matter how outlandish the schemes, the cat always came back, as our audience quickly caught on.

At midnight the *chef* took us to the tent that had been prepared for us, five cots with sleeping bags and blankets around the periphery, a table and two chairs in the center. A wash basin, pitcher of water, and kerosene lamp had been put on the table. He sat on the edge of a cot for a minute while we chose our places and thanked him for his extraordinary thoughtfulness.

"You will sleep well, *mes belles enfants*."

"Very well, thank you, *mon chef*."

"You must have no fear," he seemed to need to emphasize it, though none of us felt afraid. "Be assured, no one will bother you in the night. You have my protection."

Before he left, he gave me his whistle to wear, just in case.

At dawn I awoke to the sound of my name.

"Jer, Jer!" Pat called in a loud whisper. "Come on, Markos, wake up!"

"What?"

"Listen," she said, even quieter.

I lay very still and held my breath. Without making a sound, I slowly brought my arm out of the sleeping bag and pulled the edge of turban back from my ear. Only a sliver of grey light crept by the edges of canvas flaps tied down over the windows for the night.

I thought I heard a faint crunching, just two or three steps. Then nothing. I lifted my head from the cot and strained to hear more. My nose and cheeks were icy. I did not want to get out of the sleeping bag.

The crunching resumed. We both heard it. Footsteps outside our tent. I sat up, careful not to rustle a thread. My hand reached for the whistle hanging, with the scorpion, from my neck. Pat tiptoed toward the sound and peeked out the side of the window flap. Her hand went to her forehead and her mouth fell open. She saw the *chef* with a rifle over his shoulder. He stopped to blow warm air into his hands, then continued his patrol around our tent. Apparently he'd kept watch throughout the night. We had his protection.

Scattered across the plains of Tit, rock cairns mark the graves of fallen fighters. It was here in 1902, that the Tuareg and the French fought the decisive battle for control of the Hoggar and the central Sahara. In truth, the battle was between the Tuareg and loosely trained and organized Chaamba Arab irregulars, led and supplied by the French. What had begun as an excursion to parade the French presence deep in the desert resulted in a bloody ambush. Badly outnumbered and divided into three scattered parties, the excitable and undisciplined Arabs under Lt. Cottenest's command were no match for the fearless and highly skilled pack of "blue giants" who charged them from atop racing camels.

At the point of what was expected to become the massacre of the Arabs, the Tuareg broke from the battle and began to pillage the supplies and steal the camels of the French convoy. The Arabs seized the moment and routed the Tuareg, firing wildly and throwing themselves into hand-to-hand combat. When the dust had settled, three Arabs and nearly a hundred Tuareg lay dead on the field. A blundering accident had turned into an historically decisive act. The Tuareg's exclusive hold on the Hoggar was broken.

We walked carefully among the cairns as we would in a cemetery. Random bleached bones protruding from the rubble were the only sign that some of the piles were shallow graves. We looked across the wind and tried to imagine the scene more than sixty years before.

Soldiers Delange and Chabannier, who had been assigned

to accompany us, told what they knew in an off-hand or elaborate way, according to our reactions. The *génie* camp was the present-day link in a long chain of French involvement on the same site. The soldiers were the direct, if disinterested, heirs of France's glorious and ignoble escapades. But these young men displayed neither pride nor reverence. They would rather have been in France, far from all the boredom and discomfort, far from the underlying fear of this hostile place. If they could not be in France, they would rather be back at the camp, instead of traipsing about the plain with us.

Despite our weeks in the desert, the vast scale of empty space stayed beyond our understanding. To my eye, the plains of Tit appeared flat in every direction. Yet a short hike out of camp brought us beyond a subtle tilt of earth, a berm of rocks, or sweep of sand, each high enough to hide a person standing, to hide a person on a camel, a *camion*, a whole camp.

We'd heard the stories about snakes and scorpions, and at first kept a furtive eye on the rocks. But only Darlene really worried about such hazards. We spread out to sun ourselves on berms.

We spread out to not have to listen or respond to conversation. I felt a tremendous pull to move away, to be out of sight of any living thing. I was torn between the terror of being lost and the excitement of being on the edge. How far could I go?

"It's difficult to keep an eye on five of you when you spread out like that," Delange scolded us.

I slid beneath the berm and followed a wadi around a gentle bend. I did not need to go far to be out of range of their voices. In a moment I had passed to another tilted plate. I settled myself on the lee side of a gravel mound and looked out on a barren universe. I sat alone on the plain of Tit, in the middle of the Sahara Desert.

The Arabs say, "The desert is the Garden of Allah, from which the Lord of the Faithful removed all superfluous human and animal life, so that there might be one place where He can walk in peace." Over the whole landscape before me there was no distraction from the resonance of my own being.

I could feel the hair on my arms rise. Perhaps it was the

wind.

We drifted back together to return to camp, all of us except Pat. We waited, then stood on a high cairn and called for her. It seemed a long time before she returned. We chided her for causing us to worry.

She was not in a mood to talk.

"I wanted to be alone," she finally said. "Do you know that if you turn around fast enough, you might see God?" As we reached camp, she looked back and added, "Now I understand why they went into the desert to pray."

I knew, too.

We pressed the *chef* for the time we would leave. He had told us he was sending a truck to Columb-Béchar to be repaired. It would bring us to the northern edge of the desert, within easy reach of Algiers or Oran. We were to have spent only the night at his camp. Now there was a delay. He was waiting for someone. Or so he said.

After supper we gathered to listen to the radio. With a tower at Tamanrasset, the reception was usually good for the BBC or VOA. This evening a driving wind created static on the transistor. M. Chabannier, the company radio operator, tinkered with the short wave.

We drank tea and bottled water and continued our conversations. The *chef* had a child, a five-year old daughter who lived with her mother and his mother near Paris. His work, he lamented, was not suited to family life. But some day… He, the cook, and M. Frich were regular army. The rest were draftees fulfilling their duty. The camp marked an official French presence within easy reach of Tamanrasset. The troops went to the town for occasional meals, but, uncertain about their status and security so soon after Algerian independence, spent most of their time at Tit, surveying and sending reports north. For the most part, they considered Tit a hardship post, but a relatively safe one. Their goal was to endure, out of the way of trouble, and go home whole.

We sang some of the songs of the previous night and added *Where Have All The Flowers Gone, I Never Will Marry, Hangman,*

Lemon Tree, Take Her Out of Pity—melancholy, wistful songs. We had sung them ourselves so often in the evenings in our house at Lott Carey.

Songs, like poems, I decided, cannot be translated perfectly.

"I have to tell you all something," Darlene began, her voice somewhere between wonderment and a titter.

We were settled into our cots for the night, yet were not ready for sleep. Gruber sat up working on her backpack in the flickering light of a kerosene lamp.

"Is it a secret?"

"You're in love with the *chef*?"

"This is serious. Do you all realize where we are?" Darlene continued.

I couldn't see her face but I knew she was lying on her back, the orange silk bandana on her head, her cheeks smiling.

"I never thought we'd actually do it. I mean, did any of you believe we'd do it?" She giggled.

This was the same Darlene who spent weeks lobbying for an easier, more familiar trip. She was the one who found it unthinkable to turn back alone at Zinder. The one who came because she had no choice. The one with the rash.

"Jerrie made us do it," Pat spoke up.

"What's that supposed to mean?" I asked.

"Well, if you really think about it, we might not be here if you hadn't bulldozed us into it."

"I thought you wanted to come?"

"Sure I did. If I remember correctly, I was the one who thought it up and sent you my cartoons about the desert," Pat continued.

"I thought it up, too, you guys," Gruber interrupted. "Don't forget, I was the one who saw the movie about Lawrence of Arabia, and I told you how neat it was, and how we really had to come to the desert."

"OK, OK, we hear you," Pat said, "but I'm talking about an attitude here."

"What's that?" I asked.

"Full speed ahead and the torpedoes be damned!" she said.

"You were crossing the desert, and we all might as well come along."

"Well, we did get to the middle of it," I agreed. "But it's not over yet."

"What does that mean?" It was Victoria, awake after all.

Each of us was sustained in different ways. Gruber liked to have tangible proof of order and readiness. The greater the stress, the more compulsive she became. She was assured when the water bottles were full, when the baskets were accounted for, when there were five of us in a row. Like a good scout, she was always prepared, and nothing pleased her more than pointing that out. While the rest of us used suitcases, Gruber had a canvas backpack. She had picked up the idea and the pack from the Swiss and German students with whom she had traveled throughout Europe several years before. Even though the tent was cold and the light dim, she packed, meticulously, as she had every day, at every opportunity.

Gruber packed out loud, for our sake as well as hers, reviewing all the neat compartments and her precise placement of every item in each compartment. She had engineered the arrangement of her belongings down to the millimeter and she was mightily satisfied to fold something in a predetermined way and have it fit where she intended.

"I can tell you where anything is," she said. "Go ahead, just ask me and I can put my hand on anything."

No one said a word.

"Let's see," she continued, "my blue robe. Now for the blue robe, I open the main zipper on top, reach down one hand length on the left side and...there it is!"

The walls of the tent shuddered in the wind, though the tent itself was surprisingly good at muffling outside sounds. I had no tolerance for the cold and wore a soldier's borrowed quilted jacket day and night. Over the sleeping bag I spread my own blanket and black woolen robe and did my best to tuck them in around me.

"Now, if I want my toothbrush, where do you think I'd look?" Gruber was still at it. "I know exactly where my..."

"Oh, shut up about your damned toothbrush!" Pat snapped.

Pat was not without her needs, but they were different from Gruber's. She dissected what others said, weighed advice and information. If a decision was properly deliberated and arrived at slowly, then it must be right. Pat would not like anyone to think she had not been thoughtful. She covered her tracks and hid her uncertainties.

Victoria listened but took no pleasure in participating. When her opinion was sought, she asked for a restating of the question. She allowed decisions to take place by skillfully reading the direction consensus had taken and announcing it. Otherwise she wanted no part of decisions, and was pained by any action which might place a share of responsibility on her.

And so, while our entering the desert may have been the result of my bulldozing, it occurred only with the complicity of the other four, whose minimum requirements were being met. We did seek advice, count supplies, refrain from pressuring Victoria, and make clear to Darlene that she was free to go home at any time—alone.

"What that means," I finally answered Victoria, "is that it's over 2000 kilometers (1200 miles) to Algiers. When the *chef* offered us a ride, he didn't say anything about having to wait for somebody to drive."

"He seems sincere," she said.

"I agree. Maybe it's beyond his control. If it is, where does that leave us?"

"At least we can stay here for free," said Darlene.

"Not for long. I'm sure these cots and jackets belong to someone. The five of us have to be a burden on a camp this small."

"How are you coming, Gruber?"

"I'm just getting ready," she replied. "Do you guys want the light off?"

"It doesn't bother me."

"The light's not the problem. It's time to rest. You don't have to pack now. We're not leaving at dawn."

"When do you think we will leave?"

9
Hijacked

"So, these are the American misses."

I had turned my head to the entrance of the tent, awakened by a beating on the door flaps. Three men in uniform strutted about, looking at us. The leader wore a grey woolen cape and carried a riding stick. None of them had removed their hats or gloves.

"Do they sleep all day?" the leader asked *chef*, who stood by hesitantly.

"Who are these guys?"

"Ah, you speak English. I also speak English," he said. It was heavily accented, but it was English. "I am captain."

Another intruder into our language. We immediately switched to our most extreme Liberian English in an effort to assess the situation, discussing them among ourselves, meeting their arrogance with passive indifference.

"Get up. I have come to take you to see sights."

"*Merci, non.* We are not tourists."

"We are French. We must care for our guests. You have heard of, *comment dit-on* (How does one say), *la galanterie française* (French gallantry)? You will enjoy your time with us."

In a rapid round of mumbling to each other we did our best to assess this new circumstance.

"What if he's a friend of the *chef*?"

"*Chef* looks bewildered."

"This just doesn't smell right."

"Maybe he's a higher rank than *chef*."

"Look at the smug looks on their faces."

"I don't like them."

"Is it French gallantry that storms into a ladies' tent before we are awake?" I said firmly to the intruders.

"Don't push it, Jer."

"I wish we knew more about the uniforms."

"Theirs is different from the *génie*."

"Who do they think they are, barging in here?"

"We don't have time to sightsee," Gruber told them, "we are late for work."

I snickered in my sleeve.

"*Au revoir, messieurs, c'est à dire* 'good-bye'. (Good-bye gentlemen, that is to say, good-bye.) We are leaving soon and do not wish to sightsee."

"Remember, I am *capitaine*. Who are the *génie* that you stay with them? You will see me again." And before any of us got nastier, *chef* moved in playfully, shrugging his shoulders and throwing up his hands in a who-can-understand-women gesture, and ushered *capitaine* and his two companions out of the tent.

The intruders were *gendarmes*, military police. The *chef* had hoped to get us on our way before they learned we were at the camp, but we were fast-traveling news. The *gendarmes* outnumbered and outranked the little band of army engineers. Their base was a permanent fortress. They had some role in military intelligence, but a greater reputation as the bully boys of the desert. The *chef* gave them wide berth. He told us not to worry, but their appearance caused him concern.

We spent a lazy day indoors, eating, reading, assessing, considering our alternatives. Unlike thick mud walls which warmed and cooled slowly, the dark canvas absorbed sunlight rapidly, turning the tent into an oven by afternoon. Dry air made us cross, and the delay in our departure, anxious. *Chef* assured us we would be leaving soon, as soon as the driver arrived.

M. Bakari, a Tunisian, built a fire in a basin on the earthen floor of the tent.

"Perfect," Pat exhaled, dropping her head back in a great sigh. She had come to the end of *Loneliness,* a book by Clark Moustakas, which had kept her in a near trance for days.

"Isn't it a little dangerous to be reading about loneliness here?" I asked.

"Perfect," she said again. "Perfectly written, perfectly whole. The perfect book to bring it together for me."

"What's it about?" asked Darlene.

"Give me a minute," Pat answered, closing her eyes with another sigh.

Bakari set out his equipment on one end of the table while the *chef* wrote letters on the other.

Mechanics Libert and Bertrand perused our Michelin map and outlined the route we would follow to Columb-Béchar. They were to drive one vehicle in our convoy. The fellow we all awaited was to drive the other. Gruber showed them our route from Liberia to Tit. They nodded. She drew a sketch to show them the rain forests of Liberia. Just a quick sketch, but from an artist's hand.

"*Formidable!*" they said.

"*Oui,*" she replied, knowing she hadn't conveyed it at all.

We passed around the *crème.*

"It's an existential view of loneliness," Pat began. "The author looks upon it as an essential human experience, central to self-knowledge and growth."

"Like what?" asked Darlene.

"Here, I'll read you some parts.

> I believe it is necessary for every person to recognize his loneliness, to become intensely aware that, ultimately, in every fibre of his being, man is terribly, utterly alone.

She flipped through the book, searching for favorite lines.

To love is to be lonely.

Loneliness is as much a reality of life as night and rain and thunder, and it can be lived creatively, as any other experience.

In absolutely solitary moments man experiences truth, beauty, nature, reverence, humanity.

"Sounds interesting," Darlene nodded. "I guess you have to read the whole thing to get it."

Bakari set a tall coffee pot filled with water on the hot coals. He arranged glasses, a cone of sugar, sprigs of dried mint leaves, a package of tea, and two blue enamel pots at his end of the table.

With their canvas flaps rolled up the windows admitted brilliant patches of light to stream across the dark drab interior.

I wrote notes to the *chef*, clarifying what we thought we understood. Writing was laborious, but we did not want to misunderstand the time events were to take place. I could not trust my French pronunciation nor my ear with some verb tenses. By this method I learned the driver we awaited was a contract civilian, an expert in the vehicle as well as the route. He had all the proper papers to travel without harassment. There were *génie* camps all the way to Columb-Béchar, where we would be welcome guests. The *chef* had already begun to write to the commanders of each post, introducing us.

I asked him to list all the men of the camp in my account book as well as their address. In a stylish print with florid capitals he wrote the names with notations by which we would remember them.

> M. Malnoux, *chef*, S/C Malnoux, Alex (Commander)
> M. Floch, *sous chef* (Second in command)
> M. Bertrand, *camion* (Truck driver)
> M. Frich, *chien* (Frich was never without a can of beer in one hand and a white dog under his arm.)
> M. Pawlack, *polonaise* (Polish)

M. Delage, *col. chef* (This must have been a joke,
   for he was not a colonel.)
M. Chabannier, *radio* (Radio operator)
M. Libert, *soutier* (Mechanic)
M. Alain, *cuisinier* (Cook)
M. Bakari, *tounise* (Tunisian)
M. Soule, *malade* (Sick)
M. Garido, *bouc* (Goat)

Pawlak, wanting especially to be remembered, carefully wrote his name again on a separate page, "SAHARIEN, Pawlak Robert." When his tour was over, he would go home a Frenchman, never to fear deportation and never to willingly leave France again.

We wanted to leave them something. There wasn't enough to make individual gifts. We emptied our bags of the French books we had bought in Abidjan. Some novels, the poetry of Baudelaire and Rimbaud. The soldiers protested. It was too fine a gift, they said. We insisted. We had nothing else. See, they are in French. Chabannier hesitantly whispered that, for the most part, they could barely read. No more was said. We left the books anyhow.

All eyes were on Bakari. He poured a dark amber stream two feet into a small clear glass and stopped at the moment the glass was full, without spilling a drop. An Arab tea ceremony was as much theater as it was courtesy and refreshment.

The day passed and the civilian driver did not come.

After supper we were to have a treat. The *chef* sent everyone away except Pawlak, who seemed ever more fragile the longer he was without his harmonica.

"If only he could understand the existential value of loneliness," Victoria mused.

"Or if they'd just give him back the damned harmonica," Pat countered.

"For true."

Chef brought out a jar of cherries. He had saved them, he said, for the most special occasion of his tour.

We gave him the bottle of wine we had carried from Agadez, the one remaining from M. Joyce's gift box.

We felt secure and comfortable with the life of the camp so we were unprepared for the arrival of the long-awaited driver. A great clamor of prolonged engine revving and horn blowing announced him. We should have been warned.

He burst into the tent, steadying himself briefly with a grip on the inner vestibule flap. We watched the room change as he demanded everyone's complete attention. He flipped a chair around and straddled it, leaning heavily into its back. He was near enough for me to catch a stale breath of alcohol, but he seemed not to notice us. The *chef* had described him as experienced in the desert; close up we saw he was not much older than we. He spoke French but in an odd coarse way that I had trouble following. I concentrated on the tone and inflection and tried to sort out the key words from the bombast.

It was hellish to understand, and I did not like the drift of the parts I could understand.

"*Il est belge* (He is a Belgian)," *Chef* inserted for our sakes.

A Belgian. Of course. That accounted in my mind for the arrogance in his attitude.

"What are these chicks doing here?" he smirked.

Chef introduced us briefly as the American Peace Corps, Darlene, Pat, Gruber, Victoria, and Jerrie. The Belgian grunted and wiped his mouth on his sleeve. He was filthy. Life in the desert assumed a closeness to the earth and a coat of blown dust. But even by desert standards he was a wreck.

"If he didn't smell so bad, he'd be good-looking," Darlene commented.

"For a Belgian," Pat added.

Others of the camp trailed in to hear the gossip he carried. Alain brought him a plate of food, which he washed down with several cans of beer. He drank more, and more desperately, than any of the others. We watched. Beer and wine (this was the French army) were available in the camp but benignly controlled by the *chef* and Alain. Even Frich, who liked his beer, drank discreetly.

"So, Peace Corps? Why are you here?" The Belgian spoke to us but performed for the benefit of the other men. "There is no peace here. Everyone must fight to survive. This is the desert. You are not welcome here."

"It is not your desert to decide whether we are welcome or not," I shot back.

He lowered his chin and glowered at us from under his eyebrows. The cold air that had rushed in when he pushed back the tent flap settled over us.

"What do you do in Liberia?"

"Teach."

"It is not possible. The Liberians are black, are they not? Blacks are savages." He put his elbows out and scratched himself under the arms in imitation of a gorilla. He laughed uproariously at his own cleverness and looked around expecting everyone to join him. There were a few nervous chuckles and a lot of eyes looking to the *chef* for guidance. "The blacks," he spit out, "they cannot learn. You waste your time."

"*Monsieur*, you are stupid!" I translated quickly so the others could understand my anger. Here was a prima donna desert rat, questioning us!

From the minute he swaggered into the tent, it was a disaster. He was too loud for the low-keyed atmosphere of the camp. He was bigoted and selfish where tolerance and sensitivity were the rule. He drank too much.

"This guy took a double dose of mean pills today," said Gruber.

"Ass hole!" fumed Pat. "I feel like punching him in the mouth."

"This is the guy we're supposed to ride with!"

"We will never ride with this—I flipped through the dictionary—jerk," I told the *chef*, "*jamais!*"

Even as we spoke, we realized there were precious few alternatives. If the Belgian had understood what we said...but by then he had slumped across the table in a drunken stupor.

"It will be better tomorrow," *Chef* assured us. "Good night, *mes belles enfants*." They dragged the Belgian out.

We took pictures of the camp. Of them. Of ourselves. We took pictures of them with us. They took pictures of us with them. Shaking hands, each with each, they smiled, we smiled.

We left behind their wonderful warm jackets. I returned the *chef's* whistle. Bit by bit, we prepared to go.

Across the camp an out-of-order five-ton truck was maneuvered onto the flat car trailer of another, larger rig. It was slowly brought in front of the flagpole. The sound of engines warming followed us into the tent for our bags and as we watched them loaded high into the cab of the broken down vehicle. Above the roar we squinted, straining to follow the instructions shouted by the *chef*.

"Two will ride with the Belgian in the towing rig. The cab of the smaller truck has a large space behind the seat. For three of you and two of my men." He held up the right number of fingers and pointed out the people. I was confused. I saw two vehicles, the towing rig and the one on top of it, the one we called *le malade*. The cab of *le malade* had already been filled with our belongings.

"The smaller truck up there?" I asked.

"No, the other one," he said.

"How many trucks will make the trip?"

"Two."

I looked around and saw only the piggy-backed pair in front of me.

"*C'est tout* (That's all)?"

"*Ah, nononon.*" He nodded toward another, similar in size to *le malade*, just entering camp. Victoria, Gruber and Pat would ride in it, Darlene and I with the Belgian.

I had carefully composed a farewell speech. Perhaps I'd waited too long to say it. The noise of the trucks was deafening. Each of us said good-bye, flowing in a line past the *chef's* words.

"Remember, you will go with these trucks all the way to Columb-Béchar. No one will bother you. You are safe with us. You will stay in *génie* camps. Everything is free. Don't be afraid. I am the *chef*."

He motioned for the small account book protruding from my purse and across from the list of his men's names he wrote:

"*Allez-vous garder un bon souvenir de l'armée française.*" (Keep a good memory of the French army.)

"*Mon chef*, we leave with tears in our hearts. Thank you." It was not the sort of message one ought to shout. I hoped he heard.

Our last *au revoirs* were lost in the din that carried us away from the camp. I looked back, longer than I had watched any place along the trip grow small and vanish. The tears in my heart would evaporate in hours of sun and miles of sand.

I was never more thankful for the distance between oases, the space in which to rest and digest.

We drove a long time without speaking. The Belgian, a much subdued person, had kept to himself throughout the morning and now respected the silence with hardly the blink of an eyelash to break his communion with the truck. He was as much stuck with us as we were with him. Perhaps he would rally and make an effort to act reasonably.

I folded my arms on the open window and wedged my chin in them to stare at a distant butte. We seemed to not move at all. I brought my eyes down steadily to the base of the butte, to the land before it, and the land before that. Closer. A bush shot by. Closer and the rocks lining the side of the road blended to a smooth ripple and were not rocks at all. Like Little Black Sambo's tiger, who chased his tail so fast that he became a pool of butter, the rocks blurred to a grey stream. Near things moved too fast. I raised my eyes. Far things moved not enough. By and by my stare settled on a distance in rhythm with the truck. My mouth shaped songs to fit the beat. Songs, speeches, all in harmony with the cadence. "My mother moved..." A poem from the past. "My mother moved through..." Then what? Not my mother. My brother? Father. "my father moved through dooms of love," I remembered, "through sames of am through haves of give," line by line, "singing each morning out of each night my father moved through depths of height." It made no more sense than it ever had, this e.e. cummings' poem, but it had the right sound and rhythm, and I said it over and over, rocking myself with the words.

"*Mademoiselle, Voilà, la bombe!*"
"What?"

"La bombe." The Belgian pointed ahead to low hills where we could just make out a light—or was it two? They appeared to be set on derricks or radio towers out of the side of the hill. He whistled long and steady while his hand crashed down against his thigh. "Wooosh!" His head slammed back from the force of his hand's explosion. *"La bombe atomique!"*

"Ah, oui oui oui. The French bomb?"

"Oui."

"He says that's the area where the French do their atomic testing," I relayed to Darlene. We couldn't see anything. It did not appear on our map. It was generally known that the French conducted their atomic research and testing in the Sahara, but I felt we had stumbled upon a great piece of intelligence. It was frustrating to not know more and to have only the Belgian as a source.

We passed within sight of a Tuareg camp, which he told us was called In Amguel. I loved the sound of the names— Ahaggar, In Guezzem, Agadez, Asekrem, In Amguel, and somewhere soon ahead, In Eker.

He began to gear the truck down, releasing a pressure valve on the right side of the steering wheel. Hisss.

"Shit. Sixteen gears," he told us. He reached for a second valve but couldn't force it open in time. Cursing, he scrambled to adjust levers that would compensate for his failure with the pressure valve. The monstrous ca*mion* hiccoughed and gagged. Through the rear window we saw our piggy-back passenger heave forward and wrench the steel cables that anchored it. Should it come loose, nothing would prevent it from crashing the window and the backs of our heads. Darlene and I watched it rock and listened to the creak of strain on the cables.

The Belgian let out a long stream of agitated words.

"Monsieur?" I reached for the dictionary.

"What good are you?" he shouted. "You learn nothing worthwhile from dictionaries."

Still trying to lower the gears, he reached across the wheel with his left hand to the stubborn second valve. Hisss. He had gotten it open, but had not moved fast enough to simultaneously shift the levers on the left. His face tensed in pain.

"What is it, *monsieur?*"

He held out his right hand. It was swollen so that he could not grip it closed.

"I have something for it," I said.

"Nothing will help."

"I have something."

"Nothing will help. What do you have?"

"I can't explain. When we stop, I will get it from our baggage." Ace Bandage was not in my dictionary.

It had been two or three hours since I'd had a snack, I thought as I reached into my handbag for a package of biscuits. Earlier ones I'd eaten had been foul-tasting and when I examined them closely what had looked like crumbs turned out to be tiny sand-colored worms. The square ones now in my hand had been mashed a bit but none of the crumbs seemed to move under its own power. Despite their sour flavor, I ate several.

The Belgian brought the truck to a stop without turning off the engine at a place just beyond a fork in the road. Ordinarily, he made it quite clear, he would have taken the route to the right which passed through the site of underground atomic testing. Now he was forced to take a long detour because we civilians without clearances could not travel that route. *Chef* had not said anything about bomb sites or detours.

The second truck pulled up behind us, and the driver came to talk to the Belgian. Biscuits in hand, I dropped to the ground. The sun had fallen to its last orange quarter. The wind was rising and the air already dry cold. After the confined heat of the cab, I was refreshed by the crisp air and, letting my turban fall lose about my shoulders, ran back to the other vehicle.

Stretching up on my toes, I passed the package of biscuits through the window.

"Thanks. How is it with the Belgian?" Pat asked from inside the hood of her yellow sweatshirt.

"His hand hurts, seems sprained. That truck can vex him plenty-o," I said in Liberian English. "It's got a lot of valves and levers that need two good hands. Certainly doesn't help his disposition."

"The biscuits are awful."

"True, but no worms."

"Oh man, you guys, I want to get out of here." Gruber was crouched in a small compartment behind the seat, looking especially uncomfortable.

"What's wrong?"

"This guy wants to play footsies and I don't want any humbug." The young soldier sharing the compartment had drawn his knees up under his chin and watched woodenly. He knew we were talking about him, but he could not understand the words.

"Ah swear, Gruber, that child?" I hoisted myself up on the running board to get a better look.

"Oh man, look how scrunched up I am, just to stay away from him."

"Woe is me, the trials of a desirable woman."

"This isn't funny. I want to trade places with somebody. I'm tired of always getting stuck."

"Don't be encouraging him, Gruber. We don't need any more trouble."

"Is there any water?" It was Victoria who asked. Easier for her and Pat to ignore Gruber's discomfort than to become vulnerable to a change of seats by acknowledging her. When no one answered, I guessed the question was directed to me.

"Some." I jumped from the truck and whirled around. It felt good to stretch and bounce. I went to the first truck for the water bottle—not the full one—and skipped back with it.

"Markos, something got into you?"

"I feel good. Have a drink."

"You can't leave the bottle?"

"We need it. Do you know what place this is?"

"The soldier tried to explain it."

"Over in that direction the French test atomic bombs. We can't pass that way because our names aren't on the papers."

"Jer!" Darlene called, "come."

The Belgian leaned over the driver's seat, waving his arms in French sign language.

"What's he saying?" Darlene sat confused between us.

"*Ah, mademoiselle*," he began. The best I could make out of his loud explanation was that for some reason the soldiers had to report at a checkpoint along the road to the restricted area. The smaller truck with all its occupants would go while we waited at the intersection. Darlene walked back to tell the others.

I took the opportunity to climb up to *le malade*. The temperature was dropping noticeably. Very soon we would need warmer clothes. But this good reason aside, I needed to climb *le malade* because it was there. The more I hopped about, the more energized I became. I was overcome by a great sense of excitement and anticipation quite clearly not shared by my friends.

Up I go. Both feet on the cab floor, holding on to the door frame. Left foot to the first ledge of the trailer. Left hand gripping the trailer frame. Right hand pushing against the cab roof. Shift weight to left. Second ledge. Both hands on trailer. One leg over the top. The second leg. Jump. Squeeze between trailer side and *le malade*. Around the front wheel. Reach for cab door. Handle falls off. Must climb to running board and open through window. Vent closed. Can't reach crank to open window. Through the cab, I see the window on the opposite side half open. Climb over the hood to the other side. Hoist up on running board. Reach through window to release door handle. Success.

Inside, our poorly-packed belongings were a scrambled mess. Baskets of food and blankets had overturned and wedged among twisted suitcases. There was no way to straighten it out alone. I satisfied myself with pulling out the black robes, a box of biscuits and an Ace Bandage and called to Darlene to catch as I threw them over the side. Before climbing down, I reached across the baggage to open the right window and put the broken door handle in the glove compartment.

Back over the hood. Turn on my stomach to slide down to the trailer bed. Up the railing, over, down the outside. Feel with right foot for cab floor. Jump.

"*Monsieur.* Here is something for your hand."

"I don't need it."

"Try. It will help."

He did not offer his hand, nor did he draw it away as I began to wrap it.

"It will be too tight."

"It can be loosened."

"My own Red Cross," he chuckled, embarrassed, yet flattered. "It will get dirty."

"It can be washed."

"*Merci, mademoiselle.*" He took off his cap and bowed.

"*Rien.*" (It's nothing.)

Within an hour the second truck of our convoy returned from the checkpoint on the route we civilians were not permitted to travel. Our friends told of the most extraordinary scene. They had gone a little way among low hills before they were out of sight of us. Soon afterwards they noticed barbed wire lining the side of the road. It seemed to go on for miles, enclosing nothing but empty space. Along the way there were signs warning of danger and no trespassing. Around a bend they suddenly came upon a barrier guarded by heavily armed *gendarmes*.

From their vantage points inside the truck they glimpsed the French atomic station at In Eker. Well beyond the check point lay a space age domed city, a surreal habitation in the dusk of the desert. An enormous complex of military and scientific installations sprawled at the base of a towering granite mountain. In the few years since the research base had been in operation, France's first underground atomic bomb had been exploded beneath that mountain. The entire complex was illuminated by powerful beams that kept the encroaching night from ever reaching it.

"They operate round the clock," the soldiers said with awe.

The dome roofs shone radiant white in their bath of light and a great incandescent glow arched upwards against the sky. If they had not all seen it, compared and confirmed it, they would have thought it had only been a wondrous mirage.

"I wish you had seen it," Gruber sighed. "It was like being on the edge of the future."

The atomic installation helped explain the presence of the

French army deep in Algeria nearly two years after independence. I, too, wished I had seen it.

After a final examination of the trucks, we boarded again. Darlene asked if I didn't mind giving her a turn at the window. It was not a question of minding, but of fair turns, so I agreed. We put on our woolen robes and were off.

At cruising speed the Belgian took a long drink from a bottle of beer. I offered him a biscuit. He brought a beer from behind the seat for us. It was surprisingly cold.

"*Monsieur*, what is your name?"

"My name, or my first name?"

"All two."

His name was Edmund. The rest was embellished with a story about his aristocratic lineage.

"Very interesting," I said from time to time, but did not concentrate enough to remember it.

I told him our names. He was especially interested in Victoria and made up a tune for "*ma-de-moi-sel-le-Vic-tor-ia.*" Two more swallows and his beer was finished. He sang. Familiar sounds. American songs. Strong and loud. Gusty syllables in place of words. It took a minute to place them. Yankee war songs. We followed, humming until we remembered the words. How did Edmund know them?

We tried to sing him a French song, but our voices were too light to be heard over the din of the engine.

And this way we passed into the first hours of night.

If the Belgian had anticipated anything along this stretch, he had not warned us. When a smattering of lights materialized in the distant left, he said only, "*la gendarmerie.*"

Darlene elbowed me. We both remembered the unwelcome encounter we'd had with the *gendarmes* in our tent at the *génie* camp. Edmund gripped the steering wheel with both hands and looked straight ahead. None of us spoke. I had been watching the lights, which seemed to stay at a safe distance from the road, so I was caught off guard when the headlights revealed something moving just ahead of us. A grey blur of a man waved his arms at us.

As we raced by, the high beams glanced more blurred figures scattered along both sides of the road. The Belgian geared down. At a slower speed the blurred figures became men in speckled camouflage uniforms, blocking the road with raised machine guns.

"I swear!"

"Jer?"

"I can't believe it." I gasped.

The Belgian stopped the truck remarkably close to the line of scrimmage. With the beams lowered, we saw more of the grey uniforms approach from the sides, pistols drawn.

So quick, we had no way to mentally process what was happening. Was this entire performance for our benefit? This armed blockade?

The Belgian was scared silent. We had no chance to ask him for an explanation.

Before the truck's valves had stopped hissing, Darlene's door was torn open. A pistol flashed between us and an angry, shouting, familiar face, the *capitaine* who had barged into our tent. The self-important gallantry with which just yesterday he had offered to escort us sightseeing was transformed into the bitter invective of a battle officer come upon a second chance at an elusive enemy.

We stayed quiet, almost polite, for in truth, we could not understand his clipped, bossy French. Our dumbness enraged him. He bandied the pistol about, and with his other hand fixed a flashlight in our eyes. Just as abruptly as he'd opened it, he slammed the door shut. With the flashlight he whipped us off the road to the left to stop just before the outer wall of the *gendarmerie* compound.

"What did he say?" I quickly asked the Belgian, who nervously played with the levers. "What do they want?"

"They want to inspect our papers..." It was all he could reply before his door was jerked open by the same word-spitting *capitaine*. Edmund was ordered out. Halfway down, he turned back to us, "Stay in the truck."

"But the engine..."

"Leave it running. It will take too long to start it again. I should not be long."

"*Oui, d'accord.*"

"No matter what," he said, "do not leave the truck!"

"I understand."

"What's going on?" Darlene asked.

"He says they want to check papers and we shouldn't leave the truck." I maneuvered my handbag between my legs and the seat and reached down to touch my passport. "Where's your passport?"

"I think it's up in my suitcase," she replied.

"Damn! Check your purse."

"There's so much stuff in here. Wait...I have it."

"Good. Hang on to it. Let's lock the doors."

"What do you think will happen?"

"I don't know. But they sure do know how to scare a person."

A hand rapped at Darlene's window and a peaked head bobbed up and down.

"What'll we do?" Darlene shivered.

"Open the door," shouted the voice of the bobbing head.

"It's Pat."

"Let her in."

Pat huddled inside from the running board.

"What the hell is happening?"

"The Belgian went to find out. What did the guys in your truck say?"

"Not much. All I got was that we had to stop. They're vexed and talking only to each other in their own brand of French, so we can't understand."

"The Belgian said they wanted to check papers, but he didn't act as if it was routine to be hijacked by machine guns."

"For true."

"He said to not leave the truck. We'll let you know what we find out when he comes back. But go back to your truck and lock the doors. Don't get out for anybody. Don't talk to anybody. The bastards!"

Pat ran into the rising wind and we locked it out again.

"I wish we were all together," Darlene said.

"Me, too."

Edmund returned, subdued.

Softly, calmly, he started. "They say we must not drive in the desert in army trucks at night. They have prepared a dinner and rooms for us. They say we must stay the night."

"*Jamais!* (Never) Tell them we have our own food."

"*Ah, mademoiselle,* I will talk to them again. But they are serious, I think."

"Then let them come here to speak to me. I will tell them myself."

"Please, *mademoiselle,* be reasonable, let us not offend them."

"Offend them! It is I who am offended. *Moi!* Do you understand?"

"Stay here and I will speak for you. I will try."

"*Bon.*"

He leaped out and was consumed by the darkness and the continuing clamor of the engine.

"Jer, what do you think they'll do to us? What do they really want?" Darlene trembled with unspeakable thoughts.

"I don't know. You can be pretty sure it doesn't have anything to do with official papers. No imagination. Damn!"

In my frightened and angry heart I shared Darlene's terror. But I forced myself to think. I had to get beyond the paralysis, that blinding streak of white light, that helpless confusion. I forced all of my senses to help me to understand, to sort, interpret and use every signal they received. I could actually feel myself focusing. I told myself how important it was to rally around strength. The strong would prevail.

"Have you got a match?" she asked.

"Here. Let me have one of those, will you?" She passed me a cigarette and soon we filled the cab with smoke.

"Do you think they're serious?" she asked. The sound of our voices thinking aloud was a comfort. "Maybe it's just a joke, you know, something to get our attention. After all, the *chef* said we could ride the *camions.*"

"Some joke. Those were machine guns out on the road. And every man I've seen here is armed." For an instant it seemed absurd. "Those stupid asses. Can you believe grown men carrying on like this?"

"Should we put this in the chapter on *The Sahara as a Mattress* or *The Sahara as a Toilet*?" Darlene followed. The silliness helped.

"That's good. But who would believe it? Can you see yourself writing to your mother, 'Dear Mom, We are having a fine vacation-o. Yesterday our trucks were hijacked by the French *gendarmes*. Love, Darlene.'"

"I think we should talk about what we're going to do."

"Any ideas?"

The Belgian came back and without speaking went about moving the truck. He ignored our questions and friendly goading. The noise was deafening. We could not see the other truck.

"Are we leaving?" I shouted. Everything we said was shouted. "Where are our friends?"

Edmund chose to be silent. I dared believe we were leaving and this silence was a joke of his. Soon he would give us a hero's speech and think well of himself for having gotten us out of it. But after a great deal of revving the engine and a bit of going backward and forward, he pulled the truck up along the side wall of the compound, stopped and turned it off.

How much our illusion of security had depended on the raging of that truck. The womb of light and sound ceased. We grew cold and frightened and very quiet.

"Our truck was blocking the entrance," he said meekly.

"What is this? What's happening?"

"*Mademoiselle*, I beg you. Do not be foolish. Cooperate."

"Speak slowly, please," I told him, "we must understand everything."

"OK. The *capitaine* wishes us to remain at the *gendarmerie*. He says you may inspect the rooms. You will see they are safe, have doors with keys."

"*Jamais!*"

"Ah! You are too stubborn. Sometimes I think you are stupid!" He stopped ranting at us and pleaded. "I will try again. Compromise. That is all I ask. Agree to have a meal.

Perhaps that will be the end of it."

"Perhaps, *monsieur?* We cannot depend on perhaps." The crisis was forcing each of our true selves to the surface. The Belgian was a coward. I didn't know whether to pity or despise him. We needed him, but could not rely on him. On top of it we had to bolster him so he would not get so frightened as to abandon us completely.

"Tell them about the *chef.* Yes, tell them we have the permission of the *chef* to ride with you at night." He slid out slower than before. "And tell them we only speak English."

Darlene and I sat in the quiet cold, no longer remembering to lock the doors. The Belgian came and went several times, trying to persuade us to compromise. One or two of the waiting minutes were spent wishing we had arrived under other circumstances. I would have liked to tour a working fortress. It was a misplaced thought.

The next time the Belgian returned he did not get in the cab. He held the door open, fumbling with his cap, pulling it forward. He mumbled and nodded us down from the vehicle. His eyes, nervous, downcast, avoiding us but aware of what surrounded them in the darkness and wanting to avoid all that as well, found no place to rest.

"*Eh monsieur*, it's cold out there. And windy!"

He paced in place. His head slumped lower between his shoulders.

"The *gendarmes* will look at your passports," he said flatly. "It is a checkpoint."

"Truly?"

He looked ghastly. His mouth hung loosely open, all the muscles of his face seemed to sag. What I saw of his eyes was dull and darting.

I slid behind the steering wheel to see who was out there. The only face close enough to recognize was the *capitaine's.* Several others hovered in the darkness. The *capitaine* began to say something in French.

"I only speak English," I interrupted in my most disdainful and uncompromising voice.

Beyond him, crossing in front of the light from the entrance to the compound, I saw Gruber, Pat, and Victoria. They were walking toward us. I told Darlene. She pulled her purse closed and tied the strings around one wrist.

"Let's get down," she said, "maybe Pat found out something."

"OK. Put up your hood and walk slowly."

"Why?"

"Never mind, the *gendarmes* left."

The Belgian said we would be notified when they were ready to see us. He shrugged and followed the soldiers into the compound.

We five were left outside the wall in the dark. The sliver of a first quarter moon did not lighten the sky or obscure the stars. Behind us was the *gendarmerie*, before us, the vast Sahara. Against the chill of our peril we found comfort in being together and in the sounds of our voices.

Pat stomped back and forth, her yellow peaked hood bobbing above her black robe. She pounded one fist into her other hand. By pacing, Pat vented her anger and converted it to courage.

"Damn, who do they think they are! Wait until I get in there. I'll let them have it." Little dynamo David was working herself up to slay the giant *gendarmes*.

"What are you going to do, charge with your cavalry?"

"Was that necessary?" Victoria, anxious, interrupted and cooled us.

"OK, but we have to agree on what we're going to do. I say we don't stay here. We don't cooperate. We only speak English."

"Why?"

"Because it is to our advantage. We have to struggle to understand them in French, and then we're never sure we're getting the true meaning. We know some of them speak English. So let them struggle. At least it will all be in our language. We lose control if we use French. Agreed?"

"Well, since I can't understand a word of French anyhow, I think it's a good idea." That was all Victoria had to say. When she and I agreed, we constituted a majority. But having said it, she began to back off. "I'd like to hear what everyone else thinks."

"It's fine with me."

"Me, too."

"Oh man, you guys, let's not waste time. So we're going to talk in English. So that's fine. See what I mean. I mean, that's fine, but what are we going to say?" Gruber was a wonder. She had been standing about two feet out from the wall and now, having spoken, she stiffened her legs and, without looking behind, leaned back, trusting that the wall would be there to catch her shoulders. Her heels dug into the sand. She squeezed a swallow of water into her mouth from her extraordinary bottle and rested it on her chest.

"Gruber's right. We have to have a plan, and we have to convince them that we mean what we say."

We all easily agreed to wear our black robes with the hoods up and to wrap our heads so that no hair showed. Ugliness could not hurt. Next was the matter of our papers. Just as we were deciding to not—under any circumstances—surrender any of our papers, a middle-aged officer summoned us inside.

Walking single-file across the courtyard, we looked at no one yet saw everything. Low mud buildings, yellow light seeping out of deeply recessed windows, walls within the wall. The peaks of our black hoods rose and fell with each determined step.

Though I'd had nothing to eat for half a day but biscuits and water, I felt energized. I floated up the steps to the porch, staring at an unoccupied place in front of me. The periphery grew hazy and melted away. I focused more intently on the center of my attention. This concentration provided me with a swagger, an assuredness to buffer my fear. By the time we entered the administrative room, I felt I had the power to stare the *capitaine* and his band of hijackers into disintegration.

In the short walk across the yard, we went from complete blackness to the harsh glare of electric light. I knew squinting gave me a stern and mean look. I kept it even after my eyes were comfortable. The room was full of tables and desks but had none of the trimmings—paper, typewriters, pen holders—of an office. It looked as if the *gendarmes* were about to vacate and only waited for the movers to take the big pieces.

Two officers in grey uniforms sat behind a table that blocked the way. One of them began to question us in French.

"We speak only English," I said.

The Belgian leaned against a door frame, joking nervously with a couple of *gendarmes*, his cowardice as exposed as the bare whitewashed walls in the yellow light.

"Very well, *mademoiselle*," said a voice entering from the right. It was the *capitaine*, the same one who had barged into our tent at the *génie* camp and who had forced us off the road. He had changed from his uniform to civilian clothes. He wore a loose white shirt unbuttoned to the middle of his chest and a silk sash tied around his waist.

"We have prepared a very nice supper for you," he said.

"I'll bet you have," muttered Pat under her breath.

"You will relax and enjoy it."

"Thank you, no. We do not want your food."

"Does the desert offer so much hospitality that you scorn that of the French *gendarmes*? No matter. Your passports, please."

The two at the table looked at each other and straightened the single sheet of paper in front of them. We took out the passports and opened them to the page with the Algerian visa and stamps.

"We travel properly," I said. "We are American citizens and all our papers are in order."

When one of the officers reached for my passport, I gripped it firmly. It was the moment of direct challenge.

"You are not authorized to travel on military vehicles. It is not permitted."

"The *chef* has permitted it. We are under his protection."

It would be a battle of wits and words. Whether bluff or truth, it did not matter. There was no higher court to hear our arguments.

"Ha!" he countered. "The *chef* is there. I am here."

"You may look at our passports all you wish, but we will

hold them."

We did not seem to be getting anywhere. Another tactic suddenly occurred to me.

"And while you're looking," I continued, "look at this." I fished in my bag for a wallet that held other identification. "Do you know who we are? We are American Peace Corps. All five," I emphasized pointing to each one of us. "See these cards? That is the great seal of the United States government. It is very official. Our ambassador is in the desert at this very moment. Tomorrow he will be passing here, and he will be very unhappy to hear how you are treating us."

I looked for a sign that a doubt had been planted.

The *capitaine* signaled to the fellows at the table to get on with their business, and he left the room. One peered closely at the personal data page of Gruber's passport. As he read, the other one wrote on the blank sheet of paper in careful school-boy penmanship.

"*Nom* (Name), K-a-t-h-e-r-i-n-e, the first of June, 1937."

And so on for each of us. That was the precious information they needed—our first names and dates of birth? They had no interest in our passport numbers, Algerian visas, or dates of expiration. We suspected that these two did not understand English very well and, once the *capitaine* left, we felt freer to talk among ourselves in Liberian. All the while we clung to our scorn.

"Tell *le capitaine*," I said when the painstaking transcribing was done, "that we will not eat here, we will not sleep here, and that he will be in a lot of trouble if he delays us."

With that speech, we turned up our noses and marched out.

Our parade across the courtyard was interrupted by a slightly-built *gendarme* with thinning hair who stepped from the shadows to tap Victoria on the shoulder.

"Just keep on walking and ignore him," someone said.

But he persisted, in an obsequious sort of way, to ask for assistance. He had a letter, which at first we thought he wanted us to deliver to someone in America. Then he opened it and held it up for us to read. It was a "to whom it may concern" from an American graduate student who wanted to come to the desert to study the wall paintings at Tassili-n-Ajjer. It was nearly a year old.

"What is this matter to us?" I barked.

He stood there rather pathetically holding his letter as if he were completely ignorant of our predicament. The absurdity of it incensed me to an irrational rage.

"Why are you showing us this stupid letter?" Pat glared at him.

"The men and I wish to…" he began.

"Men? I see no men at this camp," I shot back, not wanting to hear another word. "Only animals! This is what we think of your animals!" I spit on the ground. "Of your *gendarme* camp!" I spit again. "And of your disgusting hospitality!" Another spit.

We stomped out of the compound in varying shades of unanimity—Darlene confused, ready to be told what to do; Gruber, angry, adamant that we stay together; Victoria, terrified, wishing it were a bad dream; and Pat, livid, her jaw clenched and her hands in tight fists.

Outside the compound it was just as dark and considerably colder than when we had left. The heat of anger and shelter inside quickly dissipated in the cold wind. In a huddle we smoked, warming our circle with the matches as long as we could.

"Oh, oh. I'm sure I'm overflowing," someone said.

It was a very inconvenient moment to think about a menstrual period, much less to take care of it.

"I need to change, too," another added.

Accompanied by a third who stood watch, the two followed the wall of the compound around the corner and out of sight. It was utterly black except for an occasional match lit by the one who kept watch and almost instantly blown out by the wind. In the course of it we all went around the corner, although in shifts to keep a presence near the entrance. Bracing ourselves against the wind, juggling long robes and baggy pantaloons, set us to laughing and wise-cracking. It was not all that funny, but we took every bit of relief-giving hilarity we could from it. We worked quickly, burying our debris in the sand, not wanting to be stranded separate from each other when the *gendarmes* returned. By the time we had all taken turns converting the side of the *gendarmerie* into a public toilet, we felt better.

It was not to last.

We waited a long time. Our woolen robes seemed like cheesecloth against the wind. We became gritty with sand. I hopped about, putting my hands in my sleeves and holding the floppy openings closed. Victoria and Darlene went to sit in the truck. Gruber worried that we were separated.

"I am going, *mademoiselle*," the Belgian said. He stole out of the compound, his shoulders slumped as if he hoped to escape without our knowing it.

"What are you saying?"

"I'm leaving, departing, getting out of here."

"Then we're all going."

"No. The trucks and drivers only."

"Impossible!"

"It's no use arguing, *mademoiselle*. I am instructed to unload your things and drive away."

"The jerk. The coward," Pat muttered.

Victoria and Darlene raced toward us. Their *génie* drivers had tried to tell them the same thing. They didn't understand the language, but deep inside, they understood the message and they were afraid.

"It's true, *mademoiselle*," said one of the *génie*. "You can disagree and insult the *gendarmes*. We cannot. We are military. They have great power over us. They will put us in prison if we do not obey. They have said it."

He was nearly as frightened as we were. Yet, defending us had no advantage for him. He had inherited us without being consulted and would give us up as required. "We have only a short time to serve. It is very bad to have your military record blackened."

Victoria shrieked and gripped my arm. "They can't leave us here! Stop them!"

Her face froze in terror. Do something!...her eyes screamed.

My heart pounded. Yet in a perverse, but very useful way, I

was strengthened by having someone more frightened than I. I would not ride the coattails of panic, and I would do my best to not let anyone else do so either.

I clutched Victoria and stared intensely into her enlarged eyes.

"Stop it!" I shouted. "We can't panic." I spoke in a firm, measured way though my mind and heart raced. "Pull yourself together. You can't break down now." I shook her as if shaking could break her trance. "Listen to me. Stop it! We're not giving up."

Victoria had never allowed herself to believe we were in danger. This was not a reality we recognized. It must be pretend. The *gendarmes* would make their demands, we would refuse. Each of us would play our part and then, like any other theater we had ever known, the lights would come on and it would be over.

But there were no lights here, only the absolute blackness, the raging cold wind, and the *gendarmerie*.

One word at a time. I dragged them out, hoping a resolution, a bolt of lightning, would come and release us. The others were numb and more or less silent. Where was Pat's fire? She quietly moved in to be with Victoria as I released her.

"We will carry your things in, *mademoiselle*," the Belgian said. "Cheer up, you may get to like it here."

"*Jamais!* If you must take our things off the truck, just put them by the side of the road. Our ambassador will pass here in the morning, perhaps even in the night. We will wait for him. We are accustomed to sleeping in the desert." It was the only thing I could think of. I had no idea whether the others agreed. There was no time to discuss it and take a poll.

"*Mademoiselle*, you are causing a lot of trouble over nothing."

"We will never go back in the *gendarmerie*! Furthermore," I added, "you will have to do all the unloading. We will not assist in our own misfortune. And now that you are the *gendarmes'* boy, you can tell them that, too."

"*Mademoiselle*, I am a simple *routier*. I drive trucks for money. I take care of myself. I don't ask questions."

"Very well. And we will take care of ourselves, without your help and certainly without the *gendarmes*. We will begin to take care of ourselves by getting out of the wind."

We climbed into the cabs in which we had come and waited, shivering and silent. Amidst the sound of raging wind, I thought I heard them climbing up to le m*alade*, the cables groaning, the thud of bags thrown to the ground. But in the faint pool of light leaking from the entrance to the *gendarmerie* I could not see them. Were ghosts unloading our belongings? Was anyone?

In less than five minutes the Belgian emerged from the compound, head high, smiling. He started the engine but said nothing. While it warmed up, he went away and returned. We were bewildered. As he put it into gear and turned on the lights, we saw the smoky exhaust pouring from the other truck. We rolled forward tentatively, then bolted away.

We raced along the *piste* for miles, dodging rocks until the Belgian let out a great whoop. "*Libre*," he sighed, then said it again with a great shout, "Free!"

10

Behold the Ladies

Spontaneous applause and wide smiles filled the cab. We were finally free.

The Belgian drove like a madman, frantically changing gears to match our increasing speed. I was starving. The flatbed, used to lumbering at moderate speeds under heavy loads, was pushed to its limit. I wolfed down the remaining biscuits. *Le malade* lurched, and the cables anchoring it creaked as they strained against the shifting weight. Through the rear window we saw a huge fender come close and recede.

In a flash I hoped I had not been spared by the *gendarmes* to be beheaded by a breakaway truck. But the worry I might have mustered had been all used up. There was only euphoria left.

Somewhere between Tit and the *gendarmerie* we had passed the Tropic of Cancer. The sun would not be truly overhead again until we returned to Liberia. I wished I had known the moment when it happened.

Random thoughts like that darted through my mind—odd bits of poems, Jim, the speeches I should have said at the *gendarmerie*, food, the racing truck, my pounding heart, missing the Tropic of Cancer—until we finally pulled off the road at the site of a stone obelisk.

For the first time in the many nights we had spent in the

desert, I sensed a danger in stopping. Our fire could attract bandits. What if we had not gone far enough from the *gendarmerie*? On such a black night nothing could be seen outside the ring of the fire. Someone could be in our camp before we knew it.

But I was too elated to spare these little alarms a place to smolder. A lull in the wind let us hear our voices without shouting. I heard the voices of the others say I didn't have to unload the truck all by myself. I heard them tell me to calm down. But the adrenaline flowed, and my pulse raced. It was nearly midnight of a long and intense day, and I was full of energy.

> We were very tired, we were very merry.
> We had gone back and forth all night on the ferry.

Edna St. Vincent Millay's rhyme played over and over in my head as I went back and forth to *le malade* to unload our things. I felt weightless and graceful as a sprite as I soared up the rail of the flatbed, swung myself over the rim, across the hood of *le malade*, fetching a bag or basket and returning by the same route. Up, over, across, pause, across, over, down, leaping with a flourish to the ground. I did it again and again, a little faster and more recklessly each time, until on an ascent, my shoe caught on a piece of protruding metal frame and broke my rhythm.

It was a small thing, catching one's shoe, but it accomplished what the looks and comments of my friends had not, what I alone had not been able to.

I carefully lowered myself to the ground and examined the right angle torn into the new green sneakers I had bought just before leaving Liberia.

The Belgian slumped against the stone obelisk, stretching his long legs to their full length. Tiny glints of flame reflected in his eyes from the fire as he absently studied a twig turning in his fingers. No one spoke. Each of us, warming in the circle of the fire, privately digested the events of the evening. It was as lovely a moment as one could ask for.

"*Desmoiselles*." The Belgian cleared his throat. I do not think he meant to speak out loud. But it happened nevertheless, and the silence was broken. "*Desmoiselles*," he said again, squinting at each of us across the pool of light. He sat up and swept his arm in a grand arc as if to present us. "*Voyez desmoiselles!*" (Behold the ladies.)

He caught himself about to say more, as if he had misplaced his thought, and instead fumbled with his cap and reached for a beer wedged among small stones. The struggle to sort out what he wanted to say worked its way across his transparent face.

"Tell me, *mademoiselle*, you have come a long way, and, without doubt, a difficult way. First from your America to live in the jungle. Then on this long journey. How long is it?"

"Some thousands of kilometers, *monsieur*."

"Yes, thousands of kilometers across Africa, through the most difficult part of the world. Most grown men would not attempt such a thing. Yet, you do it, and you do not appear afraid. Not afraid of the place or the people."

In French his description made us sound even more astonishing.

"You know no one, yet they help you, want to help you. They would never help me. I assure you, I take care of myself. That is the way it is. But you are not prepared to take care of yourselves. Myself, I do not think you are fools. You have good luck, certainly, but you also have great courage. *C'est formidable.* Do you know what it is *formidable?*'"

"*Oui, oui, oui, je sais.*"

"Then tell me, how is it possible?"

I tried a fast translation, but the others had already caught the tone of his speech. A little shiver passed across our smiling faces, a shiver of delight.

"Tell him we are five together, not just one person alone."

"Tell him we're Americans, Peace Corps Americans-o."

"Tell him we don't ask for privileges, we respect the ways of different people and they respect us."

"Tell him God has chosen to protect us."

"Tell him we're nice to people, not like some Belgians we know."

"Tell him we have lived in Africa for eighteen months and are used to the ways."

"*Monsieur*, look at us. We are young, healthy, and have good sense. We live as the people do and are not a...a...*comment dit-on?*..." I couldn't remember the word for 'threat' and looked it up quickly in the dictionary. "That is to say, we are not a threat." The word in French was *menace*. In fact, we were not a threat or a menace.

"We come with good will and trust others to see that and treat us with good will. It is very simple. Of course we know fear, but we are not afraid because we are not afraid." We actually had many fears but not the big fear that prevented us from trying. It was not simple at all. I didn't know how to explain. "It is like wishing it to be so." If it sounded naive, it was because we probably were, though we did not think it. Nevertheless, it was the whole truth.

"Ah, yes, *mademoiselle*. But there have been other Americans, French, Belgians—it does not matter who—with good sense, health, youth, who lived many years—no matter how many—in Africa. Even five together, or fifty, with the desert what does it matter? They found fear, misfortune, cruelty, deceit, even death." He remembered the beer he had been toying with and tilted back his head to finish it in one gulp.

"*Non, non, non, mademoiselle*, there is something else. Something you surely know—for you are not fools—and do not wish to admit as your real secret. But I will say it."

"And what is that?"

"The life of the desert is for men, and in your case all that matters is that you are young women, and in general, it doubtless works to your favor..."

My attention was distracted by the crack of toes exposed by the hole in my sneaker. How silly it was to have torn it that way.

When they asked me what he said, I remembered something about pretty. Yes, "in general, it doubtless works to your favor that you are very pretty."

Much later, far from the euphoria and giddiness of that evening, I couldn't be sure whether he had said that we were, in general, very pretty or not very pretty. French is like that. You have to listen carefully to get the negative. The others never knew of this small doubt for either could have doubtless worked to our favor.

A chance to eat and rest was all the reprieve there would be from the wind. Just as we began to get comfortable, gusts of sand swirled by. A few feet away from the fire the air was icy. We were trying to figure out how to best arrange ourselves for sleep when the Belgian stood up and kicked sand into the fire.

"Let's go," he said.

The weather rapidly turned worse. Wrapped in blankets, we boarded the trucks and started off. I hoped he knew what he was doing. Perhaps there was a shelter ahead. Any memory of the mellow hour we had just experienced vanished in rising wind. We moved slowly, ponderously. Windshield wipers were useless against the storm of sand. The tire tracks we had been following disappeared. The sand blew too thick to see the rocks marking the edge of the *piste*. It was impossible to go on.

The moment the engine was turned off, I was overcome by a rush of the same feelings I'd had in the sudden silence in front of the Amenokal Hôtel, the same feelings of lost protection at the *gendarmerie*. But this time there was a difference. The engine was off, but the world was not silent.

Outside the wind raged. Sand scraped the windows and bombarded the metal cab which enclosed us. The truck shuddered and rocked. From time to time we rubbed our fingers and toes or tucked them under the blankets, but it was impossible to warm them. We could not stretch, or lie down, or move about. And so we huddled, Darlene, the Belgian and I, sitting up through a sleepless night of nature's fury.

When at last the wind subsided, it was dawn. First light revealed a coat of sand that had crept through the vehicle's invisible crevices. Black robes had become grey. Granules fell from our hair. We moved carefully, brushing fine grit from our eyebrows and cheeks, testing our cramped legs.

The foul night had not done much for the Belgian's disposition. If we had not been there, he could have stretched out and slept as he was meant to in his own truck. I looked at him blankly and did not respond to his stupid grumbling.

I longed for the sun to warm us. I longed for a hot drink. By and by, we got out of the cab and shook out the sand as best we could. But it had penetrated every fiber. I felt it chafe under my clothes, in my underwear. In the other truck the experience had been similar with the added bother of Gruber's harassment by the soldier. We all spent a few minutes stretching. Not much was said. We boarded and drove another hour before the trucks needed attention, giving us an opportunity to eat. We were tired, dull and grimy. The five of us crouched in a circle a short distance from the trucks. The sun shown as if nothing whatsoever had happened. It was out of place to be numb from a sleepless night. After an uninspired combination of sardines and canned peaches, I finished the canteen of water disguised with sweetened orange syrup, which was still mercifully cool from the night. It was simply an act of sustenance.

Before we reboarded, Gruber tied a small American flag to the outside mirror of the lead truck. Surely we would soon cross paths with the American ambassador.

On the morning of the 22nd of February, four days after we had expected to arrive in Algiers, we came to the Foreign Legion outpost of Arak, nearly a thousand miles short of our destination.

The fort straddled the narrow mouth of the gorges of Arak, protected by an outer string of rooms and high walls built across and hard against the sheer rock canyon. Behind the fort, red rock mesas, hundreds of feet high, hid more narrow canyons. In front, a guardhouse, striped diagonally in red, white, and blue, lent an incongruously festive air. High across the entrance a red, white and blue arch bore the words *Légion Étrangère*. How the French love their arches. How unequivocally an arch says, "This is the place. See how important it is."

Officially there were no longer any *légionnaires* this far south in Algeria, but they were there nonetheless.

The Belgian chatted easily with several of them across a low stone wall in the open, away from us and the fortress. It was much the way the driver from Zinder had spoken with the men at the wells, as if they were old friends. From time to time the Belgian gestured toward us, waiting in the trucks. He was, no doubt, telling the story of us, punctuated by the slap of his hand on his knee and a shake of his head. It was the beginning of our legend, as the Legion was a legend, a grain of truth embellished by repeated tellings.

And so, legend to legend, the *légionnaires* offered the Peace Corps women a late breakfast and showers, and we accepted. We were careful, however, to take our showers in shifts, with someone always keeping a close eye on the trucks so that they did not leave without us.

The *légionnaires* at Arak fed us and the French soldiers but did not eat with us, so we had only a passing impression of them. There were only a few, young and smart in their uniforms. They were friendly in an odd sort of way, shifting from curious to indifferent, with darting eyes and no pause for conversation. We left once the Belgian got fuel for both trucks.

Three times around the stone landmark, an Arab grave, was necessary, the legend said, to ensure a safe journey. We had come more than 200 miles from Arak over the Plain of Tidikelt and within the hour would arrive at the oasis of In Salah. Behind and before us the *piste* went straight to the horizon. But at the old stone it bulged into a ring.

The desert clings to its rituals and its stories. With so few people in so vast a space, every person has value, every act entered in history. In a place where the bones of a battle more than sixty years before lie visible under their rock cairns, where abandoned vehicles remain a part of the roadside for ten or thirty or more years without rusting, where the earth does not change its face to mark seasons, in such a place the myths and rituals become as fixed as the landscape. There were no tracks cutting across the circle. This was not the time to test the fates. And so the great flatbed carrying *le malade*, followed by the five-ton army cargo truck, fell in with the tracks of hundreds of predecessors three times around in a wide circle.

I don't know what I expected of the French Foreign Legion—perhaps that it be made up of men who were worldly, mysterious, deep, and well…manly. At least that it would be French. The few young *légionnaires* we'd briefly met at Arak had not prepared us for what was to come.

The contingent at In Salah was largely German, Austrian and Russian with a few Swiss and "others." There was no aura of military discipline or an officer corps' propriety. Instead, the Legion seemed a refuge for the pot-bellied, the scrawny, the balding, the awkward, and the short. Most of them had bad teeth. To a person, they had darting skittish eyes, as unsettling a characteristic as it had been with those at Arak.

The officers at the mess were rowdy in a self-conscious sort of way, full of exaggerated greetings and gestures. They stood around the table, and at some signal, undetected by us, picked up their empty wine glasses, turned them upside down and shook them. It was the custom, one of them said, "to shake the sand out of the glass." That was all the effort any of them made to acknowledge we were present. The rest was performance ritual for their own benefit. A little wine was poured into each glass. They stood again and toasted, "to our friends who are in the sand." It was meant to be said together, but the voices of a few stragglers trailed after most had finished. They drank the wine in one gulp and slammed the glasses on the table. Again, there were stragglers and some tried a second time with an even greater whack. It made for a lot of pounding.

"Do you know who he is?" one of them asked, pointing to the middle-aged fellow beside him. "Eh, eh, do you know?"

"I don't know," I admitted. "Is he important?"

"Important! He's a para. Surely you've heard of the paratroopers' revolt?"

"*Oui.*" Yes we'd heard. By their passionate support of the right-wing *colons*, the paratroopers of the Legion and the French army sabotaged France's intention to withdraw from Algeria, prolonged the conflict, and delayed independence for probably more than a year. The last action I'd remembered was a coup led by General Challe during which a few specialized regiments occupied important buildings in key northern cities but failed to persuade the regular French soldiers to join in. After a few days the rebel leaders were arrested and their units disbanded. But that had all occurred several years before.

"I was there," the para spoke up for himself. "I was Challe's man in Oran. I am one of the 1st Parachute Regiment, the famous ones. I made history. Everybody thinks we're finished. After the coup they scattered us to weaken our power. But we are the best. We will come back. We have no fear. We will fight to the death. The paras everywhere, even at this moment, are plotting our next move. De Gaulle has given up Algeria. We have not given it up. Algeria will be restored to France."

It was February 1964. Algeria had been independent for nearly two years. The Legion's historic headquarters at Sidi-bel-Abbes had been closed in the fall of 1962. Yet here was a Legion paratrooper clinging to his fantasy, full of bravado, devoid of reality.

There was still no food in sight. The mood seemed agitated with *légionnaires* shouting across the table in several languages. I worried that the pounding and slamming of glasses would lead to a brawl.

One of them called for attention, cleared his throat and began to sing a slow, measured song, _Le Boudin_ (Black Pudding).

> In the course of our faraway campaigns,
> Facing fevers and bullets,
> Let's forget, along with our sorrows,
> Death, which never forgets us...
> Here's the blood sausage,
> the blood sausage, the blood sausage,
> For the Alsatians, the Swiss,
> and the Lorrainers,
> There's none left for the Belgians
> 'cause they're the shirkers...

They sat together, stood together, shouted in unison, pounded the table, and sang a dirge that was their anthem. It was like a fraternity party, with spilled food and broken glasses by the time it ended.

Pat winced as she held a glass of tea to her lips. She daubed more salve on the crack in the corner of her mouth. It was a small thing, just dryness we agreed, despite how uncomfortable it might feel.

"Wrap your turban across your mouth to keep it moist."

"Take an extra vitamin C. Maybe you're just suffering from a lack of fresh fruit."

We gave Pat a lot of advice, having little else to offer. Extremely dry conditions had been hard on our skin but were also known to promote healing. We washed when we could and covered ourselves in thick *crême*, but generally felt the desert gave us a reprieve from the skin diseases so prevalent and persistent in the tropics.

At Columb-Béchar there would surely be a doctor to treat Pat's sore. The Belgian was a little vague about how long it would take to get there. We knew it was to the north and west. Our reading of the map indicated two or three days. When asked if that was right, he said, *"C'est possible,"* and shrugged his shoulders.

We had become accustomed to the Belgian's strange ways and paid no special attention to his sullen avoidance of our questions.

Our first glimpse of In Salah, barely distinguishable from the high dunes that surround it, had been in the late afternoon, when the angle of the sun separated the earth into golden shapes and shadows. The town differed from the dunes only in the geometry of its forms. The dunes undulated, mounded, rippled. The oasis rose in rectangles, squares and arches. The texture of each was the same granular earth. The color was the color reflected from the course of the sun.

The dunes had been planted with palm fronds along their ridges to retard the drift of sand into the oasis, like a snow fence I thought. We walked at sunset, Victoria and I, out of In Salah, into the desert.

A French scientist we met at the *légionnaires* dinner accompanied us to a high place from which we could look out over the red gold horizon, over a grove of tamarisk growing out of a dry wadi, over the flag of Algeria fluttering from a parapet, over the little cluster of cubicles strung along in a sink of dunes.

"And people ask why I love the desert," the scientist said.

Colors changed as we watched, but the change took place across the entire tableau, never disrupting the aesthetic balance.

After hundreds of miles of bleached rocks and only the most subtle earthen tints, there was a place in our senses that accepted dunes. The monochrome of mounds and ripples flowed to the bleached earth oasis itself. It was a change we could understand. Not so the incomprehensibly lush *palmerie* (palm grove).

The link between water and life was direct and profound. Fat date palms grew out of ditches flooded from a permanent underground supply of water. Their broad crowns of fronds, deep green, created a fluttering canopy. Water, trees, food, shade, life. One could swoon from such extravagant greenery. But an inch beyond the irrigation ponds the sand swirled, menacing, a constant reminder that this fragile life could not be taken for granted. I understood why the oases are not part of the desert. Just as an island is not a part of the sea. One leaves the island to go to sea. One leaves an oasis to go into the desert.

Out of In Salah, due north, we drove through the gusts and eddies of the wind over the absolutely flat Tademaït Plateau. I liked the idea of going "into the desert." Oases were good for refueling but quickly felt confining. As we moved deeper into the culture of North African Moslems, we stood a greater chance of getting into trouble in oases where we might be the only uncovered women. We were freer in the desert.

At a small *génie* camp near the water hole of Igosten, the Belgian came to life long enough to regale the troops with the story of us. A pattern was being established. He was indifferent to us except when he had an audience. Then he became possessive and proud, like a carnival barker with his own five-headed freak.

Once again, as he had at Arak, and then with the *génie* and the *légionnaires* at In Salah, he told of our encounter with the *gendarmes*. Each time, the tale got a little taller, our feat more extraordinary.

"I love you," a teen-aged soldier said to me as we ate their breakfast rations. "In thirty-seven days I will be finished here. Marry me, and I will take you to Paris."

"Have you seen the American ambassador recently?" I asked. In order to have arrived in Tamanrasset as expected he had to have passed by this camp a couple of days before.

"I don't believe I have seen the American ambassador ever."

"They say he is driving to Tam, and we have been watching for him."

"Very unusual. Ambassadors don't drive. They fly in, have their pictures taken with a Tuareg, and fly out the same day."

"This is the <u>American</u> ambassador, you know, good will, people to people."

"I'll believe it when I see it."

The fact that the ambassador's entourage hadn't been seen was perplexing. We were on the route directly south of Algiers and if they had come into the desert, they would have been spotted by now. There was no way to take a secret motor trip in the desert. Perhaps they'd broken down. We would continue to look out for them until we turned west toward Columb-Béchar, perhaps the next day.

Afternoon shadows stretched to twice the height of the truck when the Belgian said there was something interesting to see not far off the road. His words interrupted the half-sleep into which I'd slipped. The winter temperature in the desert rose and fell in daily extremes of 70 degrees or more. We slept fitfully during freezing nights and nodded off easily on dry, hot afternoons.

He veered to the west and in the time it took to refresh myself with a drink of water and a dose of eyedrops, we came upon a scene that might have come straight out of Saharan cinema.

Like an abandoned temple, the mud blockhouse of Fort Miribel stood blinding white on a knoll above the flat and desolate Tademaït Plateau.

Miribel and its sibling, Fort MacMahon, about a hundred miles to the west, had been conceived as toeholds for the French penetration of the desert. They were built before the turn of the century near the northern edge of the territory controlled by the Ahaggar Tuareg. The French believed a contingent of their Saharian troops and *tirailleurs,* (riflemen recruited from freed black slaves) set up at Miribel, could protect the traffic between El Goléa and In Salah from nomadic raiders. Instead they became stationary targets for raiders themselves.

So desolate, so hopeless, and so boring was Miribel that even the Legion refused it. Its occupation was brief. From a military standpoint it was a disaster; as a penal colony, a horror.

Fearing soft sand on the sloping approach to the fort, the Belgian stopped at the base of the knoll. He invited us to explore the fort. The engines were kept running. We hesitated.

"And you, *monsieur,* will you come along?"

All of us hiked to the top of the mound and entered the fort. Squinting beyond the sun spots that danced before my eyes and feeling sick in the intense radiating heat, I moved slowly through the courtyard and imagined a life confined to the rectangle of rooms and cells that enclosed it. After more than seventy years on its utterly exposed site, Miribel was, like most mud structures in the Sahara, wind-weathered but without age.

The dirt floors of the cells had been dug out to two or three feet below grade, creating the semblance of a dungeon. Instead of a parapet, narrow slits high in the outer walls afforded observation and defense. In modern time an erector-set watchtower had been added outside a corner of the fort.

Something about the bleached ruin called for reverence. And so, even though there was no one within a hundred miles, we trespassers trod lightly and spoke softly. For the two *génie,* Miribel was clearly an awesome experience. They peered tentatively into the cells and remembered the tales of torture from which few prisoners survived.

There was a contradiction in the message of Miribel. Despite a frightful exposure to the world's most unforgiving elements and its own gruesome history, the fort cast an image of purity and order. What doors, shutters and other furnishings there might have been had been stripped away long before. Only the mud structure remained, earth to earth.

There was no water and no vegetation and there never had been. Without water of its own, Miribel had had to be supplied from El Goléa, a four to five day camel trip, one way. The fort had been laid out in a formal plan detailed with arched roofs and doorways. Yet it had no water. Simple forms repeated themselves in a powerful aesthetic. It had harmony. Symmetry. But no water. The hand of the architect had tried to civilize this tiny plot. It looked like a place one could live. It was an illusion. No water, no life.

We arrived at El Goléa after dark, drawing a lot of attention to ourselves. As if the roar of engines were not enough, the Belgian used the horn to startle a herd of goats corralled in a corner of the market place. He drove too fast for the dark narrow lanes. A few lanterns and small cooking fires blurred in the dust stirred by our vehicles. The Arabs crouching about their camps watched but did not respond.

It was a relief to reach the *génie* compound. The five of us were clearly unexpected, not to mention very tired and hungry. Yet the *chef* of the camp engaged us in leisurely conversation. It wasn't clear whether he would offer us rooms until, after what seemed a long while, he stepped aside for a private message from an aide. He then insisted that we accept his hospitality. The rooms were full of personal belongings and had been hurriedly vacated for our use. We hesitated. But not long. We were so tired. This night we would knowingly be a bother. Tomorrow we would deal with it.

We were awakened by a lot of racket and shouting.

"*Au revoir, mademoiselles!*" a voice called, or we thought we heard a voice call.

"What is it?" Darlene stirred.

"Shh. I don't know. Listen." Lying very still did not help. There was too much noise. Engines. Banging on our door.

"Oh man, you guys, what time is it? Where are we?" Gruber asked as I was trying to answer those same questions for myself. Our room was dark.

"*Au revoir, mademoiselles. Je vais maintenant,*" the voice

shouted.

I turned toward the door, and I saw shafts of bright light breaking through cracks in the shutters. We had slept in. I pulled a *lapa* around myself and rushed out the door.

It was the Belgian, already given up on us, walking toward his truck.

"*Monsieur*, here I am," I called. On the ground beside the truck were heaped our belongings. "What's going on?"

"I am going now."

"We'll be ready in a few minutes."

"I say good-bye, *mademoiselle*. *Bon voyage*. Good luck. That's it. I alone am going. Unless, of course, *mademoiselle* Victoria with the blue eyes will come with me. I will make an exception for her."

"What are you saying? You can't leave us!" Standing barefooted on the dirt veranda in my pantaloons and *lapa*, I actually tried to reason with the Belgian. "The *chef* said we were to ride with you to Columb-Béchar."

"The *chef* is in Tit. I have had enough of you. Here are all your things. That's it." He continued toward the truck.

"Wait!" I screamed, keeping an eye on him while I ran back to call the others. "Wake up! Wake up! The Belgian's leaving us."

"Where are the *génie*?" I shouted above the deafening engine, grasping at anything I could think of to delay him. "What about the *génie*?"

"They stay here a few days and return to Tit."

Gruber walked by me in the most casual way, out past the pile of baggage signalling him with her arms. "Hey you, Belgian guy. *Attendez*. I mean wait a minute."

"Gruber, look out! He's backing up."

"I say? You have something of mine."

He could not have heard her, but he stopped as she picked up her pace past his door, waving her arms. It was just a few seconds' pause, just enough time for Gruber to retrieve her flag. Then he drove away.

11

La Piste est Finie

"**H**ere—we—sit—like—birds—in—the—wilderness, birds—in—the—wilderness..." someone began tentatively, half singing, half reciting.

"Cute."

"Do you have something better to contribute?"

"Knock it off. Let's deal with getting out of here."

"I can't believe the Belgian just left us."

"Believe it."

"We're lucky he didn't leave us in the desert."

"The ass hole."

"We don't even know what this place looks like."

We had gathered in one of the rooms in which we'd spent the night to sort out our changed circumstances. The local *chef* had sent pots of coffee and hot milk, which we had with biscuits and canned fruit from our own supply. The soldier whose room it was came in for his shoes and asked in an impatient way how soon we would be out.

"Gruber, you were really smart to remember the flag."

"For true. It's a good sign." We ferreted out good omens. Clung to them. Repeated them out loud.

"We just have to find a ride."

"You know how long that takes. We're already behind

schedule."

I privately held no hope for finding a ride quickly. Things were not done quickly. There were courtesies to be exchanged. We had yet to learn who had the power and the inclination to help us.

"Do you suppose anybody misses us?"

"Maybe they're searching for us right now."

"Who?"

"You're right. We'd have to be gone a lot longer before anybody would actually notice."

"Well at least we're together."

We packed, once again, so that we could go at a moment's notice.

"How's your mouth sore, Pat?"

Pat shrugged her shoulders and winced. No one said it, but the sore looked worse. It was only a little larger but had turned red-brown and raw. It did not seem to be responding to our treatment.

"If we don't get a ride, we'll have to find another place to stay."

"You're right."

"Why? I don't see what's wrong with this. It's free."

"It's also somebody else's room."

"I think Pat should keep her cup and spoon separate so we don't spread whatever she has," Victoria said, looking away from Pat. It was the first interest Victoria had ever shown in the mechanics of our trip.

We took an inventory of our food—sardines, a small canned ham, three packages of dried soup, a few cans of fruit, a little oatmeal and powdered milk, half a jar of relish, a can of baked beans, and a few items fallen to the bottom of the basket. If we added some bread, it would be enough for several days.

Money was a greater problem. Among us we had about $200 in a combination of dollars, new and old French *francs*. Not quite $40 each. The rides we had paid for had been about $10/person, but the distances between oases varied so, there was no way to predict what the last five hundred miles would cost. *Campements* had been under a dollar each but did not seem to be available any longer. Hotel rooms, even the sparest, would get more expensive as we moved north to the more populated areas.

"What we need are a doctor to take a look at Pat, some bread and maybe some oranges, and a ride to get us out of here."

Darlene accompanied Pat on her search for a doctor. Victoria did not go with them. In her terror and loathing of bodily imperfections, Victoria was turning away from Pat.

El Goléa, the Citadel, the oasis with water enough for a *palmerie*, fruit orchards and the eucalyptus and tamarisk that shaded its squares and lanes. We would not have the peace of mind to explore El Goléa and enjoy the advantages of its sweet water. The sun was high by the time we set out from the *génie* compound. The *chef* of this camp had not been very helpful. He was new to the oasis, and, he was quick to point out, since independence the policy of France was "not to fraternize, not to mingle with the Arabs or the nomads." Under those circumstances, and since he could not offer us a ride himself, our chances were weakened by association with the French military.

We located the *sous-préfet* and explained who we were and what we wanted. He regretted to tell us there were no lorries or other public carriers.

"Of course, but there are trucks. Surely someone could take us at least to Ghardia." The market was busy with traffic. A merchant had told us a load of sheep would probably be ready to leave that afternoon. We asked the *sous-préfet* to find out if this was true and to negotiate a ride and a price for us. He was aghast.

"It is impossible. You must be patient. Perhaps in a day or two I will find you a suitable ride."

He meant well and spoke about "suitability" as if he were talking to women with the resources to buy protection and comfort. Although we bargained hard and were appropriately shocked at prices, we could not reveal to anyone how very low in money we really were. We felt perilously dependent and could not risk losing the control over our lives that making our own decisions appeared to give us.

Once again we hashed over our options. Pat stood stiffly, eyes staring behind her green tinted lenses. Her posture begged that she not be asked to participate. The French army doctor she had found gave her another salve, but she fled from his boozy breath. Her sore was not larger than a dime, yet it was big enough for her to retreat behind. I remembered the speck in my eye and understood.

Gusts of sand menaced the market, turning the air grey. The sheep bawled, and the men herded them with impatient shouts and prods which only made the sheep more irritable and stubborn.

"*Mademoiselle*, you should not do this. It is not right. These people are low-class. They have no manners," the *sous-préfet* pleaded.

"Our friend is sick. We must get to Algiers. We cannot afford a long delay. Please understand that we are grateful for your concern."

The sand that had swirled throughout the oasis all day blew into a thicker cloud, shrouding the sun and bringing an early dusk.

We should have read the evidence. If we had not been so desperate to move on, we would have hesitated at the battered old truck. We would have been wary of the uncommunicative driver. The baggage went in a four-foot wide section partitioned across the front of the cargo area to separate it from the sheep. We should have been suspicious when the greaser and the half-witted teenager who came with the sheep grinned stupidly and did little to help us load our things.

Patient Pat and nurse Darlene rode in the cab. The rest of us sat on the baggage with the greaser and the boy. It was crowded and precarious. We had to have our legs up out of the way of the sheep while constantly holding on to a piece of the frame in order to not fly off the truck.

It was not going to be wonderful, but we were toughened to discomfort. Most importantly, for $5 each we would get to Laghouat, at the edge of the Atlas Mountains, more than half way to Algiers.

The one thing we had not reckoned on were the sheep themselves. They smelled. They were frightened and highly agitated. They made a hell of a racket. Sheep may be cute scurrying across a market or grazing in a field, but they were dangerous in a moving vehicle. They had no way to steady themselves. With every lurch of the truck all fifty sheep were thrown as if they were a single projectile to one side, then another. They could easily crush a person caught in the surge. The driver was clumsy, the *piste* rutted and the truck virtually without springs. The sheep were constantly thrown about. At times it seemed the mass of sheep would turn the truck over on its side.

Gruber, Victoria and I crowded together to keep warm, but also to mark our territory atop the baggage. An unoccupied space of more than a foot clearly separated us from the crew. It was not to last.

"Oh man, you guys, I think I have a feeler," Gruber shouted above the din of engine and sheep.

I looked past her and saw the greaser staring indifferently ahead.

"It's your imagination. You probably just got thrown closer to him in the last pot hole. Move over here."

"For true, you guys. I moved and he followed."

"Kate Gruber!" Victoria scolded, "can't you see the situation we're in?"

We were all shouting to be heard, clinging to the truck for our lives, and trying to protect ourselves from the cold and wind-blown sand. And now this harassment.

"Here, I'll change places with you," I offered before I had thought through how that could happen. My legs had fallen asleep. I untangled one, then the other, flexing to get the circulation back. I so needed to stretch. The only way was to stand down with the sheep. I kicked one out of the way to make myself a space, but another moved into it. They were stubborn, bleating animals. They also weighed more than I expected. My kicking was for nought. The sheep moved only when they chose to or when they were thrown out of control. I waited for an opening, hopped down and hoped to not be crushed. Gruber slid left to my space and I climbed up onto hers.

I made as great a show as possible of wrapping my legs under my robe and turning my back to the greaser. In no time he fell against me. I turned and glared at him. He was smiling lasciviously. I belted him in the chest with my elbow and screamed at him in English. The boy, who all along had been straddling the rail or hanging from it over the side of the truck, was highly amused. Then I realized that the greaser had opened his pants and was fondling himself. I swerved around, planted both feet against him and tried to push him off the truck. It got his attention, and he settled onto his own side of the baggage to recover.

The sheep truck and its occupants were the nadir of our journey.

We rode long into the night without a single break. Stiff, hungry, and fearing that we might fall asleep and bounce overboard, we had to get the driver to stop. Gruber lay forward over the baggage and beat on the roof of the cab, shouting until the truck began to slow down.

The driver said nothing. We could not determine whether the stop was to be just a short rest, time to eat, or camp for the night. More than anything, I hated stupid uncommunicative people.

We took down a little food and kept a close eye on the movements of the Arabs. When they finally built a fire, we brought down more food and our blankets. For the first time in thousands of miles we ate separately from our fellow travelers.

We laid our blankets within reach of each other very near the truck. Should we take turns keeping watch? Would the sheep ever shut up? We tried to talk about these things, to sleep, and to stay alert.

Not until the driver sternly called, did we realize we had drifted off to sound sleep. It was black, the fire was out. In the middle of the night we boarded the truck and took off. It was crazy. We were too tired. The driver had to be tired as well. But there was no discussing it. In the hours before dawn we did our best not to fall off the truck or into the sheep.

Throughout the morning there were numerous stops. Stop to change a tire. Stop to water the sheep. Stop to tinker with the engine. Despite hours of bone-jarring driving we had made little progress. The sheep truck was slow. Whereas we had previously averaged twenty-five or more miles an hour, even over the worst *piste*, we now barely did twenty. At that rate it would be days before we reached Laghouat.

We couldn't stand it any longer. We had to get away from, as Gruber called them, "these horrid people, these horrid sheep, this horrid truck."

Late in the morning we stopped at a junction where several other trucks had pulled in by an adobe rest house. Out of the maze of tire tracks there was a clear pattern of heavy use going off to the east. Our driver and his two assistants unloaded their sleeping mats, an indication that this would be a long stop.

"*La piste est finie* (The track ends here)," he said, nodding north.

Off on the horizon a grey break in the sand marked the edge of paved road. That was as deep into the desert as it had come. Suddenly the Sahara seemed tamer, the wind breezy instead of raging, the sky clear, the sun at a friendly angle. Before us was a paved road. It couldn't be very hard or very long now. In no time we would be in Algiers.

But even as we excitedly tried to confirm this with the driver, he shook his head blankly.

"Algiers? Who said anything about Algiers?"

"Not immediately, of course, but after Laghouat."

"Perhaps. I'm not sure I will go to Laghouat. First I will visit my family."

"Wait a minute," I said to the others, "I better listen closer. I think he said he was going to visit his family and not to Laghouat."

"Where is your family?"

"Ouargla," he said pointing to the track running to the east.

"Oh shit!" Pat said quite firmly without even moving her lips.

We did not want to go to Ouargla. It was hundreds of miles out of our way. Why had the driver told me back in the El Goléa market that he was going to Laghouat? I hated all this messy communication. I was disgusted by the sheep people.

They napped. We ate and squatted in a cluster, scratching patterns in the sand, struggling to invent a solution. The paved road led somewhere, but we could not walk it. There was a shelter at this site, but one empty adobe building was not an oasis. We could not stay here. Most of the trucks that had been here when we arrived had gone. The sun crept from late morning to mid afternoon. We shifted position to keep it at our backs.

Two shiny oil tankers pulled up across the road, aloof from the rest of the common Berliez cargo vehicles and as far as possible from the battered sheep truck.

"Maybe we can get a ride with them," I said on an impulse. "I'm going to find out where they're going."

The *pétroliers* (long distance oil drivers) were the princes of desert transport. Better educated, better paid than any other class of driver, they enjoyed very high status. I didn't know any of that as I ran across the sandy plain and climbed up to the cab to get the driver's attention.

"*Bonjour, monsieur. Ça va* (How's it going)?"

"*Pas mal, et vous?* (Not bad. And you)?" He showed only the slightest amusement and no surprise at a young white woman bobbing up at his window.

He stepped down out of the cab, and I explained who we were and that we wished to leave the sheep truck and go to Algiers. At best he could take us to Ghardia, but he had to confer with his colleague for they were a convoy. The other driver was hesitant. Women were bad luck.

"*Monsieur*," I said, "You have very beautiful trucks. I see they are Shell. Shell is an American company. Owned by my countrymen. Surely the owners would be pleased that you had assisted their sisters. As you can see, it is impossible for us to continue on the sheep truck." I don't know how it all flowed out of me. I just kept talking. I made it up. I opened my mouth and trusted that what I needed would flow out.

He was sympathetic, but not convinced. They would discuss it.

I ran back to the others. The sheep men were loading to go.

"Ask them to wait until we know if we have the other ride."

"You ask them."

"I don't care if we have it or not. I'm not going another mile with that sheep truck and those creeps."

We were caught.

"Even if the oil guys don't take us, there is bound to be someone else in a day or so. We have enough food and water to last."

"Hey, this is really hitchhiking."

"Oh-my-God," shrieked Darlene, "if my mother could see me now. They'll never believe this in New York."

"Wait, wait!" The driver was starting the engine. "All our stuff's still on there!"

"Jer, go back and try to persuade the oil guys. We'll get our stuff off the sheep truck."

I hesitated.

"Don't worry, we'll get yours, too. Just do your job and talk good. We'll get it all."

I went back to the intensely hard work of chatting with the *pétroliers* in an easy rambling sort of way, watching for signals, reinforcing points they seemed to respond to. After fifteen or twenty minutes, I returned with good news.

The plain was quiet except for the rising wind. The sheep truck had gone. The four of them stood solemn and wind-blown beside a heap of baskets and suitcases.

Something had happened. I looked at them and they at each other.

"Guess whose baggage was left on the sheep truck?" Darlene said at last.

"Nobody's," I said, not wanting to hear it. "Nobody's was left on there because you all made sure every piece was taken off."

"For true, we missed one."

"Mine?" I jumped in before anyone could answer. "Do you mean to tell me while I was working my brains off getting us a ride, you left my bag on the sheep truck?"

"Not yours. Is that all you can think of?"

"The pack got left because it blended in, it was hard to see at the bottom of the baggage compartment."

"Gruber's pack? Is this a joke?" I searched their faces for the first one to dissolve into laughter.

"It's only a material thing," Gruber said slowly, wanting to believe it, testing herself in this moment of loss with a truth remembered from childhood lessons.

"It's only a material thing," she repeated of the pack she loved, the pack in which she had taken almost obsessive pride. In her care and attention it had become a comfort, a friend when the rest of us were tired of her organizing and her frantic, tangled energy.

"We can't allow ourselves to care too much about material things. See, I'm OK. Really."

"Oh, damn, Gruber, it's terrible."

I asked about her passport, her camera, her money. All of these things were safely in the purse she carried with her.

"How about your film?"

"It's in my pack, in the main compartment, way at the bottom since I didn't think I needed to get to it until we got back to Liberia."

"Damn, damn, damn! All those rolls of film."

"You can have copies of our pictures."

"And I have something you can wear."

"In the next oasis, we'll get you a new toothbrush."

We wanted so much to make up for her loss. What if it had happened to us? Would we accept it with such equanimity? Not likely.

"Hey, you guys," she held up her hands to stop us. "It's really all right. I know you all mean well. But it really is only a material thing," she repeated firmly, almost squaring her shoulders with the strength she felt in believing. "See how lucky I am to have you guys as friends? I mean, it isn't everybody who has such good buddies like you guys."

She meant it, and that only made us feel worse.

The oil rig was a joy. Stainless steel tank and shiny chrome trim. A cab easily held four across, so with three of us in one rig and two in the other, *nous cinq* entered the modern world. As we cruised along the paved road, the *pétrolier* demonstrated the air conditioning, the radio. He was clean, confident—unlike the grubby stupid sheep haulers—an Arab of the future, in a modern expansive industry. He was the cowboy of the desert, independent, a man with a machine he was proud of. I felt we'd passed through a time warp.

We admired all the features of the cab. Indeed, it seemed too much luxury for a truck. I felt awkward, a little out of place. I resisted taking too great a pleasure in it. Perhaps it was because we had simplified our lives to such a rudimentary level. But more likely I resisted because I did not want to be reminded of an underlying reality. For us, the slick oil rig and paved road represented the beginning of the end of the desert.

We rode in comfort and stopped before dark to make our camp.

On what was to be our last night in the desert, I longed for cooked food and offered to make our supper. All I needed was a free hand. I may not have been a very good cook, but I could put together something interesting. There was not much left in our basket. The centerpiece had to be the last canned ham. Alone, it was just more cold finger food. But if I cooked it in a sauce and added vegetables.

"Just keep it simple," they warned.

"Yeah, no 'creative' combinations. We want to be able to recognize what we're eating."

"Don't worry. Leave it to me."

They were tired. I seemed to be the only one with energy that night. I understood their reticence to experiment. That took energy. The meal would be terrific. They'd realize their worry was groundless.

The only ingredient in the basket in which to cook the ham was the dry soup mix. No one liked reconstituted split pea—yet it was the only one left, and I knew it would be wonderful with the ham.

They hated it. All four of them were angry, wouldn't eat my

concoction and wouldn't speak to me.

Other trucks gathered at our camp that night, each at a little distance from the others. Under an unobstructed dome of stars the lights of one or another truck came out of the distance and quietly claimed a space. Even on the paved road, it was a wonder to encounter other vehicles.

In the morning we took a short side trip to an oil camp where we brushed our teeth in the water gushing out of a four-inch hose. The sound of water running was deafening. We let it run over our hands and wrists. We splashed it on our faces. The hose just lay there, pumping water into the sand as if there were no end to the supply.

The sore in the corner of Pat's mouth had not improved. She was frightened.

"She wants to get out of the desert as soon as possible," Victoria said, "even if it means being flown out."

There was probably an airport at Ghardia, but the idea of flying seemed so foreign, so inappropriate. To simply get on a plane and fly out would discredit all we had done.

"She wants someone to go with her," Victoria continued.

We looked at each other and at Pat's eyes imploring from behind tinted green lenses.

"I don't see why she told me. I'm not responsible for her. I've come all this way, I want to finish overland. Everyone is free to do what she wishes. But just because one person wants to give up, I don't see why anyone else should." Victoria said all of this right in front of Pat, looking away from her as if she no longer existed.

The subtle shift of Pat's attention from concern for Victoria to concern for herself altered their relationship. With the flow of support to her fortress self ended, Victoria pulled up the drawbridge.

By late morning we approached Ghardia, a crowded oasis that had long been a trade center of North Africa and the northern Sahara.

The majority of people were M'Zabite Berbers whose ancestors fled the domination of the Arabs in the tenth century and settled on the limestone plateau between the Great Eastern and Western Ergs of the northern Sahara. Of the seven oasis towns they built, five were nearly within sight of each other, strung along on a row of hills and linked by rock bridges which permitted the torrential floods of occasional rains to sweep by them.

Though not the oldest or the most revered, Ghardia was the largest in modern times of the seven towns of the M'Zab.

"How large is it?" I asked.

"Two hundred thousand date palms," the *pétrolier* told us with undisguised pride. He drove faster and smiled a little with the excitement of the sight before us. Moreover, he was going home.

Bleached earthen houses crowded the mound on which the town had been built. Here and there pastel blues, lavenders or pinks decorated a wall or portal. Otherwise the palette ranged from blinding white to shades of sand.

The flat-roofed buildings clung together about a minaret which rose above all else at the pinnacle of the hill. They encompassed a *palmerie* at the base and continued to the edges where the town ended unequivocally with nothing but the desert beyond. There was no drifting off as our cities do, with their dense downtowns, loosely packed outer neighborhoods and suburbs, then rural space inhabited only here and there over great distances as if there were only so much force the center could muster to hold the whole together.

The M'Zabite builders never lost sight of the primary purpose of a town—the protection of its inhabitants. Ghardia began inside a wall and, as it grew, additional walls expanded the circle. As a result, the oasis is as dense in all parts as it is in the center. Whether for dwelling or commerce, every building touches another with a common wall, a shared courtyard, a connecting roof or covered passage. Ghardia is so compact it is possible to go off a little distance and photograph the whole oasis.

A community of Jews, also believed to be of Berber ancestry

and also traders, coexists within the walls of the oasis. Although present in Ghardia nearly as long as the M'Zbites, the Jews have, until recently, been required to live and conduct their business in a strictly segregated quarter.

Ghardia was North African as no other oasis had been. The music, the veils, the fez, the twisting cobbled lanes, the bazaar, the network of market streets known as *suks*. Yet the architecture remained true to the desert.

Spontaneous architecture of the earth, Le Corbusier called it, functional and protective, without extraneous embellishments. It had endured unrelenting sun, ravishing wind and freezing winter nights in the same place, in the same way, for centuries.

On a trip into the desert, Le Corbusier was so impressed with the purity of form, with the aesthetic of simplicity, and the human scale that he used the architecture of Ghardia as the model for his chapel at Ronchamp, in eastern France.

Ghardia was four hundred miles from Algiers, deep into the desert for most Westerners coming from the north. But from the time we arrived, we felt the end approaching. There was very little money among us. Pat's sore grew worse. Our schools in Liberia were to start their new terms on Monday. We had to get to Algiers. And yet . . .

What would Le Corbusier have thought if he had gone on to Agadez?

We had to leave as quickly as possible.

We stayed in a plain hotel that faced a large open area where the oil tankers and desert traffic passed.

The innkeeper was a Frenchman who seemed to spend his time at a small table in the passageway between the lobby and the dining room. He passed the early part of the day drinking coffee with hot milk and the later part drinking red wine with his cohorts. Easily annoyed, he roused himself from the table reluctantly to accept new guests or scold his Arab servant. Nevertheless, as soon as we arrived, even before we had gone to market, we enlisted his help in finding a ride to Algiers. We were also very hungry.

"This is not a regular meal hour," he protested. "There is no cook."

Over plates of greasy fried eggs and loaves of bread, we tried to remember our last good meal. There was the disastrous green soup and ham incident. There had been breakfast with the Legion at Arak and then the dinner with all the pounding and singing *légionnaires* at In Salah. Otherwise, we had eaten out of our basket since leaving Tit. Now it was hard to eat really well when we had to count every *centime*.

"A *camion* of some kind," I replied when the innkeeper asked how we planned to leave Ghardia.

"Impossible," he said, "this is civilization. The people would not stand for it."

"Then what? A public bus perhaps?"

"*N'existe pas,*" (It doesn't exist) he shook his head. "On Sunday you can fly to Algiers."

"We can't afford to fly nor can we afford the wait. We must leave very soon."

He shrugged.

Since few streets could accommodate them, motor vehicles clustered along the outer edge of Ghardia. The row of buildings in which the hotel stood separated the outer from the inner worlds. In front of it we would find our way out of the desert. Behind it we made our way along the narrow streets of the past. Black-veiled women dashed by with only one exposed eye to guide them along the cobblestone passages of the oasis which they were never permitted to leave. They peered at the bareheaded infidels who brazenly strolled in public and bargained alone with the men of the market. Along the way the sound of nasal Arab songs poured out of transistor radios and drifted from open doors, songs as plaintive and monotonous as the solitude of the desert.

We were drawn through lanes so narrow one could touch the walls of both sides at once. The passageways wound round blind corners and up cobbled steps. Nothing more than slits between buildings, they forced our eyes to shift abruptly from stale dim tunnels to the blinding reflection of sun against a whitewashed wall. Men stood in the doorways and sat on ledges. We were foreigners here, and their comments were not always friendly.

"Jerks."

Silly boys, we said to ourselves to keep our courage. Their public insults unsettled and angered us. That tenuous balance between a respect for their ways and respect for ourselves was tested with every gesture. The black wool robes we had gotten in the habit of always wearing outdoors covered us from our shoulders to our toes. But they were men's robes. And we did not go out of our way to cover our heads. We gave them, we realized, an ambiguity to consider. And the pause it extracted was long enough to allow us to pass. I was mightily relieved to come to the open space of the main market. Whereas in the *casbah* we were met with derision and abuse, in the open we were treated with curiosity and amusement.

A colonnade of arches surrounded the main market, granting precious shade to the merchants crowded under its roof. Others had set up tents or lean-tos to mark their space in the open square. The market had operated on this site for nearly a thousand years yet all but the site itself was as temporary as any desert camp. We made our way past dusty herds of goats and kept out of spitting distance of camels.

Ghardia's reputation as a trade center was based here, amid the ubiquitous flies and the great array of merchandise. Straw mats, printed cloth, enamel pans, baskets of grain, dates in pyramids of half-dozen each, solid cones of sugar, rubber tire sandals, tea, robes, rounds of flat bread—the necessities of everyday life we had seen in every desert market. But here were also extravagances from the north—transistor radios, carpets, embroidered cloth, oranges, silver jewelry, leather sandals, brass trays and urns, scented soap, chewing gum, and on a rough table in an arch of the colonnade, blue enamel tea pots.

Our bags and baskets were already a burden and we had little money to spare. Yet I had to have a teapot. Just as there was one kind of architecture in the desert, and one kind of dress, there was one kind of tea pot. And for me these little pots with their cone-shaped lids and curving spouts evoked the grace and cold of nights in the desert. After a good bit of haggling, of walking away and coming back, of studied indifference—until I knew I couldn't bear the sun and the flies any longer—I had my picture taken buying a blue enamel tea pot.

All the elements of life in the oasis were known and fixed as they always had been. The only difference was that for this brief moment we were there. Buying the pot and having the picture taken sealed the moment. It was one of the few times I felt like a tourist in an exotic place and I didn't mind.

In a shop in a *suk* Gruber tried to buy a change of clothes, for she was still wearing the ones she'd had on when her pack was left on the sheep truck. But her heart wasn't in new clothes. Day by day we had absorbed the model of the traditional desert—where change may be endured but is not sought out, where there is comfort in the known. The idea of clothing for the sake of novelty or fashion seemed odd, frivolous.

The woolen robes hung on us by now according to our shapes, the stiff creases of newness erased by constant wear. Pat had worn her pale green knit skirt, now stretched and sagging, every single day. Our Western hearts added an element of sentiment, of tokens and symbols. What we wore became an extension of us, cherished for having shared a special time, and, like not wanting to wash away a memorable kiss, we did not want to abandon these outer skins.

The next day we saw one of the drivers who'd brought us to Ghardia in conversation with the innkeeper. That was the day we discreetly took pictures of political slogans sprayed on walls. It was also the day we came upon a building with a big opening, like a garage. Stacked along the back wall were one hundred pound sacks of wheat. In the center, a table and scale. The sacks were printed: WHEAT. DONATED BY THE PEOPLE OF THE UNITED STATES OF AMERICA, in English, and we assumed, the same message in the Arabic written on the back. The keeper of the garage was repacking the wheat in smaller quantities and selling it. We took another discreet picture and determined to tell someone about it. We bought an empty sack as evidence.

The women in the *casbah*, covered entirely with enormous

white or black sheets, scurried by, reminding us that these were the first Moslem women we'd encountered and how few women of any kind we had seen across the desert. We would have liked to talk to them or go to their homes, but they just hurriedly peered at us through their single exposed eyes, hissed and ran off.

It was like a play. Or a tale of long ago and far away. But it wasn't any of those. It was their real life, confined for a thousand years to this oasis, having lost the memory through their mothers' mothers of any other place, marrying their cousins and taking the veil. This was 1964! Did they even know that? Did they care?

Returning to the hotel, we faced our real life. One more night in the hotel would take all the money we had left for transportation to Algiers. We ate in our rooms, quietly considering our fate, until someone whispered the unthinkable.

"A taxi!"
"We can't go to Algiers in a taxi."
"It must cost a fortune."
"I never thought we'd arrive in Algiers in a taxi."
"What did you expect, riding in glory on a camel?"
"I never thought we'd get there at all."

It was happening too quickly. Agreeing to make the rest of the trip by taxi meant we would be leaving within hours. We had always known it would end. And yet.

"Tomorrow Algiers!"

12

Algiers

We sped north under a full moon.

The old taxi was just noisy and bumpy enough to fill the invisible space between us. There wasn't any conversation. We'd had enough of each other. And now, body to body, bag to bag, we remained separate.

I rode as long as I could with the window open and the fast-cooling wind against my face. In the midst of crowding and sharing, of constantly being together, we had confronted the solitude of our separate selves. It was that profound solitude of the desert that I heard in the nasal, plaintive songs of the Arabs. The slow winding solitude of camel trail, the hot naked solitude of sun, the easy sober solitude of the people of the desert, the dry bitter solitude of wind, the insidious solitude of sand. Put these into song. Add no-time, nothing to indicate beginning or foretell the end. No time or all time, time past, time eternal, the frail singular truth of time now, inert, changeless ever-since and to come. It is a song of stoicism. Unsentimental. Confident. Enduring.

The taxi had been sent to us by the *pétrolier*. It belonged to his Chaamba kinsman, who drove as if he were fully possessed by the raiding bandit blood of his ancestors. He had come to the hotel in the afternoon, smiling away our skepticism. Certainly, he assured us, the taxi could make it the 600 km (400 miles) to Algiers. Certainly, there was room for the five of us and our baggage. Certainly, we would leave that very day. The agreed upon price was $60 for all.

It was dusk by the time we were loaded and stuffed into the taxi for the overnight drive. A familiar mixture of loss and expectation accompanied us out of Ghardia. It was not yet time to think of Algiers and what we would do there, penniless and not knowing a single person. We would think about that in the morning.

"Stop! Stop!" I called to the driver as we passed by the edge of the Great Western Erg, the vast dunes of the Sahara.

"*Je veux prendre du sable.*" (I want to get some sand.)

"Some sand?" He asked as if he doubted he heard me correctly.

"*Oui, si possible*, at the side of the road, near here."

He slowed down and zig-zagged back and forth across the road, scanning the shoulder with the headlights. Even on the well-traveled route between Ghardia and Laghouat, traffic was rare and the road ours. The driver braked the taxi, opened his door and pointed to the left.

"The sand?" I asked.

"*Non, non, mademoiselle, pas le sable, le sablon.*" (Not ordinary sand, fine sand.) He left the motor running and walked over to the dune.

"*Le sablon le plus fin du monde entier!*" (The finest sand in the world.)

I sank into a glorious dune, moonlit and cold. Glittering wind-whipped grains swirled about me. How could I take it with me? I needed a container. A big container. I would have filled a basket but the others wouldn't stand for it. My turban? No, no, I needed that. At last I laid out a red kerchief and scooped the finest sand in the world into it.

"Don't any of you want any sand?" I called to rest of them hovering in the taxi.

Darlene hung another scarf out the window and asked me

to fill it for her. Pat was annoyed by the delay. The whole matter was beneath Victoria.

I spread the second kerchief and pushed sand over it, as slowly as I could. My fingers grew so cold I had trouble tying up the ends of the scarf. Just as I thought I had it, the wind tore the bundle open, spilling the sand, and I had to start again.

I knelt deep into the dune, letting cold sand fill my sneakers and blow against my woolen robe. It was the last time I would be on the ground in the Sahara. I wanted to stay as long as I could. Perhaps...What if...Whatever my inner voices whispered, the sound of the motor won out over the inexorable drift of the sand. It was impossible to carry the bundles without losing precious grains. I used the stiff crown of my upturned straw hat to support them and tottered to the taxi, the wind to my back. We settled in for a long night of cramped riding.

"Soon we'll be home," Darlene said, by and by.

"I was just thinking about that."

"Hey, you guys, I'm not so sure I want to leave the desert. I mean, it will be easy for you guys to go back to Liberia. I'd look forward to it, too, if I didn't have to make this decision," Gruber replied.

"What decision?"

"I thought the trip would help me make up my mind, you know, make it clear, one way or another. But tonight I feel really panicky."

"What are you talking about?"

"Well, there's this guy in the the new group of Volunteers."

"What guy?"

"Just this guy I met three weeks before we left."

"What guy?"

"Oh man...It's Will Easterbrook."

"Oh yeah?"

"Do you know him?"

"I know who he is."

"Is he that tall guy with the glasses?"

"That's him. But tell us, Gruber, what's this big decision?"

"He wants me to marry him."

"You're kidding!"

"Come on! Stop interrupting. Let Gruber finish."

"Well, that's all there is," she continued. "He kept coming over every single day and asking me to marry him. He said I could give him my answer when I got back."

"But you don't even know him."

"For true. But he said he wants to get married and I have a lot of good qualities. He said we can get to know each other afterwards."

"Good grief!"

"You don't sound very happy about it."

"Why didn't you mention it before?"

"I think it helps to at least like a person you marry."

"Are you speaking from experience?"

"Is that necessary? Gruber's really upset."

"Oh man, you guys. I didn't mention it because…well… I sort of forgot about it. This trip has been so great, I didn't want to think about it. Also, I didn't know you guys all that well. I didn't know how you'd react."

"Personally, I don't see why you're so upset. Who could take an offer like that seriously? It's so cold."

"Right. This isn't a business contract. You actually have to live with the person."

"But wait a minute. There are lots of places where marriages are arranged and the two people hardly know each other."

"I think it depends on how Gruber feels about it. What are her expectations?"

We listened for her response. Instead, the silence was filled with the rattling of the taxi and the raging of the wind. We could all talk about our druthers, but none of the rest of us knew what Gruber's mind and heart had to contend with. We didn't say any more about it that night. Though from time to time over the next days we did. We laughed when we could, to ease that look in her eye.

"Laghouat soon," the driver announced.

Then we saw the roadblock.

"Sooner than I thought," he muttered, still smiling.

Roadblocks made my heart quicken. We had proper papers, we were not involved in any political or criminal activity. Why did I feel so defensive? Even though reason said we had nothing to fear, my mind raced through a dozen scenarios. I had seen the scary movies where the good people were in peril from evil border guards. I remembered the hassle entering Niger. How to act? What to say? Be alert. Try to understand. Remember the *gendarmes*. Should I attempt to speak French or is ignorance best? Pull the turban across my face. Is this a routine traffic check or are they looking for someone? Deal in reality, don't let imagination run wild. Are they angry? Can they read? What is the driver saying in Arabic?

I reflexively touched my amulets—the Tuareg cross and the scorpion hanging from my neck, the Saint Christopher medal in my purse.

Young men in fatigues and rifles scanned our passports. A flashlight passed across our faces. They asked the driver to get out. They looked in the trunk and under the hood. We sat very still. They came back with the flashlight. Perhaps we were too strange to be believed, too unexpected to be accounted for.

In a few minutes they waved us on, and it was over.

That was all we knew of Laghouat.

We slept fitfully across the Atlas Mountains, cold and cramped, pulled side to side by the endlessly winding road. I awoke once to glimpse a pool of snow—blue in the moonlight— and I remembered that it was still winter. Other images of low stone cottages and rocky horizon silhouettes filtered into my semi-consciousness. A man wearing baggy pants and a long brown coat sat very still astride a donkey in the mist by the side of the road. What was he doing on a lonely mountain road in the middle of the night? Did I imagine it?

I wanted to see the route. I couldn't see it. I couldn't stay awake. In that way we crossed the Atlas Mountains, passing from the desert to the land of milk and honey without knowing the portal.

It had rained in the foothills. A frightening downpour that must have reached Algiers as well, for when we got there the streets were freshly wet. At the embassy gate, we unloaded in a misty pre-dawn. It was still dark and hours before the staff would arrive. We tried to delay his leaving, but the taxi driver, ever smiling, wanted to be paid and go to sleep.

The marine on duty let us wait indoors while he called the *chargé d'affaires*. "He'll be expecting us," I said.

Indeed he was.

The wires we had sent from Agadez had been badly garbled and created so much misunderstanding that by the time we arrived numerous cables had flown among Monrovia, Washington and Algiers trying to clarify who we were and what we were up to. Our ambassador in Liberia decided we were nothing but trouble. He informed Algiers that if we ever did arrive, he wanted us deported from Algeria and forbidden to return to Liberia.

"He can't do that!"

"We'll deal with it later." I didn't know whether he could or not, but I needed to sleep before I could think about it.

At the Embassy they asked us a few questions. They were very clean and lively. We must have looked odd to them, in our dusty turbans and long woolen robes. We had so much to tell them, but I sensed it might not be possible. We had long answers, they wanted short ones. They farmed us out to board with resident Americans.

The first day two of us went with Louise, a middle-aged officer from the embassy. Her apartment was perfect. Precious French furniture with spindly legs and velvet upholstery. English china. Ironed tablecloths and napkins. A showcase. Perfectly ordered, perfectly controlled. All perfectly kept by Maria, a French/Algerian maid in a uniform.

Before she returned to work, Louise showed us to her room with a large four poster bed. She had Maria move her things into a smaller guest room. We showered and slept and were delirious with the luxury of it. In the early afternoon the others called from the places they were staying, and we invited them to join us for lunch.

We later overheard Maria crying on the phone. She could not endure it, she said, between sobs. The towels, the water. She had not hired on to a hotel. And there was no end to the amount of food we and our friends could eat. We got on the phone with Louise. She was terrified by the possibility of losing her maid. In a few hours our presence had come close to destroying the perfect world the two of them maintained. I promised we'd try to be good.

In the afternoon I took Pat to an American hospital where a young doctor cauterized her mouth sore. When they heard how we'd gotten to Algiers, some of the staff came around and looked at us. A nurse invited us to her going-away party.

We returned to the embassy to arrange to borrow the money to get back to Liberia and to find out what happened to the ambassador's trip into the desert.

We stood among the white columns on the marble floor in our black desert robes and were interviewed and photographed by the Algerian press.

Apparently the ambassador really did make the trip along with an entourage of six Land Rovers, short wave radio, tents, a medical doctor, cook, auto mechanic, body guards, assorted embassy staffers, translators, and—here is the curve—a reporter from the *New York Times*. The trip was a classic in how a turn of fate can thwart the best laid plans.

President Kennedy had been a supporter of Algerian independence. In the wake of his assassination and amid the political turmoil of post-revolutionary Algeria, there was concern among the Algerians that the United States would shift its attention and its material aid elsewhere. The posting of this ambassador affirmed America's continued support and met with a great deal of favor.

The ambassador had shown a real interest in Algeria. He was competent in Arabic and highly visible at other than official functions. He expressed enthusiasm for people-to-people programs and sought out opportunities to get out in the field. He treated the Algerians and their culture with respect and was well thought of in return.

When the ambassador went into the desert, pampered and

protected by his entourage and equipment as he may have been, he nevertheless broke precedent by going among the people at some discomfort and risk to himself. It was fair of him to take along the reporter from the *New York Times* because his effort merited attention. And so, even if his trip was, well, "ambassadorial" and conspicuous from our point of view, we were inclined to think well of him and looked forward to meeting him.

It was not to be.

We had not run across the ambassador as we traveled north because he had taken a different route south. He arrived in Tamanrasset, his southernmost point, a few days after we left. From then on he seemed to be following us, arriving a day or two after we were gone from each camp and oasis along the Hoggar route. At each stop he was welcomed well enough, but he was also regaled with stories about the five American women who had just been by.

The *New York Times'* reporter heard and made notes, and when they returned to Algiers he sought us out. A story of our trip appeared on the front page of the *Times*. The ambassador was not mentioned. Worse, he was not amused.

We were naive enough to think he would enjoy swapping stories with us as we would have with him. Instead he had a pout. During the five days we were in Algiers he remained "unavailable."

Once the *Times* story broke, a reporter and photographer from *Life* magazine came to Algiers to see us. We had international phone calls. Articles appeared in *Newsweek*, *Paris Match*, numerous papers and an Arabic magazine we couldn't read. We became guests at every meal and were smothered with attention from the American community.

Louise was disturbed by my going out at night. It wasn't safe she was quite sure, and her neighbors would gossip. One must be above reproach, she told us. When I left that evening to go dancing with Pat's doctor, she gave me a set of keys and asked me to let myself in through the back door at the foot bridge without making a ruckus. A key for the outer gate, one for the inner gate, one for the dead bolt and one for the door.

By the end of the second day, Louise and Maria couldn't stand us any longer. She wanted to be a perfect hostess, and we were making her a failure. We kept doing what we wanted to, coming and going as we pleased. It was impossible. We moved into the house of an AID (Agency for International Development) couple with whom Gruber had been staying. They spread cushions on the floor and fed us couscous and lamb stew.

The level of activity in which we found ourselves was exciting and isolating. For so long we had dealt only with each other and with the need to look after ourselves. The problems of eating, sleeping, toileting, finding rides, changing money, keeping warm were straightforward and consuming. In Algiers it seemed we had become the center of gossip for hordes of people.

When we slipped away on our own, we found the public Algiers to be a male city. We had crossed a desert populated by men, but this was different. Men crowded the tables of coffee houses and outdoor cafes. Near the University, where the rare female student dressed modestly and moved quickly and discreetly, we defended ourselves against swarms of hooting, leering, pinching Arab males. Crowded, idle, volatile. This urban male culture had a great deal of leisure and seemed just a spark away from mob mentality and mob actions.

The Americans warned us about riding public buses—only the natives did that. They chauffeured us among themselves and to a hairdresser. (The hairdresser cut and set our hair just like that of the embassy wives she was accustomed to doing. Fortunately, the set washed out, and we could continue looking a little like our own selves.)

"Aren't you glad you won't be needing these baskets anymore?" our American protectors said as they shuttled us about Algiers. "Here, I can get rid of all these old rags," one assured me as he rummaged through our treasures.

I folded and packed our *lapas* and the MADE IN THE PEOPLE'S REPUBLIC OF CHINA blankets in my suitcase, safely out of sight.

But our food baskets became lighter and the wonderful hat

Carolyn had given me in Khorogo disappeared. We felt less in control of our lives and our belongings than we had among foreigners.

Two young men involved in an AID agriculture project took us to the *casbah*. They had been here before, they said, and we shouldn't be afraid. It hadn't occurred to us to be afraid. Now, amid the narrow cobblestone lanes, the two AID fellows stayed near us and looked over their shoulders. They didn't want us to worry, they said, and personally they thought there was too much fear among the American community, especially about being in public. But the rumors and mystery of the *casbah* were so powerful. Despite their reassuring words, they watched us and fretted.

After more than a year and half of living in foreign countries, trying to understand other values and ways of thinking, we were most bewildered by our own people. Only a small part of the attention we got was genuine. People escorted us because they wanted to control our activity, they housed us because they were assigned, they fed us—well, we did have to eat—to interrogate us and confirm their deep suspicions.

We paid our way by being honest and amusing.

We talked and talked and told of the experiences we'd had and people we'd met. We wanted everyone to know about Abidjan, the third-class train, dancing with the Upper Voltain students, Barbara of USIS, the Englishmen, Graham and John, and the boulders of Zinder, *les camion*, Agadez, the Tuareg, Mme. Dodet, Aboubakar, Tamanrasset, Mme. Florimound, Zoro, the *bordj* of Father de Foucauld, Asekrem, the *chef* and the *génie* camp at Tit, the *gendarmes*, Fort Miribel, the sheep truck, the Foreign Legion, the cold nights, the space-age city at In Ekker, the camels, the locusts, and the mountains of peanuts. We wanted to tell them of all the wondrous things we had seen and of all the generosity and kindness of the people who helped us.

The more we tried, the more we realized how much was lost. In the comfort of a warm apartment or the elegant lounge of an international hotel, our stories and pictures were just stories and pictures, not the experiences themselves. We had been in another place. And it was now a part of us. The change was within and set us apart from almost everyone else.

"Now that you're back in civilization, what would you really like?" a well-meaning countryman asked at a party.

"I'd like to turn around and go back into the desert," Victoria answered. And she said it so plainly and so quietly, he was embarrassed to have asked.

Within a week Sargent Shriver, Director of the Peace Corps, was including his version of our journey in speeches he made across Europe, calling it the true example of the meaning and spirit of the Peace Corps. Secretary of State Dean Rusk intervened on our behalf and somehow arrangements were made to return us to Liberia.

I walked along the balcony of the hospital with the young American doctor. Fields of perfect spring green spread across a gentle valley and onto the lower slope of the foothills. Beyond were the Atlas Mountains.

"You are very remarkable," he said. I felt satisfied, but not remarkable. "What an adventure you've had."

"It was not an adventure," I insisted. The idea of an adventure seemed so trivial compared to our experience. "It was just one day after another. So many people helped us. It was really their tolerance and kindness, their permission that made it possible. We were so vulnerable, we could have been done in at any time."

"Do you know why you're getting this mixed message from the other Americans? They're fascinated—as I am, who wouldn't be—but they're envious, too."

"They can do it as well."

"That's the point. There isn't an American or a European here who isn't intrigued by the desert. They're dying to go. They talk about it endlessly, make plans, gather information, you know the sort of thing. When is the best season, the best route, should I take my own water? They probably know a lot more than you do about the tribes, the history, what to do in a sandstorm. They'll sit here and look at those mountains and fantasize."

"I guess we benefited from our ignorance."

"But you actually did it. And they can't stand it. You and your rag-tag bunch just damn well did it!"

He had been to Viet Nam, and I had barely heard of it. He wanted me to know he was not like the other Americans. In a way, he said, he was closer to the Peace Corps, a contract civilian doctor seeing the world and doing good. But he was thirty-two years old, a responsible adult, virtually middle-aged I thought, and I was leaving Algiers in a few days.

I sensed a change I couldn't identify. At first I thought it was the fresh sea air or the trees and flowers that made me so comfortable in Algiers. But it was more subtle than that. The quality of light was indeed different. Late winter sun lay mellow and clear against whitewashed buildings. I no longer winced in anticipation of a blinding, harsh outdoors. I sensed the change from high rise balconies, in the midst of the *casbah*, walking through the bazaar.

Of course. The wind had stopped.

Postscript

I have heard that Algiers doesn't work any more. They say the people are without skills, without discipline, without understanding of what it takes to maintain a modern city, disdaining elegance for utilitarian socialism, rejecting the trappings of colonialism, rejecting the style of the French. Whatever the reasons, they say it's neglected, run down, clogged with people, short of resolve, colorless, oppressive, every negative thing.

I don't want to believe it. The Algiers of my memory is lively, colorful, white buildings stepping nicely up hillsides, palms, ferns, fresh air, and giant geraniums blooming in pots and bougainvillea cascading over walls, everywhere views of the mountains and the Mediterranean, as beautiful a city as one could ever hope for.

We left Algiers with the reporter and photographer from *Life* magazine. It wasn't easy to get to Liberia from Algiers. During two days of seven airplanes—each smaller than the one before—and six countries, we hopped around the western bulge of Africa and returned to the steam bath of Liberia on March 6, 1964.

The *Life* people expected a great crowd to meet us. We knew that was silly. Great crowds, even of your dearest friends, do not come out to cheer you for living your ordinary life and going about your ordinary business. Nevertheless, it seemed to mean a lot to the journalists to photograph us coming down the stairs from the airplane at Roberts Field as if we were celebrities. Despite the suffocating humidity, we cooperated by putting on our desert robes for a few intolerable minutes. What attention we did get was from bystanders who thought we'd lost our senses. The Peace Corps sent someone to the airport to get us and the sight of them and the blue Jeeps was wonderful.

We felt we had been away a very long time.

"What's the news?"

"A couple of new staff people. The guy who tried to rescue Phyllis and Faye from their walk through the bush—the one with the new leather "bush" boots—ended up in the hospital and went back to the States. Oh yes, and we're going to have a wedding next week-end."

"Who's getting married?"

"Will Easterbrook and one of the new girls."

Gruber smiled.

There was mail, and, as I had been afraid to hope, it having been so long, letters from Jim. One was written after a few weeks filming a road-building project up-country:

> *2-25-64*
>
> *Leaving tomorrow for Sinoe and probably will return the end of March. But of your trip— such a book or film—even the letters were fine. You should really put it together.*
>
> *'godamnwomen' is what George said upon hearing of your luck and energy and skirts. True, at the same embassy where we were told to get the hell out of the shower, you were whispered to like babes. True, you made friends where we made enemies. True, you managed well where*

we merely tried. But, altogether, it sounded as if you had been there and come through with something that we missed, or spent little time getting—an adventure and a love. On the map your trip looks a bit amazing, but from your letters, which I saved for the stamps (but now perhaps for other reasons) it could be seen that a foundation of connections and friends were forming to see you through. My best to all the travelers. See you next weekend.

Friends in Monrovia gave a party for us on the roof of their apartment.

"You may regret having done all of this," one of them said a little wistfully. "Now the rest of your life will be anticlimactic. This will be the pinnacle to which you'll look back. Nothing can top it."

Some people resented the fact that we had been singled out for publicity when their travels had been as meaningful and often more difficult. They were right. It had been a matter of chance and circumstance.

But the most surprising and hurtful reactions came from a number of male Volunteers who went out of their way to discredit our trip because we were "just a bunch of girls." Now they stood at the bar, fortifying their wounded maleness by trying to lessen what would have been the supreme adventure for them. "You know you wouldn't have made it if you hadn't been a lot of skirts." These were people I had thought of as friends.

We returned to our classes and our students didn't know we had become famous until we showed them our pictures in *Life*. "For true. Da' your picture-o," they agreed.

I did not regret having crossed the Sahara, and my life since then has been anything but anticlimactic. But the Peace Corps days did profoundly mark my consciousness and become both the ballast and the prism for the rest of the journey.

Crossing the Sahara as we did had little to do with skirts. I believe we succeeded partly because the desert was there, the season was right and we allowed it to happen. And partly because we overcame our apprehensions, our instinctive resistance to the unknown, with a greater faith in the genuine humanity of the people among whom we passed.

We walked softly with no sticks at all. We brought our curiosity, our respect and our terrible vulnerability. They accepted this ultimate trust and responded with generous charity. To all of them who taught us so much about ourselves and the quality of life, I am gratefully indebted.

Many people have been curious about what has become of the women who made this journey. Despite the intensity of the time we spent together, I have had no contact with three of them for more than twenty-five years. The following facts come largely from others and are often not first hand reports. Of the five of us, two made careers of teaching, one never married, one was widowed, two divorced, two had children, two never again lived in the communities in which they were raised. While some have traveled, none has lived abroad again.

Of the countries through which we traveled, Upper Volta is now known as Burkina Faso. Nearby Dahomey is now Benin, and Spanish Sahara has become Western Sahara while its statehood continues to be in dispute among its various neighbors and nationalist defenders.